IRRESISTIBLE
Invitation

RESPONDING TO THE
EXTRAVAGANT HEART OF GOD

IRRESISTIBLE
Invitation

RESPONDING TO THE
EXTRAVAGANT HEART OF GOD

MAXIE D. DUNNAM

Abingdon Press
Nashville

IRRESISTIBLE INVITATION
RESPONDING TO THE EXTRAVAGANT HEART OF GOD

Copyright 2008 by Abingdon Press
All rights reserved.

This book is printed on acid-free, elemental-chlorine–free paper.
Original art, cover, and page designs by Joey McNair.

Library of Congress Cataloging-in-Publication Data

Dunnam, Maxie D.
  Irresistible invitation : responding to the extravagant heart of God / by Maxie Dunnam.
      p. cm.
  ISBN 978-0-687-64879-5 (binding: adhesive, perfect : alk. paper)
  1. Christian life. 2. Spirituality. I. Title.
  BV4501.3.D855 2008
  248.4'876–dc22

                              2008003863

ISBN: 978-0-68764-879-5

Excerpt from "The Dry Salvages" in FOUR QUARTETS, copyright 1941 by T. S. Eliot and renewed 1969 by Esme Valerie Eliot, reprinted by permission of Houghton Mifflin Harcourt Publishing Company.

Unless otherwise indicated, all Scripture quotations are taken from the Holy Bible, NEW INTERNATIONAL VERSION®. Copyright © 1973, 1978, 1984 by International Bible Society. All rights reserved throughout the world. Used by permission of International Bible Society.

Scripture verses marked NRSV are from the New Revised Standard Version of the Bible, copyright 1989, Division of Christian Education of the National Council of the Churches of Christ in the United States of America. Used by permission. All rights reserved.

Scripture verses marked TNIV are taken from the Holy Bible, TODAY'S NEW INTERNATIONAL VERSION®. Copyright © 2001, 2005 International Bible Society. All rights reserved throughout the world. Used by permission of the International Bible Society.

Scripture quotations marked NKJV are taken from the New King James Version®. Copyright © 1982 by Thomas Nelson, Inc. Used by permission. All rights reserved.

Scripture verses marked NEB are from *The New English Bible.* © The Delegates of the Oxford University Press and The Syndics of the Cambridge University Press 1961, 1970. Reprinted by permission.

Scripture quotations from *The Message* Copyright © by Eugene H. Peterson 1993, 1994, 1995, 1996, 2000, 2001, 2002. Used by permission of NavPress Publishing Group.

Scripture quotations marked NLT are taken from the *Holy Bible,* New Living Translation, copyright © 1996. Used by permission of Tyndale House Publishers, Inc., Wheaton, Illinois 60189. All rights reserved.

The New Testament in Modern English, rev. ed., trans. J. B. Phillips. Copyright © J. B. Phillips, 1958, 1959, 1960, 1972. The Macmillan Company.

The Bible: James Moffatt Translation, copyright © 1922, 1924, 1925, 1926, 1935, HarperCollins San Francisco, copyright © 1950, 1952, 1953, 1954 James A. R. Moffatt.

08   09   10   11   12   13   14   15   16   17   10   9   8   7   6   5   4   3   2   1

MANUFACTURED IN THE UNITED STATES OF AMERICA

CONTENTS

ACKNOWLEDGMENTS

No book is a private enterprise. More often than not, a number of people have made very important contributions to the process. Since this book reflects a gleaning of much of my writing and preaching, I am indebted to countless people who have contributed to my life and ministry through the years. I am who I am because of the people who have loved me, believed in me, and who have been mentors even unawares. I thank you.

More specifically, this book is the product of the thinking and praying of a number of people. I am especially indebted to an editorial team that conceived the project: Fiona Soltes, Andrew B. Miller, Mark Jacobs, Nancy Wise, and the leadership at the United Methodist Publishing House. This book is the outcome of our conferencing and praying.

Fiona Soltes, a talented writer with a special anointing from God, has helped bring this project to fruition, along with the help and guidance of Andrew B. Miller and his staff at Providence House Publishers: Kelly Bainbridge, Darlene Chaney, Holly Jones, Melissa Istre, LeAnna Massingille, Joey McNair, Maren Minton, Lane Rosencrans, and Nancy Wise. Their writing, editing, advising, guiding, and questioning were indispensable. In fact, without their work, this book would not be. My deepest gratitude to them.

My daughter, Kim Reisman, challenged me and kept me centered. Thanks!

As with everything I have done, my wife, Jerry, has been my chief encourager. She knows I am "cutting back" when I work fifty rather than sixty hours a week. To have that kind of understanding gives me the freedom I need to be creative and productive. If I knew a better word, I would use it; I don't. So, Jerry . . . *thanks.*

INTRODUCTION

I t is with great boldness that I have written this book. The title is as bold as it gets—*Irresistible Invitation*. Your immediate thought might be, *How can an invitation be irresistible? I am free to respond however I choose to any invitation that I receive.* I wrestled with the same feelings as our team of editors pondered the possibility of this title. Then I went to the dictionary and found this definition: "Irresistible: impossible to successfully resist." That definition erased all my reservations. Of course we are free; we can resist. But we can't "successfully" resist God's incredible grace.

It is mind-boggling, really . . . that God would desire a loving relationship with me. As staggering as the thought is, as unbelievable as it appears on the surface, this is the very heart of the gospel: *I am loved by God.* There is a place in God's heart that only I can fill. Denying this truth is a great sin of disbelief. The Bible, when we read it extensively, makes it unmistakably clear. God loves each one of us as though we are the only person in the world to love. It's in the book!

Don't you remember? Jesus said that not even a sparrow falls to the ground without the Father taking note of him. And you, he said, are of more value than a sparrow. Jesus went even further than that; he said the very hairs on our heads are numbered. Each of us is a unique, unrepeatable miracle of God. So, we are not just saved *from* our sins but *to* a personal, intimate relationship with God.

This book is about God's irresistible invitation to enter into relationship with him. It is about grace—God acting in our lives to accomplish, with our willing response and participation, what we cannot accomplish on our own.

In writing this book, I have gone back through what I have preached and written during my many years of ministry and have provided the information and guidance you need for the journey. There is a sense in which this is the best I have offered, and the very best I can offer today.

After each day's reading, you will have the opportunity for reflection, guided by questions that get to "the heart of the matter." Please spend prayerful time responding to those questions.

Community, where conversation and communion take place, is essential for Christian living. My hope is that you will share with others on this journey and meet weekly to encourage and challenge each other as "one heart sets another heart on fire."

I remember the words from Walker Percy's novel, *The Second Coming*: "If the good news is true, why is no one pleased to hear it?" I believe the good news is true, and I believe people are pleased to hear it when it is proclaimed in its radical essence: the incredible possibility of living a life in Christ, shaped by his indwelling Spirit and expressive of his presence in the world. So I invite you on a forty-day journey of considering the irresistible invitation and responding to the extravagant heart of God.

Week One

COMING HOME TO GOD

INCANDESCENT AMAZEMENT

Day 1

*In the beginning
God created the heavens and the earth.
Gen. 1:1*

The singer Mary Martin used to say that her grandmother, who lived to be ninety-nine years old, spent her life in a state of "incandescent amazement." Isn't that a marvelous term? It's what I feel when I ponder God's eternal nature, and when I read that first line of the Bible: "In the beginning God . . ."

Few phrases have stimulated the mind and imagination as much as this opening verse. Numerous poets have tried to find words for the day that Shelley describes as "when God first dawned on chaos." Philosophers have written volumes reflecting on its wisdom. Scientists continue to debate aspects of its truth. And theologians—that's us, when we think and talk about God—find in these words both the beginning of God's story and our own story. We begin here as we explore our relationship to God, what the Christian faith is all about, and how we live out that faith day in and day out.

When asked in 1989 what book most influenced her during the past year, author Madeleine L'Engle responded:

> There is no question that the book that has been most influential for me this past year is the Bible's first one: Genesis. . . . The marvelous story of the creation is for me filled with incredible joy . . . the words shouting all things into being in a great cry of joy. Genesis is also filled with marvelous

3

> people—flawed and human—and underlines for me that God
> does not choose "qualified" people to do the work of love. . . .
> Genesis has everything—all the human vices and glories, love
> and hate, murder, sacrifice, and a great story. There is no end
> to plumbing its depths.

She's right. There is no end to plumbing its depths. In the first eleven chapters of Genesis, you have God's version of the human story and also our version of God's story.

You may wonder why I refer to only the first eleven chapters. As you read the book of Genesis, you will find there is a distinct, though unannounced, change of tone that begins at Chapter 11. It is there that the story of Abraham and his descendants begins. William M. Logan reminds us:

> From that point on, the record has a more concrete sound. It
> moves more slowly and gives more details. It does not cover a
> thousand years in a single breath. It slows down to a pace with
> which we can keep up as it traces the life story of men and a
> nation. In contrast, the first eleven chapters of Genesis are epic
> in their scope. Their sweep is tremendous. Incomprehensible
> periods of time are covered in a few words. Stupendous events
> are described with brevity and matter of factness of a child's
> fairy story.

This is history, not in the sense of the chronological recording of people and events, but rather the nature of humanity and our spiritual journey. These chapters explain history not in terms of what, when, and how things happened, but *why*. Here's more from William Logan:

> The stories are told in such manner that when I read them, I
> realize that I'm not reading an account of history; I'm looking
> in a mirror! This is not Adam I'm reading about; this is myself.
> This is not a tower built long ago in a faraway country: this is my
> own society in action, and I am part and parcel of that society.

GOD IS ETERNAL

Perhaps you've heard a child ask—because just about every child asks at some time or another—"Who made God?" The answer is, "No one." God has always been, God is and will always be. God existed before the world and before human history, and God will exist after the world and human history are dissolved.

Someone once asked Martin Luther what God was doing before the world was made. The old reformer replied, "Cutting switches with which to flog those who ask foolish questions!" Foolish or not, this question certainly makes us think. God is eternal, and when we begin to understand that, our relationship to God comes into clearer view.

There is something more we need to rest on: in the beginning, God *created*. Listen to the second verse: "Now the earth was formless and empty, darkness was over the surface of the deep, and the Spirit of God was hovering over the waters" (Gen. 1:2).

> *The world in all its complexity did not come into existence by chance; the odds are too great for that.*

It's interesting to note that the Hebrew word used here for *created* is one that is used only in reference to God in the Bible. The truth is, the word implies work that is utterly beyond human imitation or comprehension. The world in all its complexity did not come into existence by chance; the odds are too great for that.

Someone has said that if you put ten pennies minted in consecutive years into your pocket, the odds of taking them out in order are one in ten billion. Can you imagine—those being the odds—that this universe, of which we are a part, could have just happened by chance?

William Herbert Carruth describes his sense of incandescent amazement at God's creation in his poem "Each in His Own Tongue":

A fire-mist and a planet,
    A crystal and a cell,
A jelly-fish and a saurian,
    And caves where cave-men dwell;
Then a sense of law and beauty
    And a face turned from the clod—
Some call it Evolution,
    And others call it God.

As we begin our forty-day journey together, I invite you to ponder these foundational concepts that speak to the heart of our Christian faith: in the beginning, God created everything that exists. God is bigger than any concept we can hold in our minds, yet God in his infinite love desires a personal relationship with us. The chaos that we sometimes feel overwhelmed by is actually an illusion; God's reality is law, beauty, and order breathed into creation in divine wisdom.

As we go about the details of living our lives, it's easy for us to lose sight of the big picture. When we're running through our days on autopilot, we can miss those moments of incandescent amazement when God reveals something beautiful to us. But if we are willing to listen, we soon realize that God is calling us to slow down and pay attention to these moments of wonder.

We might hear truth in a song lyric, glimpse the divine in a flowing stream, or see the face of God in the eyes of a child. If we tune in to God and open ourselves to seeing the creation with fresh eyes, we'll begin to experience more and more moments of incandescent amazement.

At this point, you might have more questions about God than you have answers. You may even doubt God's great compassion, or God's willingness to be intricately involved in your life. That's okay; you're far from the first person to feel this way. But if you'll agree with me right now that God could literally change your life through this study—that you'll allow God to teach you new things and reveal himself in new ways—there's no telling what could happen next.

THE HEART OF THE MATTER

※ What do you feel when you reflect on the first few lines of Genesis? How does this feeling color your perception of God?

※ How could a deeper understanding of the creation story affect your relationship with God? Does this story challenge any of your previous assumptions?

※ Have you experienced moments of incandescent amazement? If so, how have those experiences informed your understanding of God?

GOD'S CREATION IS GOOD

God saw all that he had made,
and it was very good.
Gen. 1:31

Yesterday, we centered our thinking on incandescent amazement. God calls creation out of chaos—and rejoices. Now let's take it a step further. "And God said, 'Let there be light,' and there was light. God saw that the light was good, and he separated the light from the darkness" (Gen. 1:3).

The writer of these first chapters of Genesis doesn't describe a God who looks down on creation as an engineer, scientist, or technician who has created a model that is flowing off some production line. No, the God of creation is an artist, painter, and sculptor—and the creation is his masterpiece.

Note that after each dimension of the creation, there is the phrase, "And it was good." We need to hang on to that phrase, because our temptation is to see the world and all that is in it as evil. When the darkness of our circumstances makes life seem dark, we grow frightened and sometimes faithless. We find it difficult to believe that God is near, and fear that God has forgotten us. We long for the light in the midst of our darkness.

Have you ever read John Keats' poem, "Ode to a Nightingale"? In the poem, Keats expresses a longing to escape from his pain-filled life and join the pleasant-sounding nightingale, which lives apart from the trials of human beings. He asks for a cup of poison to drink, and says:

That I might drink, and leave the world unseen,
And with thee fade away into the forest dim:

Fade far away, dissolve, and quite forget
  What thou among the leaves hast never known,
The weariness, the fever, and the fret
Here, where men sit and hear each other groan;
Where palsy shakes a few, sad, last grey hairs,
Where youth grows pale, and spectre-thin, and dies;
Where but to think is to be full of sorrow
    And leaden-eyed despairs;
Where beauty cannot keep her lustrous eyes,
Or new Love pine at them beyond to-morrow.

Keats had felt the emptiness, darkness, and hopelessness of life. We all feel this way from time to time: the darkness of our particular circumstances makes us believe that all of life is dark, and so we become frightened and faithless.

What we need to know, however, is that God owns the darkness as well as the light, and that God is present in the night as well as in the day. There's a marvelous verse in the book of Isaiah which says, "I am the LORD, and there is no other. I form the light and create darkness" (Isa. 45:6–7). Isaiah knew—because he believed the creation story—that the entire universe belonged to God. No aspect of human experience is without God's presence. The psalmist knew it too, so he could sing:

If I go up to the heavens, you are there;
if I make my bed in the depths, you are there. . . .
If I say, "Surely the darkness will hide me
and the light become night around me,"
even the darkness will not be dark to you;
the night will shine like the day,
for darkness is as light to you. (Ps. 139:8, 11–12)

Not only does God bring deliverance from darkness; sometimes God reveals himself most vividly in the darkness. We may not understand it or be able to explain it, but we can know full well that God is in the midst of everything.

> *We may not understand it,*
> *but we can know full well that*
> *God is in the midst of everything.*

Of course, the providential care of God does not protect us from the bumps and bruises of life, nor from the struggle—and sometimes tragedy—of living. Brothers betray brothers. Husbands desert wives. Good people lose their jobs. Teenage girls get pregnant. Teenage boys use drugs. The young die too early. The old live against their will through feeding tubes and breathing machines. Hurricanes devastate cities. Tornadoes destroy trailer parks and rivers flood towns. An earthquake in the middle of the ocean causes a tsunami a thousand miles away.

As such, it may not always seem apparent that every part of God's creation is good. But we can be confident that God is always working out his magnificent plan of redemption.

We have to be honest here and say that sometimes people— the height of God's creation—don't act according to the image in which they were created. But what a wonderful surprise when they do. We finish today's study with a beautiful example of God's creation reflecting his glory—and his great compassion.

Some time ago, the Associated Press carried the story of Manuel Garcia. Garcia was a poor man who suffered from cancer, and he needed to be treated with chemotherapy. He had always been proud of his full head of hair, but now he had to surrender to its loss.

When the time came for Garcia to leave the hospital and return home, he felt embarrassed by his baldness. As he entered his house, his five-year-old son came running to him. The little boy threw his arms around his father and shouted, "Daddy, I love you!" Garcia was surprised when he realized that his son was completely bald; he had shaved off his hair so he could look like his father.

Then, in a few minutes, the doorbell rang. Garcia opened the door to find some fifty neighbors and friends standing on his front lawn. They had all shaved their heads in a sign of solidarity and support. What a picture of God! God may not save us *from* our troubles, but he will save us *in* them. God's creation may sometimes seem dark and evil, but in the full picture, the long view, it will prove to be good.

THE HEART OF THE MATTER

❈ Have you been aware of God's presence in a time of darkness and suffering? Describe your personal experience.

❈ Have there been times of hardship in your life that, looking back, you are able to recognize as forming your character for the better? Are you aware of a purpose in those times of struggle?

❈ Have you given or received a show of love like the one described in the story of Manuel Garcia? If so, how did that experience affect you?

A GRACIOUS GOD

I have come that they may have life,
and have it to the full.
John 10:10

We've all been there: uncertain, unqualified—even, at times, unfit. It doesn't matter our position, our calling, or our training; sooner or later, we all experience that sinking feeling that we're absolutely, completely in over our heads.

I've been known to feel that way during the seemingly simplest of tasks: heading to the grocery store to pick up one or two items for my wife. Let's just say that the grocery is not exactly familiar (or comfortable) territory for me, and I get there only when a state of near-emergency is declared at home.

But there have been other times far more serious. I remember, in particular, when I was called to join the staff of The Upper Room, charged with directing a ministry, calling people to a life of prayer, providing direction and resources for growth in that area, and giving structure to a united expression of prayer by people around the world. Feeling very much the novice, I recall telling Dr. Wilson Weldon, then the editor of *The Upper Room*, that the search committee—and the church as a whole—must be in desperate straits to consider me for the job, I was such a novice in the area of prayer life and its development.

Looking back, though, I have to admit something: God met me there in a profound way. The responsibility forced me to be even more deliberate and disciplined in my own life of prayer. But it also introduced me to a wider dimension of spirituality than I had ever known.

I became intensely interested in the great devotional classics. The Upper Room had published a collection of little booklets—selections from some of the greatest spiritual teachers of the ages, whose names I barely knew and to whose writings I was a stranger: Julian of Norwich, William Law, Francois Fenelon, Francis of Assisi, Evelyn Underhill, Brother Lawrence, and an array of others. I began a deliberate practice of "keeping company with the saints," seeking to immerse myself in their writings which have endured through the centuries.

I have continued this practice for more than thirty years now. As I have kept company with the saints, I have observed some characteristics they have in common:

* They passionately sought the Lord.
* They discovered a gracious God.
* They took Scripture seriously.
* They experienced a living Jesus.
* They practiced discipline, at the heart of which was prayer.
* They were convinced that obedience was essential to their life and growth.
* They didn't seek ecstasy, but surrender of their will to the Lord.
* They were thirsty for holiness.
* They lived not for themselves, but for God and for others.
* They knew joy and peace transcending all circumstances.

The first two lessons are connected. The saints passionately sought and discovered a gracious God. That is what this forty-day study is about . . . the irresistible invitation that flows from God's extravagant love.

THE GOD OF ALL COMFORT

In the Bible, Paul opens his second letter to the Corinthian church by offering the grace and peace of "God our Father and the Lord Jesus Christ" (2 Cor. 1:2). He continues:

> Praise be to the God and Father of our Lord Jesus Christ, the Father of compassion and the God of all comfort, who comforts us in all our troubles, so that we can comfort those in any trouble with the comfort we ourselves have received from God. (2 Cor. 1:3–4)

Paul crowns his greeting to the believers in Corinth with this illuminating, encouraging, and challenging word. He emphasizes the primary nature of God in order to keep the truth of God's compassion alive before the people: "the God of all comfort" comforts us.

James Atkinson shares this thought from the great reformer Martin Luther in his *Daily Readings* series:

> All the many countless blessings which God gives us here on earth are merely those gifts which last for a time. But his grace and loving regard are the inheritance which endures throughout eternity. . . . In giving us such gifts here on earth he is giving us only those things that are his own, but *in his grace and love toward us he gives us his very self.* In receiving his gifts we touch but his hand; but in his gracious regard we receive his heart, his spirit, his mind, his will.

What does it mean that God gives us his very self? That's really what this study is about. God so graciously offers us not just divine assistance, but also infinite wisdom, love, guidance, and purpose.

During this journey—especially in the first couple of weeks—we'll have the chance to immerse ourselves in the goodness and generosity of God and the expression of his extravagant love in Jesus Christ. The hope of it all is that Jesus, who is our Savior, will truly become our Lord, and that we will understand what it means to live our lives in response and witness to the grace that has been given freely to us.

> *God loves us enough to allow us to walk into new life one step at a time, always by our side.*

We have to remember, however, that immersion takes both time and effort. It flies in the face of the instantaneous world in which we live. Just as God has done throughout the ages, he invites us to "Be still, and know that I am God" (Ps. 46:10). When we are willing to do that, we find the depths of all God is.

Yes, God is gracious enough to give us new hope and new life, but the idea that all we have to do is turn toward God and everything will be just fine points to the fallacy of the "instant-fix" mindset. The reality is that God loves us enough to allow us to walk into new life one step at a time, always by our side. It is in that daily seeking, trusting, and growing that we become the people God meant for us to be all along.

CAN WE REALLY BE GOOD?

From the dawn of time, we human beings have been both attracted to and repelled by the idea of being "good." We lift people up as heroes and saviors, yet relish the moment when they are exposed as having feet of clay. We spend countless dollars on books, videos, programs, and workshops, hoping that they will help us be all that we can be. Yet we deliberately sabotage those very efforts with bad habits that have infiltrated our daily living. We want to be good, but we aren't always able. We don't completely like being bad, but we sometimes don't mind it. As Paul expressed, there seems to be a battle going on within us between our desire to follow goodness and the allure of evil that surrounds us.

It is a universal issue, but there is good news that goes along with it. God's infinite mercy includes the gift of power over sin. We can start with the very word "virtue," which comes from the Greek word *arete,* meaning "power." This is a major hint in answering the question of whether goodness is possible. God not only gives us tools in virtues like wisdom, courage, justice, and temperance, but God gives us power to walk in them, as well. The virtues are the evidence of God's love, of God's grace.

Thomas Aquinas was one of the great champions of cultivating the virtues in our moral life. He described them as a source of power in developing our character. But he also considered the virtues to be habits. Like all habits, good and bad, they are developed through repetition and exercise, formed in the laboratory of daily life by the countless choices we make in each moment.

It is only through the power of God's grace in the virtues, and our own disciplined exercise of them, that we are able to strengthen our character and move toward the good person God created us to be. Like Aquinas, then, we can believe that living a life of moral virtue is possible, though not without God's help.

NOW CHOOSE LIFE

We must understand that our individual relationship with God is all about choice. The choice is not whether we will become a new person or not—that is a matter of grace. Christ alone holds the power to make us a new creation. Our choice is whether we will choose to start to become a new person. Do you see the difference? We do not choose to become a new person; we choose to *start to become* a new person.

A theme which echoes through the Old Testament is, "I have set before you life and death . . . now choose life" (Deut. 30:19). Here *life* and *death* don't signify existence and nonexistence; rather, they hold a promise that existence can be enriched and thereby become real life. You can choose either a dead life or a real life—one that is lived in confidence, hope, and gratitude made possible through the miraculous working of God's Spirit.

John's Gospel explains that Jesus came to abolish death and to open the possibility of abundant life to all people. *Death* in this context speaks of a weakness or a nulling of the life experience rather than actually ceasing to exist. *Life,* on the other hand, suggests a higher state of existence. This higher state, this aliveness, is available only through God. Remember Paul's word to the Ephesians: "But because of his great love for us, God, who is rich in mercy, made us alive with Christ even when we were dead in transgressions—it is by grace you have been saved" (Eph. 2:4–5).

Living in a joy and peace that transcends all circumstances requires the same habits today as always: prayer, discipline, surrender, a thirst for holiness, and the knowledge that Jesus is alive in our experience. Just like Martin Luther and the saints of the ages, we can also know God's presence in our time of need and God's grace in our time of challenge. It's all there for the choosing, offered to us with extravagant love.

THE HEART OF THE MATTER

❋ Think about your habits, good and bad. How have they shaped your life as a whole?

❋ Have you chosen to "start to become" a new person? Why or why not?

❋ What does it mean to you to choose to be in relationship with God? Do you make it a habit to seek God's company each day?

THE PICTURE
OF GOD

Every good and perfect gift is from above,
coming down from the Father. . . .
James 1:17

A divinity student was having a difficult time describing his relationship with God, so his counselor asked the young man to draw a picture to illustrate God. The student said he couldn't draw very well, so he would take it home and bring it back when the class met again the following week.

It happened to be around Christmastime, and when the seminary student returned, he brought an artist's drawing of a scene from Charles Dickens' story *A Christmas Carol.* In the picture, the angry, demanding Ebenezer Scrooge sat behind his desk with pen in hand, his debit-credit ledger before him. In front of Scrooge, standing in terror, was his clerk, Bob Cratchit. Pointing to Scrooge, the young man said, "That's God." Pointing to Cratchit, he said, "That's me."

Here was a young man getting As in theology, describing God as a skinflint Scrooge and himself as a cowering Cratchit in God's presence. But let's not be too hard on the young man. In all of us, there is probably some difference in the way we talk about God, in our mental and philosophical concepts of God, and how we feel deep down about God. Another way to say it is that the God of our minds may not be the same as the God of our feelings.

The verse from James which began today's reading, in other translations says "every endowment and every perfect gift," or "every generous act of giving" comes from the Father. The ultimate example of God's extravagant love is the gift of his son, Jesus. During this study we'll focus on Jesus, as he provides the perfect picture of God.

James gives us another interesting image of God:

> Don't be deceived, my dear brothers. Every good and perfect gift is from above, coming down from the Father of the heavenly lights, who does not change like shifting shadows. He chose to give us birth through the word of truth, that we might be a kind of firstfruits of all he created. (James 1:16–18)

These words of James say two things about the nature of God. First, God is defined as "the Father of lights." This is a reminder that God is the Creator of the universe. Second, the text declares that with God is no variation or "change." The *Moffatt* translation says that there is "no shadow of turning with God." This teaches us that God is eternally faithful. Turning is what casts shadows; it is because the Earth is turning that the sun goes down, and shadows of the evening are spread out. But with God there is no shadow of turning.

Now I want to put these truths about the nature of God together and out of them sound three affirmations. One, God never lets us down; two, God never lets us off; and three, God never lets us go.

GOD NEVER LETS US DOWN

God is the Father, James says, and the love of God the Father never lets us down. Listen to Jesus as the authorized spokesman of God, and look at what Jesus did as the life of God, and you can't deny that instead of letting folks down, Jesus was always lifting people up.

There may be times when it seems that God lets us down. We pray for a healing, and it doesn't come. We pray for a job, and it goes to the other candidate. We ask to be delivered from some crippling circumstance, but nothing seems to change. We seek a detour around the road with a cross at the end of it, but find all of the roads are closed. Sometimes it does seem as if God lets us down. It even seemed so to his own son, once. "My God, my God," he cried from the cross, "why hast thou forsaken me?" (Matt. 27:46 KJV).

> *Though God never promised to save anybody from trouble, he does promise to save us **in** trouble.*

Isn't it true that the reason we think God lets us down is actually our own self-centeredness? We put ourselves at the center of the universe and expect God to regard us as such, to make it his chief business to look after us. We consider God our personal nursemaid, if you will, who has nothing else to do but to watch our interests and save us from trouble. Whenever we mash our finger or have a flat tire, the cry goes up that God has let us down.

That is to misunderstand God. God never promised to save anybody from trouble, not even his own son. We are not the center of the universe. God is the center. His eternal purpose, not our personal pleasure, is the big thing.

Though God never promised to save anybody from trouble, he does promise to save us *in* trouble. God never allows temptation, trial, or suffering to come upon us for which he does not provide a way of escape or strength to withstand. That is a promise you can count on, and it will not let you down.

Toyohiko Kagawa was a great Christian activist and social reformer in Japan in the early twentieth century. When he was threatened with blindness and lay for months in the dark with a terrible pain in his eyes, doctors told him his health and sight were gone. He responded:

> As I lay forsaken in this dark room, God still gives light. At the center of things there is a heart. On yonder side of darkness there is light. To me all things are vocal. Oh, wonder words of love! God in every inanimate thing speaks to me! Thus, even in the darkness, I feel no sense of loneliness. . . . In the darkness I meet God face to face . . . I am being born of God . . . I am constantly praising God for the joy of the moments lived with Him.

What an amazing witness to God's everlasting faithfulness. Kagawa was able to testify to the truth: God never lets us down.

GOD NEVER LETS US OFF

Just as God never lets us down, He never lets us off. I like the way John Redhead expresses it:

> The love of God is not soft like a jellyfish. It has backbone. It is built on certain standards, and when those standards are not met, the penalty falls heavy and sure. God is a Father whose love never lets us down. The God who never lets us down is also the God of moral holiness.

James called God the "Father of Lights." Light suggests openness and judgment. Under God's light, everything is illumined. We can't be sentimental about it. God is not a soft, sentimental "yes" man, who winks at sin and says it doesn't matter. When you look at God through the person of Christ, you know that along with the tenderness of God comes also the terror of God. It is not that God finds any pleasure in punishing sin. It is just that there is something in God called holiness, and that holiness sets up a law which says that right is right and wrong is wrong, and wrong must be punished. Not even God can repeal that law.

Paul understood this divine law, as we read in his letter to the Galatians: "Do not be deceived: God cannot be mocked. A man reaps what he sows" (6:7). Do you want to know what that means? Again, Redhead explains it so clearly:

> It means that hangovers always come on the morning after. It means that the man who sows his wild oats will have his out-come tax to pay. It means that punishment is tied to sin like the burned spot to the blaze. It means that if a man eats salt herren, not even the grace of God can keep him from getting thirsty. It means that not even God can give a man a pass that will let him through the gates of sin without paying the price. It means that while God is always compassionate toward the sinner, He is never complacent about the sin. It means that while God is a Father whose love never lets us down, He is also a Father whose love can not let us off.

GOD NEVER LETS US GO

"God never lets us off" is a word of warning for people who would play fast and loose with sin, deluding themselves with the falsehood that they can get away with it. Know this: God is a Father whose love never lets us go. That is a word of hope for those who think they are past all hope.

Here is the greatest word that can be spoken about love: it keeps on loving in spite of everything. It takes no account of the wrongs done against it. No matter how often its offers are spurned, no matter how often its favors are refused, no matter how poignantly it is wounded, or how far away the loved one wanders, love always holds on, never gives up, never lets go.

When you look at God through Christ, this is the one thing you see standing out above all others. You remember when our Lord was criticized by self-righteous Pharisees for associating with people like the publicans and sinners, who were considered outcasts, he answered them by telling three little stories. A woman lost a piece of money—a poor woman who couldn't afford to lose even a penny—so she went through the house, moving the chairs and tables, taking out the rug and sweeping out every dark corner, looking for the coin. God is like that woman.

A shepherd had a hundred sheep, and when one strayed and was lost, the shepherd left the flock and went out on the mountains wild and high, seeking until he found it. God is like that shepherd.

A father had a son. The son showed himself ungrateful for his father's favor, turned his back on his father, went out to a far country and threw his life away. But that father always kept his candle burning in the window, and always kept watch, too. One day, there was a speck down the road. Gradually it got larger, came nearer. Down the stairs, through the open door, out through the gate—when he was yet a great way off, his father ran to meet him, embraced and kissed him. God, says Jesus, is like that father.

THE HEART OF THE MATTER

🌸 If you were asked to draw a picture of God, what would it look like?

🌸 Of the three affirmations you just read about—God never lets us down, God never lets us off, and God never lets us go—which one challenges you the most? Why?

🌸 Think of a time in your life when you experienced a consequence of sin. How did that affect your relationship to God?

COMING HOME

Do not be afraid, little flock,
for your Father has been pleased
to give you the kingdom.
Luke 12:32

Have you ever heard the one about the unhappy nun? No, it's not a joke. It's a story I read some time ago, and if you're already wondering what it could possibly have to do with your life, I hope you'll let me explain.

This nun had been raised in a very strict Catholic home. She had attended a parochial school, and all during those formative years of her life, she was terrified of the all-seeing eye of God. Her parents and her teachers had taught her that God was watching her all of the time. Unfortunately, they used the concept to frighten her into good behavior and to make sure she never got out of line. As a result, by the time she was an adult, she was a very fearful, intimidated person.

One day she was talking with another nun, a beautiful, happy person who had not grown up in a negative environment at all. She told this nun about her story and about how frightened she was of that eye of God that was watching her all of the time. But the other nun's sensitive and wise response was this: "Oh, my sister, you've got it wrong. God does see you all of the time, but do you know why? It is because he just can't take his eyes off of you!"

How clearly this nun understood the gospel. How sad that so many of us relate more to the first nun than the second, holding tight to a harmful and punitive understanding of God. We may not be conscious of it, but we often picture God as a judge, policeman, or prosecuting attorney. Admittedly, there are Scripture passages that suggest such an understanding. But the dominant witness of the Bible says something else: God is good, caring for people as a father or mother, offering grace, forgiveness, love, acceptance, and even new life with a generosity that can sometimes be hard to comprehend.

Again, that's exactly what this book is about—God's extravagant love. God's generous nature is not just a big-picture theory; it can be relevant and empowering every day of our lives, allowing us not only to give more of ourselves, but also to receive all that God has for us.

For some, this is a challenging concept. Like that nun, we may believe instead that God is out to get us. With that, we choose not to accept God's forgiveness, and find it terribly difficult, even next to impossible, to forgive ourselves for our failings, too. As a result, we spend endless days wandering, thinking there must be more, that we somehow could—or should—be better husbands or wives or sons or daughters or church members or friends or employees or Christians, but not having any idea about how to make it happen.

It can be a devastatingly painful life when we can't forgive ourselves for something we have done or something that has happened to us. Worse yet, it can keep us so focused on ourselves that we miss the ways God wants to use us in the lives of those around us. If we don't fully understand God's goodness, we'll be hard-pressed to pass it on to anyone else. Our Christian walk will be, at best, a hobbling one.

NO LIMITS

It is true that sometimes goodness can be produced by less than righteous folk, even evil persons. We can, however, expect limitless goodness from God. We talk a lot about the mystery of evil; what about the mystery of goodness? We receive daily gifts of God's grace, poured out freely without regard for our merit. God still makes the sun shine on the evil and the good, and the rain fall on the just and the unjust. But even more mysterious is God's Spirit at work bringing good out of the actions of weak, fallible, and sinful human beings. Joseph recognized that mystery when he confronted his brothers, who had sold him into slavery in Egypt. Joseph said, "You intended to harm me, but God intended it for good to accomplish what is now being done, the saving of many lives" (Gen. 50:20).

These days, though, acts of kindness, mercy, and generosity rarely become news. We live in a time when newspaper headlines and television news shows are dominated by stories about deceit, selfishness, immorality, corruption, catastrophe, murder, rape, drunkenness, hatred, and suspicion. Through some perverted sense of the dramatic, it is assumed that evil alone is news. This point of view warps our judgment and leads us to the pessimistic view that there is little good left in the world, and that few people have the capacity for goodness. To be sure, if we know our own hearts, we cannot deny the existence of evil, but we also cannot deny the presence of goodness.

Both are illustrated in the often-told story of the prodigal son, found in Luke 15. It's a familiar tale, and may even resemble our own. The son ran away from home, only to squander his wealth. Yet no matter how far that son wandered, God was in that far country, too, continuing to extend his hand no matter how evil the son had become. How do we know? First, the prodigal realized that he was in need. God's grace awakens us to our need, and that awakening is the first step toward our repentance and recovery. Second, the prodigal found a way to survive until he could decide what to do next: "So he went and hired himself out to a citizen of that country, who sent him to his fields to feed pigs" (v. 15). No work could have been more loathsome to a Jew, but this young man wanted to live. God gives us the will to live. But still the prodigal's situation was desperate. "He longed to fill his stomach with the pods that the pigs were eating, but no one gave him anything" (v. 16). So finally, when the prodigal fully realized where he was and what he had become, "he came to his senses"—and that was a supreme act of God's grace.

When we come to our senses, we face the life and death decision of, "What shall I do now?" The prodigal remembered his father and his father's house, so that's where he went . . . back home.

There has been debate about whether this son was truly penitent. Was he still motivated by self-interest, combined with the memory of where he could get three square meals a day? He probably didn't know himself. Can any of us be absolutely certain about our motives? Most sins provide some attraction or satisfaction, or we wouldn't indulge in them. To focus on our sins and to search our souls trying to convince ourselves that we are truly sorry for every moment of sinfulness, however, is not helpful. The important thing is to turn away from sin and to turn toward Jesus. The word *convert* means literally "to turn around." The important thing here is that this young man turned around, left the far country, and returned to his father. There comes a time to leave the past behind.

DAD ON THE DOORSTEP

You may find yourself at such a crossroads, and you may wonder what the reaction of your "father" will be. In the case of the prodigal son, he had enough recognition of his wrongdoing to rehearse his speech of confession. But instead of building on this good work of reform already begun, the father completely ignored it. How consistent that is with the God of Paul's testimony in Romans: "But God demonstrates his own love for us in this: While we were still sinners, Christ died for us." (5:8). Paul goes on to describe how that love works to lead us into new life. "For if, when we were God's enemies, we were reconciled to him through the death of his Son, how much more, having been reconciled, shall we be saved through his life!" (v. 10). The saving work begins when we return to the Father's house and are received with open arms.

In seeking to understand God's love, then, we must also understand that he wants to share that love with us. And we must be willing to turn around, wherever we are, and approach that doorstep of grace. David did so with an anguished cry for forgiveness in Psalm 51:

> Have mercy on me, O God,
> according to your unfailing love;
> according to your great compassion
> blot out my transgressions.
> Wash away all my iniquity
> and cleanse me from my sin.
> For I know my transgressions,
> and my sin is always before me. . . .
> Create in me a pure heart, O God,
> and renew a steadfast spirit within me.
> Do not cast me from your presence
> or take your Holy Spirit from me.
> Restore to me the joy of your salvation
> and grant me a willing spirit, to sustain me. (vv. 1–3, 10–12)

Do you feel the throbbing intensity of that prayer? There is nothing perfunctory about it. It is no surface recitation of some pious words. There are no pet phrases packaged mechanically together and tied with the dainty ribbon, "In Jesus' name, Amen." This is true prayer, the heart-cry of a broken man, one who knew his need for God.

Ancient editors say that Psalm 51 is David's plea after he had faced up to his blatant sin with Bathsheba. The prophet Nathan confronted David with his lust, adultery, intrigue, pretense, and shame. He reminded David of how he had schemed to get his trusted servant Uriah murdered. The king of Israel had deliberately broken five of the Ten Commandments.

At that point, David had no escape; the secret was out. Yet as we read the psalm, we feel that there was a kind of relief. The hidden thing had surfaced. The cancer that was eating David's soul away was now exposed and labeled for what it was. The need for subterfuge and deception was over.

Finally letting go, it seems, brings the relief of no longer having to hide and no longer having to lie. That's the meaning of confession: the end of pretension, the coming out of hiding.

Today, then, is a day for all of us to do the same. Finding the extravagant love of God—and stepping into the reality that yes, there really is more to life—begins with the simple choice to believe that God is for us and not against us. God's love is greater than we can imagine. It is greater than our sin. And his willingness to forgive is the open door to a new life.

Shall we approach the doorstep together?

THE HEART OF THE MATTER

❁ When you hear the story of the prodigal son, found in Luke 15, how do you feel? Do you identify with the son, the father, or even the older brother who is challenged by the prodigal's return? How so?

❁ Are there any challenges in your life that might be hindering you from coming home to the open arms of the Father? If so, how do you think you can overcome them?

❁ Are you more likely to think of God as demanding and punitive, or loving and good? Why do you think that is? Give an example of a time you experienced the goodness of God.

A ROADMAP FOR THE JOURNEY

Your word is a lamp to my feet
and a light for my path.
Ps. 119:105

For some, the Bible is an intimidating book. This view may stem from a misconception that the Scriptures are merely a rule book, a list of dos and don'ts, or a collection of stories about people who lived so long ago that nothing from their lives could actually speak to us today.

Nothing could be further from the truth. The Bible is considered living and active because it is the inspired Word of God, and since God is the same yesterday, today, and forever, the same can be said for the wisdom, promises, and guidance that God has so graciously offered through his Word. When considering the goodness and love of God, then, we can choose to view the Bible as simply one more way that God demonstrates his divine love. God has provided us, in essence, an ever-relevant guidebook for the Christian walk.

The beauty of the Bible is that it is a down-to-earth book written out of human experience. It is an account of people who came to know God and were known by God; who came to know others and to be known by others. It's a story about people who learned how to live a life of relationships, then shared their experience with others. The psalmist, for example, reached into the depths of his soul, pulled out his most intimate feelings, and laid them out for us to know and share. He spoke out of the gut-level of his experience. The fact that God knew him made him quiver!

"O LORD, you have searched me and you know me," he said in the first verse of Psalm 139. That's a frightening thought, that we are known by God. It's unnerving to sense that God knows everything about us, including our desires, our innermost feelings, our fears, our shortcomings, all of it. It can be equally as scary to be truly known by fellow humans. So we play hide-and-go-seek in our relationships, stretching our imaginations for fresh ways to remain hidden.

The Bible, however, has a way of exposing our hearts, all so we can overcome our fears and get beyond our self-centered discomforts.

SEEKING VS. TRUSTING

I remember an especially dry time a while back. Outwardly things were going well. All my children seemed to be at a good place in their lives. My wife and I were in excellent health and were enjoying each other and our stage in life. Asbury Theological Seminary, where I was serving as president, was thriving. We had our largest enrollment ever. The spiritual vitality of the students was inspiring. Our trustees had made the decision to establish an extension campus in Florida. I should have been "on top;" but not so.

I came dragging to my morning time of Scripture and devotional reading and prayer. I felt like the psalmist: "My soul thirsts for you, my body longs for you, in a dry and weary land where there is no water" (Ps. 63:1). I could have prayed with the psalmist:

Why, O LORD, do you stand far off? (Ps. 10:1)

How long, O LORD? Will you forget me forever?
. . . Give light to my eyes, or I will sleep in death. (Ps. 13:1–3)

My eyes fail,
looking for my God. (Ps. 69:3)

Concentrating during my time of devotion and prayer was difficult. I would realize that I had a read a passage of Scripture and not know what I had read. Or my mind would leap about as I sought to pray for a person or about a particular issue. But then I came across a passage from Julian of Norwich's *Showings*:

> And this vision taught me to understand that the soul's constant search pleases God greatly. For it cannot do more than seek, suffer and trust. And this is accomplished in every soul, to whom it is given by the Holy Spirit. And illumination by finding is of the Spirit's special grace, when it is his will. Seeking with faith, hope and love pleases our Lord, and finding pleases the soul and fills it full of joy. And so I was taught to understand that seeking is as good as contemplating, during the time that he wishes to permit the soul to be in labour. It is God's will that we seek on until we see him, for it is through this that he will show himself to us, of his special grace, when it is his will.

The passage reminded me that I had been seeking the Lord, but I did not *trust him completely*. Over a period of about three weeks I worked on my trust. I went back to my initial Christian commitment when I accepted Christ as my Savior and was baptized. I rehearsed some of those trying, testing, and troubling times when I had trusted the Lord and was delivered. And gradually the confidence and the emotional experience of Christ's presence returned.

Part of understanding the Bible for the gift that it is, then, involves reading it with trust and faith, believing that it can—and will—change our lives. Every time we read it, it offers a revelation and an encounter with the living God. There are many gods, but in the Bible we encounter the living God: the God of creation (Gen. 1); the God of covenant (Gen. 12:1–7); the God of Abraham, Isaac, and Jacob (Exod. 3:1–6); the God of deliverance (Exod. 9:1–7); the God of compassion who binds us in love (Hos. 11:1–4); the God of justice and mercy (Mic. 6:6–8); the God of pursuing love who seeks us in love even to his own death in Jesus on the cross.

In our own lives, we serve many gods: wealth, materialism, money, greed. But the Bible says, "What good is it for a man to gain the whole world, yet forfeit his soul?" (Mark 8:36).

We worship the god of sex and pleasure, but the Bible says, "Do you not know that your body is a temple of the Holy Spirit, who is in you, whom you have received from God? You are not your own; you were bought at a price. Therefore honor God with your body" (1 Cor. 6:19–20).

We are tempted to serve the god of power, prestige, and worldly influence. However, the Bible says, "But many who are first will be last, and the last first" (Mark 10:31).

Some even serve the god of narrow, selfish nationalism, but the Bible says that God "made every nation of men, that they should inhabit the whole earth; and he determined the times set for them and the exact places where they should live" (Acts 17:26).

In addition to offering revelation and a personal encounter with God, the Bible is an invitation to life. The Bible is gospel, literally translated "good news," and not just Matthew, Mark, Luke, and John. The whole of it is gospel.

The great events of the Old Testament—creation, covenant, and exodus—all reflect the gospel. The movement of God is always a movement of love toward us, a love that knows no limits. The big story of the Bible is the story of God staying with us through his grace, wooing us, loving us, seeking to restore us to our created image and bring us back into fellowship. The last verse of Psalm 23 says it well: "Surely goodness and love will follow me all the days of my life, and I will dwell in the house of the LORD forever."

If we miss that invitation in the Old Testament, we can't miss it in the New. It is an engraved personal invitation, personally delivered by Jesus Christ. He pictured it for us in the series of parables we discussed yesterday: the lost coin, the lost sheep, and the lost son. You will find all of them in Luke 15, one of the most beloved chapters in the Bible. It has been called the "gospel in the gospel," because it contains the distilled essence of the good news Jesus came to share.

> *In addition to offering revelation and a personal encounter with God, the Bible is an invitation to life.*

And when we read these stories, no matter how long ago they were actually penned, we can find direction and guidance for our everyday lives. A word of caution about guidance, however, and a reminder that guidance in the Christian life is a matter of grave concern and a place where discipline is sorely needed.

One of the most bizarre distortions of guidance was seen in Jim Jones and the Guyana tragedy. Hundreds of people died in a ceremonial suicide following the instruction of a man who claimed to be divinely led. There are many far less dramatic examples of the distortion of guidance. A student who has neglected her studies and comes to the final exam, praying for divine guidance. An athletic team prays for divine guidance to show them the way to victory. Persons who give little thought to how God would have them spend their money seek God's guidance in making money and accumulating wealth. You can add to the list good people seeking God's guidance for questionable enterprises and even bad people brashly seeking divine sanction and guidance for the unrighteous direction of their lives.

As a result, we must consider the issue of guidance carefully. But note two clear facts. One, Scripture not only promises guidance; it assumes the fact of guidance throughout its pages. And two, Jesus also promised guidance through the gift of the Spirit:

> I still have many things to say to you, but you cannot bear them now. When the Spirit of truth comes, he will guide you into all the truth; for he will not speak on his own, but will speak whatever he hears, and he will declare to you the things that are to come. He will glorify me, because he will take what is mine and declare it to you. All that the Father has is mine. For this reason I said that he will take what is mine and declare it to you. (John 16:12–15 NRSV)

God's wisdom and guidance, then, come to us in a variety of ways. There are those rare times when God speaks dramatically in a vision or a dream or even in an audible voice, as with Paul and Peter and others whose experiences are recorded in the book of Acts. Other times, our wisdom and guidance come through the still, small voice of God within us, as we allow the indwelling Christ to be vibrantly alive in us. That still, small voice can be heard by those who listen obediently, by those who want passionately to do God's will, and by those who are about the business of giving their lives over completely to the Lordship of Christ. And most certainly we receive wisdom and guidance through God's Word.

Since the beginning of time, God has spoken through prophets and poets and dreams and visions and angelic messengers. We have the record of that in the Scriptures.

Then, too, God gave himself to us in Jesus Christ, and that story comes alive through the pages of our New Testament. So as we immerse ourselves in God's Word, we will hear the still, small voice as the Spirit causes that Word to energize all our thoughts and actions.

The central source of God's guidance is in the Scriptures. If God's wisdom and guidance are going to be ours in an ongoing way, if guidance is not to be a hit-or-miss, frantic seeking of God's will in particular situations, then we must immerse ourselves in the Scriptures. When we are familiar with God's Word through daily reading, meditation, and study, we will seldom flounder for want of guidance.

Knowledge of Scripture gives us a poise and a confidence about the will and ways of God that enable us to respond with certainty to that inward nudging, those intimations and intuitions that we feel so deeply. The inward assurance that we need to act on that nudge and those intimations is often confirmed by the Word of God. And it is our personal fellowship with the Lord in prayer and through the study of God's Word that is the ongoing source of wisdom and guidance that James says can be ours by faith.

THE HEART OF THE MATTER

❋ How does the Bible fit into your walk with God?

❋ What stands in the way of you having a deeper understanding and appreciation of the Scriptures? How could that challenge be overcome?

❋ How do you think God could use the Bible to help guide, encourage, and esteem you?

TAKING IT ALL IN

Shout for joy to the Lord, all the earth. . . .
For the Lord is good and his love endures forever;
his faithfulness continues through all generations.
Ps. 100:1, 5

I n receiving an award from the Religious Public Relations Council, newsman Bill Moyers said, "I've given up on the beat of politics . . . I've given up on the beat of international affairs because I want to cover this beat [the religious beat]. It is the biggest story of the millennium."

Moyers was talking about the spiritual quest of the American people. Then he addressed his colleagues in journalism with this challenge: "You must fasten on to what is the story of the twenty-first century, which is looking for a new human story, laced with God." In his closing remarks, Moyers said, "I sense such a deep and powerful stirring in the world that is religious in nature, exciting and hopeful. I'm hoping that my colleagues in journalism sense this and report on it, because it is the story of the next fifty years."

I like Moyers' line—"a new human story, laced with God." Not a bad vision.

Over the past few days, we've covered a lot of bases in terms of who God is—as opposed to who we think God is. It's an important work. It's not surprising that many Christians know who God is and what God is like; and yet, deep down, at the level of their emotions, there exists a very different feeling and picture of God. That deep-down feeling prevents us from experiencing lasting spiritual growth and victory in our lives.

Joseph Seka has written a helpful article, "Will the Real God Please Stand Up?" In that article, Seka lists some of the faulty concepts and feelings about God found among both Christians and non-Christians:

> First, there is the legal god. This god keeps account of what we do and waits for us to step out of line. . . . Second, the "Gotcha god" resembles Sherlock Holmes. . . . Like a private investigator, he's always following and gathering evidence. Third, there is the Sitting Bull god. This god sits in the yoga position and expects burnt offerings. . . . . Fourth, there is the philosopher god. . . . He is distant, cold, too-busy, and has a "Do not disturb" sign on his office. Last, there is the pharaoh god. . . . He is harsh and demanding, and says, "Make more bricks."

Not many of us would describe God in any of these ways, but isn't it true that at the feeling level, we have perceived God in at least some of these ways? We could imagine a God who keeps account of what we do; a God who expects us to try to please him all the time; a God who has a "Do not disturb" sign on his door; a God who is always demanding more than we can give.

The truth, however, is this: developing a healthy, authentic experience of God, harmonized in thought and feeling, is an ongoing growth process that comes with maturity in Christ. And that begins by recognizing God's goodness and love, and remembering that God really is for us and not against us.

This week, we've considered a few of the ways God has demonstrated his great love for us. But it is only a start. Creation itself provides a clue about how God relates to the world and what it means to us and our adoption.

Grace, which is the dynamic, radical love of God, is demonstrated in creation; in fact, creation *is* grace. To be sure, a lot of debate swirls around the notion of creation. But whether we follow a particular scientifically oriented concept of creation or give a literal interpretation to the creation story in Genesis, there remains a creative moment that is integral to the relationship between God and the world. The traditional belief that God created everything from nothing is very helpful because it describes the relationship between God and creation as one of sheer love.

After each act of creation in bringing the world into being, the Genesis writer says, "And God saw that it was good." When all was finished with the creation of Adam and Eve, the response is, "It was very good."

God, in utterly free love, created the world, and the climax of that creation was man and woman: "So God created man in his own image, in the image of God he created him; male and female he created them" (Gen. 1:27). That means that you and I, because he created us, are walking, talking examples of his love here on earth. And that love can play out in the way we love ourselves, love others around us, and love God in return.

In coming days, we'll continue to consider the divine aspects of love and goodness and how they can affect us on a highly personal level. But before we get there, a review would be in order. The innate goodness of God must be an established fact in our hearts and minds before anything else will make sense.

Remember that you and I are not always good, but God is. Even though human goodness is sometimes produced by wrong motives, by less than righteous persons—even by evil people— we can, nevertheless, expect limitless goodness from God.

God offers us, as we have seen this week, the ability to run into his open arms and be forgiven; the chance to start over with new life; direction and guidance through his Word; the opportunity to communicate with him through prayer; and above all, his very self.

Have you made the choice to accept God's invitation to new life by acknowledging Jesus as your personal Lord and Savior? If you'd like to learn more about that, turn to page 304 now.

As you read through highlights from the lessons of each day, consider looking back at your answers to the Heart of the Matter questions, and prayerfully contemplating what the next steps of growth in each area might be. Prepare yourself for the weeks ahead, as well. Next we'll consider the incredible gift of the gospel, and how the reality of the life of Jesus can be an example for our own.

INCANDESCENT AMAZEMENT

The first day of our study started with the big picture: it invited us to focus on the amazing fact that God is the sovereign Creator of the universe; that God is bigger than any concept we can hold in our minds, yet in his infinite love desires a personal relationship with us; and that the chaos that we sometimes feel overwhelmed by is actually an illusion—God's reality is law, beauty, and order breathed into creation in divine wisdom. Infusing it all is the idea of "incandescent amazement," the wonder and awe of all that God is, all that God has done, and all that God is yet to do. We may begin with lots of doubt and questions, but if we will focus our thinking on the beautiful miracle of creation, we can begin a new conversation with our Creator.

GOD'S CREATION IS GOOD

We read about how the God of creation is an artist, painter, and sculptor—and the creation is his masterpiece. Sometimes we feel distant from God and doubt God's love for us because of challenging circumstances, yet God has promised to deliver us not *from* our troubles, but *in* them. God owns the darkness as well as the light, and God is present in the night as well as in the day. Although we want to walk in the light, sometimes God reveals himself most vividly in the midst of our darkness. Have you reflected on the presence of God in your struggles and challenges? Is God showing you places where you can open up to a new awareness of his love?

A GRACIOUS GOD

God gives us not only a listening ear and an understanding heart; God freely gives us his son, his very self. Yes, God loves us that much. We must understand, though, that our personal relationship with God is all about choice. The lives of the saints are an example of the habits of holiness that become embodied in our lives as virtues. If we will choose to make it a habit to seek the presence of God, we can know his grace in our times of challenge. Have you chosen him?

THE PICTURE OF GOD

We all carry images of God that may be distorted from the truth of who God really is. We may imagine God to be an angry judge or a referee keeping score of sins. But if we will look again at the witness of the saints and the words of the Bible, we'll discover a God of extravagant love and sheer joy who longs for communion with us. Jesus described God's deep love in the parables as a woman who swept her entire home just to find one lost coin, a shepherd who searched the hillsides to retrieve his lost sheep, or the father who received his prodigal son with open arms. Are you able to stretch your imagination to include this radical picture of God?

COMING HOME

Remember the story of the prodigal son as told in Luke 15. No matter how far the son had wandered and no matter how many sins he had committed, his father was waiting on the doorstep for his return. All wrongs were instantly forgiven. God offers the same grace to us. No matter who we are, no matter where we are, we can always come home to the idea that there is a loving Father ready to receive us. Are there any places to which you haven't yet "come home," or admitted your need for God's love, grace, and acceptance? If so, take a moment and bring them to God in prayer. He is ready and able to hear whatever you have to say.

A ROADMAP FOR THE JOURNEY

The Bible is so much more than a rule book. It is, instead, living and active, offering us relevant guidance for today. Remember that it is a down-to-earth telling of human experience, an account of people who came to know God and were known by God. As such, reading the Scriptures on a daily basis can help us know and be known, as well. The Bible offers us hope, wisdom, knowledge, promise, joy, direction, and more. All we have to do is open it up and believe that it was inspired by God, just for us. So how is that daily dose of Scriptures coming? Have you been able to develop a regular diet of the Word that can help you grow? If not, what's standing in your way, and what can be done to remove those obstacles?

Week Two

A LOVE LIKE NO OTHER

THE HINT
HALF GUESSED

No one has ever seen God, but God the One and Only,
who is at the Father's side, has made him known.
John 1:18

J ust as modern painting is defined by Picasso, and modern music by Stravinsky, modern poetry is most often associated with a brilliant master: T. S. Eliot. Born in St. Louis in 1888, he was raised by doting parents and four older sisters. Eliot was a precocious child who spent a year in a Massachusetts boarding school to polish his rough edges before going to Harvard to earn several degrees.

At Harvard, Eliot began writing poetry and was recognized early by the famous young poets of the day. He couldn't see how he could make a living writing poetry—and indeed he didn't, until he won the Nobel Prize for Literature in 1948. His most famous and dramatic breakthrough as a poet of renown was "The Waste Land." Some critics and scholars consider it the most important English-language poem of the twentieth century. It is a commentary on modern civilization, the triumph of materialism, and a generation that had lost its soul.

Countless college undergraduates have quoted "The Waste Land" to give voice to their alienation, existentialism, and contempt for a society that seems bent on either getting rich or blowing itself up. T. S. Eliot's poetry expressed the despairing cynicism of a generation who had lost their way, their faith, and their hope.

Imagine the surprise of other poets who had championed his work, imagine the surprise of graduate students writing dissertations about the meaning of Eliot's poetry . . . imagine their surprise when he converted to Christianity!

This is one of our most distinctive convictions as Christians: God became flesh, the divine became human.

On the morning of June 29, 1927, having completed several months of instruction, T. S. Eliot was baptized in a small parish church in the Cotswolds. The next day, he was confirmed in the Christian faith by Bishop Thomas Banks Strong. For the rest of his life he remained a "high church" Anglican, attending morning mass nearly every day.

Had Eliot changed his mind about humanity, about the emptiness and soullessness of our times? No. He still despaired of human nature. He still agonized over his own sins. But he came to sense another presence—something sacred and holy, something occasionally breaking through into our realm of time and space, toil and trouble. God never overwhelmed him, never gave clear and unmistakable signs. It was just "hints and guesses" as Eliot says in "The Dry Salvages," a segment within *Four Quartets:*

> Hints followed by guesses; and the rest
> Is prayer, observance, discipline, thought and action.
> The hint half guessed, the gift half understood, is
>   Incarnation.

Don't you wish you had said that? I do! "The hint half guessed, the gift half understood, is Incarnation." This is one of our most distinctive convictions as Christians: God became flesh, the divine became human.

THE GOSPEL OF JOHN

John expressed it, "And the Word became flesh and lived among us, and we have seen his glory, the glory as of a father's only son, full of grace and truth" (John 1:14 NRSV). The Nicene Creed, in order to make clear the heart of our Christian doctrine, puts it this way:

> We believe in one Lord, Jesus Christ,
> the only Son of God,
> eternally begotten of the Father,
> God from God, Light from Light,
> true God from true God,
> begotten, not made,
> of one Being with the Father;
> through him all things were made.
> For us and for our salvation
>   he came down from heaven,
>   was incarnate by the Holy Spirit of the Virgin Mary. . . .

But what does it all mean? Incarnation. Eliot called it "the hint half guessed, the gift half understood."

I reached for the dictionary to look up the word *hint*. Had I been misusing the word? How was this world renowned poet using it? I found two definitions. The first: "An indirect suggestion or implication; subtle or covert illusion." The Incarnation—subtle? *Like a sledgehammer,* I thought. The second: "A slight indication or trace." The Incarnation—slight? Trace? Only if flesh and blood and bone—a full human being—is a slight trace of anything.

I was winning my argument with Eliot. How could he refer to the Incarnation as a hint? This is something so explicit that it is almost impossible to miss. Then I realized how foolish I was—how futile to ever argue. Eliot was a poet, and preachers are poets—that is, when we are at our best we are poets. Some of the most meaningful passages of Scripture are poetry. The message of God is spoken in parable, images, hyperbole. The language is often metaphorical and poetic, not scientific and rational. Listen to the psalmist: "I feel like an owl in the desert, like a lonely owl in a far-off wilderness" (102:6 NLT). Or this: "Let the floods clap their hands; let the hills sing together for joy at the presence of the LORD" (98:8–9 NRSV).

Listen to the prophet Jeremiah: "Oh that my head were a spring of water, and my eyes a fountain of tears, so that I might weep day and night for the slain of my poor people!" (Jer. 9:1 NRSV).

Listen to the words of Jesus from John's Gospel:

- ❋ "I am the good shepherd." (10:11)
- ❋ "I am the light of the world." (9:5)
- ❋ "I am the way, the truth, and the life." (14:6)
- ❋ "I am the gate." (10:7)
- ❋ "I am the bread of life." (6:35)

Listen to Peter: "Come to him, a living stone, though rejected by mortals yet chosen and precious in God's sight, and like living stones, let yourselves be built into a spiritual house . . ." (1 Pet. 2:4–5 NRSV).

Listen to the prophet Malachi's word about the coming Messiah: "But for you who revere my name the sun of righteousness shall rise, with healing in its wings. You shall go out leaping like calves from the stall" (Mal. 4:2 NRSV).

And listen to Luke talk about the Messiah Christ who has come: "By the tender mercy of our God, the dawn from on high will break upon us, to give light to those who sit in darkness and in the shadow of death, to guide our feet into the way of peace" (Luke 1:78–79 NRSV).

Poetry, image, metaphor, parable. Eliot was in good company—in company with those who penned our treasury of Holy Scripture. So instead of examining the poet's words, I started meditating and reflecting. "The hint half guessed." Yes, that's the Incarnation in our experience. Not from God's side, but from ours. God was presenting himself as clearly as he could. But we do the guessing, don't we?

We're guessing at the meaning of this child, this man, this life, this death, these hints wrapped up in ancient stories replete with angels and shepherds and stables and rotten kings and disinterested bureaucrats. Think about it, in the way Methodist preacher Bob Olmstead reflected on it:

> It is not the way of the sacred to overwhelm us with instant revelation; God gives only hints. And it is easy to miss the hints when we're in the midst of troubled marriages, financial hardships, and physical disease.
>
> It is even easier to miss the hints when all is going well, when our tables groan with abundance and we have more wealth than our grandparents ever dreamed of. It is especially easy to miss the hints of divinity when we take realistic stock of our own shortcomings, our faults and failings, the urges and desires we admit to no one, and only occasionally to ourselves.

Incarnation, God coming to us in Jesus. It's a mystery, a "hint half guessed" by most of us, "the gift half understood." But it's still real and powerful. Even a half receiving of this gift offers more meaning than any other promise of fulfillment for our lives.

THE HEART OF THE MATTER

❋ Has God ever revealed himself to you through hints or guesses? How has your understanding been shaped by such revelations?

❋ What is your favorite verse of Scripture? How does it speak to you with poetry and images?

❋ How does Jesus' Incarnation offer hope and meaning for your life?

WHY WE STILL
PREACH THE CROSS

Jesus said, "Father, forgive them,
for they do not know what they are doing."
Luke 23:34

Some years ago, when First United Methodist Church in Dallas erected a huge, crude wooden cross in front of their church for Lent, it was viewed as an eyesore. As the story goes, there was even a phone call emphatically asking the pastor, "Can't you do something with that dreadful cross?" The woman had apparently visited the Dallas Museum of Art across the street, and was bothered by the contrast between the loveliness of the culture in the museum and the ugliness in front of the church.

"Can't you do something about that dreadful cross?" It's a question that hits close to home, and has throughout the ages. What can—and what will—we do about that "dreadful" cross?

Even the great English poet John Milton, master of words, couldn't say. He wrote his ever-lovely "On the Morning of Christ's Nativity" in 1629, and hoped to offer a companion poem called "The Passion" a year later. But the challenge was too great; after toiling over some eight verses, he finally gave up. Completely unsatisfied—and feeling the subject was "above the years he had"—he left it unfinished. Milton had been able to write meaningfully and beautifully about Christ's birth, but when it came to his suffering and death, the language escaped him.

And what of us? Many of us are powerless to understand the cross, much less put it into words. We grasp for meaning, we hope for clarity, but like that Dallas church, we find ourselves confronted with the question: can't we do something with that dreadful cross? Is it enough for us to simply put it aside as Milton did, walking away with it unfinished?

Personally, I don't think so. And the reason is found in the words Jesus himself uttered while nailed there: "Father, forgive them, for they do not know what they are doing" (Luke 23:34). To be sure, those words from Jesus' last pulpit confront us with the sins in our own lives. Sin is the reason Jesus was there, and sin is the issue he was addressing in these words.

"Father, forgive them."

IMAGINE THE SCENE

Imagine the scene, if you will. The sentence had been passed. The soldiers had mocked Jesus with a crown of thorns and a purple robe. They saluted him with the taunt, "Hail, King of the Jews." They spat upon him and knelt down in mock homage. They led him through the gawking crowd and pressed Simon of Cyrene into bearing his cross up to the crest of Calvary, and there they crucified him.

What a mixture of emotion and response. Evil and good were doing battle. The holiness of God and the sinfulness of humankind were locked in struggle. Two robbers hung on either side of Jesus, so even in death, he was set amidst human need and sin in its most desperate expression.

The crowd continued to mock. They didn't understand what was going on. Though they taunted, "Let this Christ, this King of Israel, come down now from the cross, that we may see and believe" (Mark 15:32). they were not earnestly grasping for faith. What mystery is here, yet what love! Rev. William Booth, General of the Salvation Army, said long ago, "It is because Jesus did not come down from the cross that we believe in him."

We must not position the cross of Christ back in the first century, nor see it as an isolated event on that skull-shaped hill. We must see it right among us, present now. The black sky brooding over Golgotha is arched above us, too. The tempest and the earthquake that terrified Jerusalem terrifies us also as we envision the cross of Christ, not as something far away, but as present now.

To be sure, it is certain that Jesus died only once: "And they crucified him" (Mark 15:24). It was a once-and-for-all death, in the year 30 AD, on Calvary's hill. Yet, it was for us that Jesus died.

The death of Jesus was an absolute necessity on God's part. Jesus was the incarnate love of God and had come to reveal the heart of God to us. Had he refused the cross, the love of God would have been limited.

No, it's not easy to talk theoretically about the profound truth of the cross, but it is essential. And it is equally essential that when we preach Jesus on the cross, we don't leave him there. The reality that Jesus died for us and yet, he lives, must be central to our Christian experience.

"I FEEL SO ASHAMED"

I remember picking up a copy of Henry C. Whitley's book *Laughter in Heaven* one early, snowed-in Saturday morning. I didn't know much about him, but discovered quickly that Whitley was a Scottish Presbyterian preacher and one-time minister of St. Giles Cathedral in Edinburgh; this was a kind of autobiography of his ministry. He got my attention in the introduction by recalling the most memorable sermon he had ever heard. It lasted just half a minute.

> The man who preached it was an old minister, white-haired, bent, but with a voice which was still strong and warming, and he had a gentle, hurt face. The church was grim and dull and

depressing, as was the "area" in which it stood, "one of the forgotten slums of Edenborough."

Whitley said that the preacher, at that time, was trying to run a boys' club in half a dozen rooms of condemned property nearby. He had gone to church that morning reluctantly; it was his opinion that the church was out of touch and woefully inadequate to the problems of suffering and despairing people with whom he worked.

> The building was three-quarters empty, the congregation included a few men and the rest women and children. . . . The service had followed the normal pattern and everyone sat back waiting for the sermon. Wearily, the minister looked around his unencouraging congregation, and then in a voice half-broken with emotion, he declared: "I have no sermon this morning, nothing would come and I've been so busy with many things—I'm not sure what I believe, except that Jesus lives. Forgive me, I feel so ashamed." The tears were now trickling down his cheeks—struggling, he pronounced the blessing and left the pulpit.

Bless that old man! The truth is, he had nothing to be ashamed of. I've been there myself—though I have to admit I've never made that kind of confession in a sermon. But yes, I've been there, feeling that inadequacy and doubt, having questions, and knowing nothing more than the fact that Jesus lives.

The fact that Jesus died for us and yet still lives is the shaping dynamic of the Christian life. And we must never lose sight of it, no matter what happens.

The cross is not only a work of redemption for our sin, but it concerns our eternal salvation, as well. The rugged, dreadful wood is a reminder of what beauty lies in store.

That's what Paul was saying to the Corinthians: "For the message of the cross is foolishness to those who are perishing, but to us who are being saved it is the power of God" (1 Cor. 1:18). It is, in essence, extravagant love. Jesus' word from the cross, "Father, forgive them," confronts us with our sin, but it is far more. Jesus is God's witness in word and deed. In word: "Father, forgive them." In deed: dying on the cross for our salvation. As a result, we preach the cross because we want everyone to know that there is more love in God than sin in us. It is the very picture of justification by grace through faith.

NOT GUILTY

I remember going to court once with a young man. I was there to offer my personal and pastoral support. It was a trial before a judge, not before a jury. The prosecuting attorney and the defense attorney made their cases to the judge; they had already submitted written testimonies and other evidence to her. After the arguments, the judge invited the young man to stand before the bar of the court. Then she began to speak to him—it was a kind of lecture. The more she spoke, the more I thought to myself, *This is it; he's going to end up in jail.*

> *We preach the cross because we want everyone to know that there is more love in God than sin in us.*

We were all surprised when the judge came to her conclusion: "This court finds you not guilty." I sighed deeply as I saw a look of tremendous release come over the young man's face. But then came the challenging word from the judge:

"Young man, because the court finds you not guilty does not mean that you are innocent."

I knew, as did the young man, that there was not enough evidence in the court of law to convict him of what he was accused, but indeed, he was not innocent.

That's a hint, however faint, of the meaning of justification by grace through faith. We are all guilty. As the Scriptures remind us, we have all sinned and fallen short of the glory of God. Not even one of us is righteous—and how well we know that deep down, don't we? But God has shown and reaffirmed his great love for us by giving us Jesus Christ as a sacrifice, a substitute, a power over sin. His death on the cross was death on our behalf. When we receive his sacrificial love by faith, we are justified; that is, we are made right with God.

Justification is a metaphor from the law courts, so when we talk about salvation as justification, the imagery is that of being on trial before God. The Greek word translated "to justify" means not to change a person's nature, but to treat, reckon, or account someone in a certain way. This is the picture: when we appear before God, we are anything but innocent. We have sinned; we are estranged; we have broken the relationship; we are utterly guilty. Yet, God treats, reckons, and counts us as if we were innocent. That is what justification means.

In the Christian view of reality, we talk about justification by grace through faith. Through our faith in Jesus Christ, and what God has done for us in Jesus Christ, we are justified. It is all a matter of grace—God's grace—God's gift of love and full acceptance of us.

The cross is the ultimate expression of God's love. It is a vivid picture of God's nature. It became real to me in a poster that moved me to tears. The words on the poster were these: "Do you want to know how much God loves you?" Jesus answered, "This much!" The picture was Jesus, his arms outstretched and nailed to a cross. So, Jesus spreads out his arms on the cross and says to each one of us, "This is how much I love you."

THE HEART OF THE MATTER

� Think of a time in your life when you were aware of being guilty of something. How did you deal with your feelings in those circumstances?

� Have you ever received the gift of forgiveness? Describe your experience.

� Are you holding on to feelings of guilt and sin in your relationship with God? If so, have you considered asking God to release you from that burden so you might fully embrace the extravagant love Jesus embodied on the cross?

HE COMES AS HE CAME

> *Blessed is the king*
> *who comes in the name of the Lord.*
> *Luke 19:38*

The *New Yorker* magazine once ran a cartoon depicting that dramatic story in the Old Testament when Moses parts the Red Sea and the Israelites pass through on dry land. To be a little more precise, the cartoon takes place at the point the water has been parted and the Israelites are moving swiftly through the passage. Moses is irritated because someone has obviously said something to him. He replies to the man next to him, "Of course it's damp underfoot, but that strikes me as a pretty petty complaint to be making at a time like this."

I don't know about you, but I can identify. I've found myself reluctant to get my feet wet when faith leads me on a new and untraveled road. Thank goodness Jesus didn't feel the same way.

Today, we're going to look at the journey Jesus took to Jerusalem; it's the part of the New Testament story that gives us Palm Sunday, and it has much to say to those of us who are on our own journeys of faith.

I'd like to look at that march, then, with the idea that Jesus still comes as he came. There are three scenes in this Palm Sunday story as Luke recorded it, scenes that depict the character of Jesus, how he came to the place of his destiny, and how he comes to the world today—and to us. Let's explore each one.

Jesus on a Donkey

Our first scene is the one normally associated with the day: Jesus riding into Jerusalem on a donkey. Palm branches are waving, and people are shouting. The excitement is so great that people have literally taken off their outer garments and spread them in the road. This, after all, is the Messiah, the Promised One. The shout becomes an uproar: "Blessed is the king who comes in the name of the Lord" (Luke 19:38). The king is coming, and no one can miss him—partly because he is riding on a donkey.

To put things in context, we need to remember that, in those days, when a king went to war, he rode a horse. But when he came in peace, he rode a donkey. Zechariah, one of the Old Testament prophets, included this image in his understanding of the Messiah. "Rejoice greatly, O Daughter of Zion! Shout, Daughter of Jerusalem! See, your king comes to you, righteous and having salvation, gentle and riding on a donkey, on a colt, the foal of a donkey" (Zech. 9:9). By appearing in Jerusalem on a donkey, Jesus presented new ideas about peace, power, and humility. Frankly, those are lessons that we still need to learn.

A colleague of mine, Dr. William Ritter, is one of the most creative preachers I know. One Palm Sunday, he preached a sermon called "Clubs are No Longer Trump." In it, he made the point that we all succumb to the notion that power is for using, and that some problems can be solved only by violence—whether it be the problem of an unwanted enemy at the border, an unwanted murderer on death row, or an unwanted child in the womb. We need to search our minds and hearts to see if we have not fallen victim to that illusion—that problems can be solved only by violence.

Jesus shows another way. It is a way of power, but not of violence. It is a way of peace that comes not by the sword, but rather by strength of will and a new set of weapons.

There is an old Chinese proverb that says: "If thine enemy offend thee, buy each of his children a drum." Commenting on that, Dr. Ritter said:

> What it means, of course, is that truly creative individuals will find ways to deal with enemies that subdue without destruction. Jesus had some suggestions along these lines that were even more radical. Return blessings for curses, he suggested, invite persecutors over for supper. If an enemy forces you to carry a pack for a long distance, carry it twice as far, and see if you can't achieve some kind of reconciliation along the way. Put your ingenuity to work, says Jesus. Put your prayers to work. Put your consistent witness for truth to work. Put passive resistance to work. Put patience to work.

Do not be deceived—the Christian who follows Jesus does not go unarmed into the daily combats of ordinary life. The Christian merely has different weapons in his or her arsenal.

JESUS WEPT OVER THE CITY

Now, back to our Palm Sunday scene. In Luke 19:41–42, we learn that Jesus has come to Jerusalem.

> As he approached Jerusalem and saw the city, he wept over it and said, "If you, even you, had only known on this day what would bring you peace—but now it is hidden from your eyes."

Jesus still comes today as he came to Jerusalem: with compassion. He wept over the city. In the days ahead, we'll reflect on compassion from a number of different perspectives.

Compassion is who Jesus is, as well as the dynamic he calls us to. But for now, register this truth: authentic love calls for compassion, and compassion is often painful, bringing us, with Jesus, to tears.

G. Campbell Morgan was a powerful man, and one of the great English preachers of another generation. As a young seminary student, he fell in love with a young woman, but he was reluctant to propose to her, explaining, "I think God has laid it on my heart to say some radical things to the church. I may not be a success; I may be persecuted. I don't want to drag you into that. In five or six years, perhaps I will be established, and then I can offer you my hand in marriage."

Her immediate reply was, "If I can't climb the mountain with you, I'd be ashamed to meet you at the top." What a picture of compassion! Compassion is love that is deep enough to "climb the mountain" with another.

If we are to follow Jesus, our love must be so deep that we are willing to climb the mountain, as well.

JESUS COMES IN JUDGMENT

Once Jesus arrived in the city, he headed for the temple. This is where we join him in Luke 19:45–46.

> Then he entered the temple area and began driving out those who were selling. "It is written," he said to them, "'My house will be a house of prayer,' but you have made it a 'den of robbers.'"

Jesus, once again, comes to us as he came to Jerusalem: in judgment. Now, I realize that judgment is not a popular word. It doesn't feel good for some folks who, for at least half of a century, have been schooled in moral relativism and the notion that what is right and good can be settled by popular vote. This sort of mushy thinking is always coming to a head in some dramatic way.

It comes to a head in the devastation of children of separated parents because we have thought too selfishly about divorce. It comes to a head in millions of unwanted pregnancies, many of which have ended in abortions because we have had sex education without moral teaching. It comes to a head in crippling financial debts because we have succumbed to the greed of our flesh without practicing fiscal discipline.

> *If we are to follow Jesus, our love must be so deep that we are willing to climb the mountain.*

These are the things you might expect me to discuss. But what about war? As I write this, the war in Iraq is tearing our nation apart. The conflict is not only destroying thousands of lives, it is costing billions of dollars that could be used for improving human lives in this country and around the world. Great pain and confusion accompany any consideration of it, and the question remains how judgment fits in.

These difficult issues cut to the core of our faith and sometimes reveal our morals in uncomfortable ways. Because our culture teaches that we should determine what is right and good by popular vote, we might feel challenged by the idea of the judgment of Jesus. But the church is not a democracy—it can never be subject to majority rule. The authority of the church comes not from the consent of the governed, but from Christ, its head, who rules through the Word of Scripture and the Holy Spirit.

Christ comes to us in the world today just as he came to Jerusalem: in judgment. So who can abide the day of his coming? Only those who are willing to lose their lives for his sake. Only those who will do "unto the least of these" because they do unto Christ. Only those who love their sisters and brothers as an expression of the loving God. Only those who move beyond saying, "Lord, Lord," to acting as the Lord would have them act.

I could go on and on, but you get the point. Christ has made the way clear, and we are to walk in it by faith. When we fail to take that seriously, we invite judgment.

Yes, Jesus comes as he came. First, on a donkey, in humility, showing us new peace and power; second, in compassion; and third, in judgment. There's a saying that you can't work for McDonald's and sell Wendy's burgers. Well, you can't! You can't go to the new Jerusalem with Jesus unless you go the way he goes, because he comes as he came.

THE HEART OF THE MATTER

❋ When you think of Jesus, how do you picture him coming to you? In compassion? In humility? In judgment? Why do you think that is?

❋ How might things have been different in Jerusalem had Jesus shown up on a horse, ready for battle, rather than a donkey?

❋ In what areas of your life do you live out Jesus' peace, compassion, or judgment? In what ways do you not?

A LOVE LIKE NO OTHER

For it is by grace you have been saved, through
faith—and this not from yourselves, it is the gift of God.
Eph. 2:8

A recent classified ad read something like this:

LOST: ONE DOG. Brown hair with several mange spots. Right leg broken due to auto accident. Rear left hip hurt. Right eye missing. Left ear bitten off in a dog fight. Answers to the name "Lucky." Reward to finder.

Lucky? Of course! That was one lucky dog. Argue if you will, but he was fortunate because even with all those things wrong with him, somebody still wanted him and was willing to pay to get him back.

That is exactly the story of the gospel. Even with all of our sin and rebellion, God still loved us enough to pay the ultimate price to win us back to himself. God's merciful forgiveness is greater than our sin. And his love is more than we deserve.

As humans, we all hunger for love and acceptance. But please get this: God's unconditional love for us is the answer to that hunger. Most of our dysfunction and our failure in wholeness stems from a self-perception that we are unloved and unlovable. Another destructive self-perception is that we are responsible for the pain and suffering of others.

The reversal of this destructive self-perception requires something like a conversion. Others may help facilitate the process for us, but ultimately it's an inside job, something we must claim and experience. It's a choice: to receive the love of God which already has been given and begin the long process of coloring our whole life with that reality.

DO YOU KNOW WHO YOU ARE?

I personally believe that one of the greatest tragedies is to die without knowing who you are. Or, you can put it this way: one of the greatest tragedies is to live denying who you are.

Can you believe me when I tell you that you are more than you think you are? I can ask the question honestly because it took me a long time to believe it for myself. For a good part of my life, I spent a huge amount of energy trying to prove myself worthy of love and acceptance. My low estimate of myself set the agenda for my ceaseless efforts to be accepted.

The cross would have happened if you were the only person in the world who would receive grace.

Charles H. Cooley, an important modern social scientist who is considered the dean of American sociology, has something to say about that. Cooley developed the concept of the "looking-glass self," and if you've ever studied sociology, you've probably been introduced to this concept of human understanding. The theory he outlined in his seminal work, *Human Nature and the Social Order*, goes like this: our self-concept is established by what we think the most important people in our life think of us. In other words, our entire self-image is shaped by what we think the most important people in our life think of us.

Here is where Christians must center. Too often, we feel that God disapproves of us and thinks we are nothing. But that couldn't be further from the truth. Our Christian journey of faith must begin with the belief that God has accepted us unconditionally. There is nothing we can do to earn or prove our worth. Our value in God's sight has been affirmed once and for all by the gift of Jesus Christ in death on our behalf. We continue on our Christian journey as forgiven and affirmed people, as we allow our lives to be shaped by the indwelling Christ who keeps affirming us in our worth and impelling us to fullness of being, the fullness of God himself.

As Christians, the most important person in our lives is Jesus. Therefore, our self-concept can be established by what Jesus thinks of us.

So what does he think of you? *Jesus loves you as though you are the only person in the world to love.* He loves you so much that he died for you! The cross would have happened if you were the only person in the world who would receive grace—that's what Jesus thinks of you.

HOW HE CALLS US HIS OWN

For a long time I missed the power of Jesus' dual designation of God as "Abba! Father!" The meaning is not simply that when Jesus prayed, he addressed the One whom we call Father in a more intimate way as Abba; the meaning is that two distinct peoples, Jews and Gentiles, are joined in the acclamation of God as Father. God has liberated us, set us free from slavery, adopted us as his children, and rescued us from all bondage. Whether we have tried to control our lives through following religious law (Jew) or through divining the stars and the order of nature (Greek), the message of Paul and Jesus is the same: the Father loves us. We no longer need to struggle with life, trying to find a way to control our fear or ensure our survival. The Father loves us. He holds our lives even beyond death. We can trust him.

I remember an experience when the notion of adoption by God became powerfully real to me. My wife, Jerry, and I were flying to Japan from Korea. When we were boarding the plane in Seoul, there were three young American servicemen who had in their care six tiny babies. We learned that an adoption agency was giving these young men a free trip home and back so that they might deliver the babies to American families.

Jerry, who is forever a mother, decided those young men needed help. They did appear rather helpless! So she volunteered to take one of the babies onto the plane and care for her until we reached Tokyo.

As the plane was taking off, I looked down at the little baby in Jerry's arms and was overcome with sadness. I thought, *She will never know her birth parents, will never know her homeland, perhaps will never visit here again, and will be forever separated from her birth family.* Then I happened to look at the baby's arm and saw a little bracelet on it. I lifted the baby's hand and read the writing on it: "Mr. and Mrs. John Mabry," followed by an address in Pittsburgh, Pennsylvania.

They have to be the adoptive parents to whom the baby is being delivered, I thought. My sadness was transformed into happiness, even joy. I knew that in Pittsburgh were a man and a woman who had such love that they were willing to take this child as their own. And I knew that, all things being equal, this little baby girl would have the love and security that a mother and a father want to provide their children. Although she would someday know the story of being adopted, long before that she would have experienced the love and care of her parents. She would know the deep meaning of having been deliberately chosen, deliberately loved.

Suddenly, the notion of God loving us enough to adopt us hit home. Adoption has to do with being secure in a relationship that is given to us. God is our Father—our Father who has adopted us, just as Mr. and Mrs. Mabry became the father and the mother of that little baby. God chooses us and claims us as his children.

To be sure, we must remember that the designation of God as Father has nothing to do with gender: God is not a sexual being. Rather, it describes a relationship of shared love and fellowship in which God pours out all his blessings on all his children. In the deepest and truest sense, we do not have to worry about our destiny or our survival by trying to divine or manipulate the elements of the universe. We have a Father who loves us and has taken us in as his own.

As our divine parent, God's love for us never ends. It is like a parent's love for a prodigal child. Even if we reject God, God will never reject us. The Old Testament prophet Hosea makes this case dramatically, as he reports God saying:

> When Israel was a child, I loved him, and out of Egypt I called my son. But the more I called Israel, the further they went from me. They sacrificed to the Baals and they burned incense to images. It was I who taught Ephraim to walk, taking them by the arms; but they did not realize it was I who healed them. I led them with cords of human kindness, with ties of love; I lifted the yoke from their neck and bent down to feed them. (Hos. 11:1–4)

How much of the heartache and devastating guilt that cripples and debilitates people would be done away with if people would believe that God's love is deep enough and wide enough to forgive and to forgive to the utmost!

Because of God's great grace and kindness, however, we can be confident of this love. And isn't that our need, to be confident? The less secure we humans are, the more we rely on superficial props such as rank, title, degree, and recognition. The more insecure we are, the more we seek to prove ourselves. My own proving game once was, "See, I am worthy of your love and acceptance."

Eventually, God's love and acceptance became unquestionably real to me. It didn't come easily or quickly, or without struggle and pain. But it came. I embraced the acceptance and love of others, and when that happened, for the first time in my life, I could stand and face the world, eyeball to eyeball. I could face the ugly and the beautiful, the stranger and the friend, the domineering and the subservient. I could stand before God and everybody and say, "Here I am, Maxie Dunnam!" Not aggressively, yet without apology. Not proving myself, but simply being.

When we try to build ourselves up without God, to elbow our way to the top, to win by intimidation, to call attention to ourselves with trappings and pomp, betraying our glaring lack of both, we still do not trust. We are still not willing to risk and be vulnerable. Our lives are still being shaped by destructive don'ts.

When we come to understand that a divine *yes* has been spoken—that God has said *yes* to us, and loves, forgives, and accepts us—we truly can be confident without being arrogant. We can walk every day of our lives knowing that we have been adopted by the most gracious Father, who will continue leading us on to wholeness.

There is a popular motto that has been printed on bumper stickers and posters. It begs, "Be patient with me. God isn't finished with me yet." And here's another: "I am not what I ought to be, and I'm not what I'm going to be, but praise God, I am not what I used to be." God simply loves us too much to leave us alone.

THE HEART OF THE MATTER

❋ Is it difficult for you to believe that God loves you unconditionally? Why or why not?

❋ How has your relationship with your earthly father colored your perception of God as a heavenly Father?

❋ Are there any areas in your life in which you lack confidence? Why do you think that is, and how do you think God can help?

THE STONE WAS ROLLED AWAY

> *They found the stone rolled away*
> *from the tomb, but when they entered,*
> *they did not find the body of the Lord Jesus.*
> Luke 24:2–3

Have you ever seen the movie *Quo Vadis?* At one point in the film, Deborah Kerr is tied to a stake in the Roman Coliseum. Angry lions are released, and they rush at her. A reporter once asked, "Weren't you afraid when those lions were loosed and came plunging at you?" She replied, "No, I am one of those actresses who reads *all* the script. I had read to the end and I knew Robert Taylor would come and save me."

In that instance, there was no level of wishful thinking. Rather, it was a true measure of hope, an understanding that before anything really bad could happen to her, she'd be rescued. Lift that to an infinitely higher level, and we find the biblical witness. "Hope" for the Christian is not hoping in the normal sense of the word, as in Kerr's case; it is not wishful thinking. It is the very substance of faith which gives us our greatest certainty. I like the word from the Epistle to the Hebrews: "But we are not of those who shrink back and are destroyed, but of those who believe and are saved" (Heb. 10:39). No wonder we sing so joyfully that magnificent contemporary gospel hymn "Because He Lives," by Bill and Gloria Gaither, which sounds the note with such challenge:

> Because He lives I can face tomorrow . . .
> Because I know He holds the future,
> And life is worth the living just because He lives.

This is the climactic affirmation of the church concerning Jesus. He was born of the Virgin Mary. He was a teacher of profound truth and wisdom. He performed incredible miracles. He suffered and was crucified. But apart from the Resurrection, he would not hold the same ultimate power.

Volumes have already been written—and more will be— about the possible meaning and mighty power of the Resurrection in our lives. It is this act that gives us hope. And though a physical stone was rolled away revealing an empty tomb, the imagery goes much further.

THE STONE OF DESPAIR

First, consider this: the Resurrection means that the stone of despair has been rolled away, allowing hope to flood in.

Before the Resurrection, hope was dependent upon the episodic breaking in of God upon human history. But now there is a once-and-for-all event. Because of the Resurrection, we can sustain a vision of hope. Hope has been given the substance of life itself. That's the reason Paul argued so forcefully in the fifteenth chapter of First Corinthians that the Resurrection was the hinge issue of the Christian faith. "And if Christ has not been raised, your faith is futile; you are still in your sins. . . . If only for this life we have hope in Christ, we are to be pitied more than all men" (vv. 17, 19).

THE STONE OF SORROW

Hope does not disappoint us because, through the Resurrection, the stone of sorrow has been rolled away and we are invited to joy.

My father in the ministry was David McKeithen. He died in the fall of 1990, and I still miss him terribly. David brought me into the Methodist Church. Under his ministry, I answered the call to preach. He was the pastor who married

Jerry and me, baptized our son Kevin, and officiated at our daughter Kerry's wedding. Our lives have been woven together in so many ways. There is not one person who has meant more to me and influenced my life more than David.

Prior to David's death, Jerry and I had a chance to go to California and visit with him. It was a painful time—I cried a lot and didn't sleep very much. Early one morning, about 5 AM, I was tossing and turning. So I slipped out onto the patio and began to pray, to relive my relationship with David, and to recall my faith journey that he had influenced so deeply.

When there was enough light, I began to read the Psalms, somewhat randomly. Somehow I got to Psalm 30. This remarkable word of praise grabbed my attention: "You turned my wailing into dancing; you removed my sackcloth and clothed me with joy, that my heart may sing to you and not be silent" (vv. 11–12). But prior to that was my favorite line in all the Psalms: ". . . weeping may remain for a night, but rejoicing comes in the morning" (v. 5).

Well, later that same afternoon, we were all in the room with David: Marguerite, his precious wife (one of God's great women); his two sons, David and Floyd (both United Methodist ministers); and Jerry and me. It just seemed right that we worship together. And we did. Some of us were seated on his bed, holding his hands; others were standing close around. We prayed and we sang hymns. Boy, did we sing! And I read a passage from First Thessalonians, chapter 4.

> Brothers, we do not want you to be ignorant about those who fall asleep, or to grieve like the rest of men, who have no hope. We believe that Jesus died and rose again and so we believe that God will bring with Jesus those who have fallen asleep in him. According to the Lord's own word, we tell you that we who are still alive, who are left till the coming of the Lord, will certainly not precede those who have fallen asleep. (vv. 13–15)

For the first time in my life, it dawned on me where the writer got the inspiration for one of my favorite gospel hymns.

> When the trumpet of the Lord shall sound,
> And time shall be no more.
> When the morning breaks, eternal bright and fair;
> When the saved of earth shall gather over on the other shore,
> and the roll is called up yonder, I'll be there.

It was a time of joy as we celebrated with David there in that room—knowing that he would not be with us much longer. The stone of sorrow was rolled away, and we responded to the invitation to joy.

THE STONE OF DEATH

How better can we say it? The stone of death is rolled away, providing a doorway to life. That means both *abundant life now* and *eternal life when we die.* Consider now a story from a primitive rural Baptist church in the South, where they still practice foot washing. A preacher friend of mine was there, and he relayed this story to me:

> Delmar always sits in the front row. His body is crippled. He sits on the corner by the aisle, in position to leave early. His face is angular; his gray hair, crew-cut. His frame is small and twisted. On this particular Sunday he was set aside by an act of grace. All of us are maimed in one way or another. On this Sunday God once more revealed how being maimed does not keep us from being His witness. Elder I. D. Black as worship leader initiated the sacrament, the washing of feet. Singing his sermon-prayer, picked up the basin. He singled out Delmar in the front-row aisle seat. "I'm going to wash your feet." As he came off the platform and knelt before Delmar, he continued his song as a sermon-prayer-hymn directly to Delmar. "God is going to dress you in a new body." Old Regular Baptists do not

avoid the realities of tragic pain. The sermon-song did not mince the reality of Delmar's twisted body, hands, and feet. But Elder Black also sang of the Resurrection and the new body God gives: a glorious body, a transfigured body. Delmar reached out and hugged the preacher's neck. They put their arms around each other and I could see from the shaking shoulders that Delmar was crying. Delmar wanted to wash the preacher's feet in turn, but his twisted hands wouldn't work right to do it. A brother member came, knelt between them and helped Delmar wash the preacher's feet. The three of them were kneeling together, singing, crying, and holding each other. There is a hymn often used in that church which sings:

> The highway leads over the mountain
> The end of the journey is near.
> At the top of this mountain is a beautiful sight.
> I can almost see heaven from here.

I could see it that morning! Delmar left ahead of the crowd. He dragged his body around and down the aisle. I saw his face. In his face on that Sunday morning I saw a glimpse of the Resurrection!

Because the stone was rolled away—because Jesus is "the Resurrection and the life"—we will not be victims of death. We will be victors. We can know the stones of defeat and death are rolled away, making way for hope, and the stone of sorrow is rolled away, inviting us to joy. And when we have hope, we can know that God is ready and able to meet us wherever we are, and give us the courage we need to face whatever is ahead.

AN AMAZING THING HAPPENED

Though the Resurrection is a focal point of hope for Christians, we must remember that God began planting

visions of hope in the minds and hearts of his people long
before. We see it dramatically, for example, when Moses and
Joshua were leading God's people out of captivity. They came
near the Promised Land, but the Israelites were in the choking
grip of negative thinking. They had a defeatist mentality and
wallowed in their despair. They complained about everything:
the food was no good and the accommodations were worse.
They were frightened of the future. They criticized Moses and
Joshua, accusing them of a subversive plot to kill them. Day
after day they moped around and complained. When they
surveyed the land God had promised them, they gave themselves the ultimate put-down—they saw themselves as
grasshoppers and their enemies as giants.

Moses, their great leader, grew weary of their
complaining antagonism. Joshua was fed up. Even God cried
out, "How long will this wicked community grumble against
me?" (Num. 14:27). To add to the despair and hopelessness,
Moses died.

Then an amazing thing happened. The first chapter of
Joshua opens with this word:

> After the death of Moses the servant of the LORD, the LORD
> said to Joshua son of Nun, Moses' aide: "Moses my servant is
> dead. Now then, you and all these people, get ready to cross
> the Jordan River into the land I am about to give to them—to
> the Israelites." (vv. 1–2)

For forty years Moses had been the leader. Joshua and the
people of Israel had depended upon him. He was the great
emancipator. Now he was dead, and the people and Joshua
were discouraged and depressed. But God said, "Arise! Get
up! Be done with this hopelessness; go over into Jordan, you
and all the people, into the land which I am giving to them."

That word ignited their hope. And you already know the amazing thing that happened. These defeated, discouraged people were transformed. Though they were the descendants of slaves with no military training at all, fortified with faith and hope, they moved into a land occupied by people with vastly superior weapons and fortified cities, and they conquered it.

Hope allows us to trust that God is at work.

Let it be noted that the victory took more than mere optimism. Optimism is not essential for kingdom reality. In fact, it can become an enemy. But optimism is not hope. Hope is altogether something else, and hope is the essence of the reign of God. It is the core truth of the Resurrection, the confidence that our Savior lives. It allows us to trust that, in ways we may not understand, God is at work, and that one day he will establish his kingdom. And thanks to the cross, death, and Resurrection—thanks to that stone being rolled away—we will be able to be a part of it.

THE HEART OF THE MATTER

* What "stones" in your life has Jesus helped you roll away? What stones remain?

* Think now of a time you've experienced unexplained hope. Describe it here.

* Think of a time when you felt more like the grumbling Israelites after Moses' death. Were you able to see beyond your circumstances and ignite a new hope?

THE GOSPEL BY WHICH WE ARE SAVED

> *By this gospel you are saved. . . .*
> *1 Cor. 15:2*

It is impossible to overestimate the importance of the death and Resurrection of Jesus. The bottom line in the gospel is the living Christ.

Chapter 15 of Paul's First Letter to the Corinthians is one of the great chapters of the Bible. Paul is the first person to record in writing what had been preached about for years. His account precedes by at least fifteen years the accounts of the earliest Gospel. Can you imagine what it must have been like before all this was written down—to hear the preaching, stories, conversations, debates . . . all part of the unbelievable story of God coming to us in Jesus Christ? How he was born as a baby to a virgin, grew up as a normal human being, became an itinerant preacher, shocked listeners with his radical message of love and forgiveness, made fantastic claims about coming from God and going back to God, was condemned to die and willingly accepted that death, forgave those who hung him on the cross, and promised to come again. Then it really did happen—God raised him from the grave, and he was alive.

None of that was written down in any form that was eventually preserved as a whole until Paul began to write his letters to the communities of faith in different sections of the world of that day. His Letters to the Corinthians were a part of the earliest written record.

Of course there were questions and debates, and we can see it here. We don't know the precise questions that prompted Paul to include the message in chapter 15 of First Corinthians. We only know that it had to do with someone, or maybe a group, questioning the veracity of the Resurrection. Paul answered the question by sharing the substance of the gospel: "I declare the gospel which I preached to you . . . by which you are saved" (vv. 1–2 NKJV).

Let's try to grasp the full meaning of this good news by which we are saved. Imagine that you and I are very close friends. Imagine that I have known you long enough to know your lifestyle and inner thoughts, your dreams and passions. We have shared questions and longings, hopes and doubts. I care enough about you to be honest. One day, we are taking a long walk together. You can sense that I am uneasy. I'm finding conversation difficult. You know I want to say something, but I'm struggling to do so. Finally, I muster my courage and begin, "You are my friend, and I care so much for you." You don't know what is coming, but you sense my hesitancy. Then I blurt it out: "You are lying in the jaws of death and hell."

You are flabbergasted. "What are you talking about? In the jaws of death and hell? Maxie, you have lost it. Age is getting to you."

After whatever response I received from you—assuming you didn't stalk off angrily and leave me to walk alone—I would remind you that sometimes it takes dramatic language and images to force us to face reality. Paul pulled no punches. "For all have sinned and fall short of the glory of God" (Rom. 3:23). "Jews and Gentiles alike are all under sin" (Rom. 3:9). "For the wages of sin is death" (Rom. 6:23).

After a little thought and my reminding you of these biblical descriptions of our plight, you might not think my words so shocking after all: "in the jaws of death and hell."

The truth is, I got that picture from William Law, one of the great writers about the nature of our life outside Christ and inside the salvation Jesus offers. Law says:

> . . . the reason we know so little of Jesus Christ as our Saviour . . . why we are so destitute of that faith in him which alone can change, rectify, and redeem our souls, why we live starving in the coldness and deadness of a formal, historical, hearsay religion, is this: we are strangers to our inward misery and wants, we know not that we lie in the jaws of death and hell.

But sooner or later we do know that, don't we? We may not talk about it in that kind of language, but we know. We know that the things we have wanted most, and the things we thought would set us free, have not done so. We still look in the mirror and know the person there is not the person we want to be, nor is it the person God has called us to be. And then, praise God, somehow it gets through to us. True faith is coming to Jesus Christ to be saved and delivered from our sinful nature. It is faith in Christ as an *infallible* Savior that frees us from the jaws of death and hell.

The word of Paul, then, the Scripture that tells us that "Christ died for our sins . . . that he was buried, that he was raised on the third day" (1 Cor. 15:3–4), comes as a joyous certainty. This is indeed the gospel by which we are saved.

HOME FROM THE FAR COUNTRY

A preacher friend recently shared with me the story of his prodigal son's return from the far country. His son was thirty-three years old. He had first become addicted to marijuana at age sixteen, which eventually led him into to the miserable, dangerous depths of almost every kind of drug use. Months would go by without any contact with his family. He spent time in jail, wandered homeless on the streets, suffered in treatment centers, and had near-fatal accidents. He would bear the marks of his sojourn in the far country forever.

> *If there is no cross, no Resurrection, no living Christ, then our faith is in vain.*

This son was drawn from the "pigpen" of his tortured life by the memory of his parents' love and the gospel message his father preached: "God loves you as though you were the only person in the world to love. He was crucified, and buried, and he rose . . . just for you." He tested that gospel in a Christian community of recovering addicts. Without letting his parents know, he participated for three months in a treatment program centered in God's love, including honesty, confession, repentance, accountability, and re-imagining his future with Christ at the center. He stayed around the community for three more months after the initial three months of treatment.

His parents had not heard from their son for nine months. Their last news was that he was living on the streets in Phoenix. About three weeks before the father shared this story with me, his son had called. No contact for nine months, and now this word: "Dad, I've found Christ and I've found myself. I'm coming home. What you have preached about God's love and our salvation in Jesus Christ is true."

Can you imagine that father's joy? We want to sing it, don't we? Well, that's what Paul was doing in his First Letter to the Corinthians. "Christ died for our sins . . . he was buried, he was raised on the third day." And, "by this gospel you are saved."

Let's focus briefly now on another word of Paul: "But by the grace of God I am what I am" (1 Cor. 15:10). Paul gave testimony to what God's extraordinary grace had done for him. Paul had not known Jesus while Christ lived on earth, but his experience with Christ was no different than those who had walked with him in the flesh. Grace gave Paul a new sense of self-acceptance, the ability to say, "By the grace of God I am what I am."

Friends, we can say the same thing! The test of our faith is Christ alive in us. Now, Paul may say this in a lot of different ways, but his bottom line is clear. If there is no cross, no Resurrection, no living Christ, then our faith is in vain. He makes the case over and over again in the second part of Chapter 15. Verse 14 tells us, "And if Christ has not been raised, our preaching is useless and so is your faith."

This brings us back to where we began: the central fact of Christian faith is the death and Resurrection of Jesus. Had it all ended with the cross, there would be no good news to share, no community of faith to bear witness. There would not even be a New Testament to teach and preach. But there is a New Testament, and there is a Gospel which saves. There is, too, the Christ who is alive in me, and can be in you.

THE TRANSFORMING EXPERIENCE OF MERCY

The very fact that Christ would choose to be alive in any of us is not only a sign of the extravagant heart of God, it's also an illuminating example of another of God's gifts: mercy. Mercy (*chesed* in Hebrew) is one of the great words of the Bible. Jesus uses it to boldly declare an aspect of the new covenant: "Be merciful, just as your Father is merciful" (Luke 6:36). It is also the attribute Jesus commended in the story of the good Samaritan (Luke 10:25–37), when the

Samaritan had mercy on the man who had been beaten and robbed. He identifies mercy with forgiveness, too, in the parable of the unforgiving servant (Matt. 18:23–35); if we lack forgiveness, we will not receive mercy ourselves.

The mercy that Jesus speaks of—and demonstrates—is always active; it is sympathy in action as pity and compassion expressed in gracious deeds. In his most descriptive word about judgment, Jesus said that our level of mercy is what will determine our place within or outside of the kingdom (Matt. 25:31–46).

Mercy is, at its core, an attribute of God. Most dictionaries define mercy as "kind and compassionate treatment," but Scripture shows that it can be much more. In the Bible, mercy is always associated with forgiveness. God's mercy, then, does not involve only kindness, but also forgiveness. God's mercy is his act of wiping the slate clean, separating us from our sin and wrongdoing as far as the east is from the west. And he did that through Jesus and the cross.

God's mercy is a powerful force. When we give it a chance, when we seek to understand the death and Resurrection of Christ and what it means for our lives, we are transformed and re-created. The gospel, then, means that yesterday does not eternally haunt us; we become new people today. God's mercy forever alters our destiny, transforming Mary Magdalene from a woman of questionable reputation into an example of precious, holy love, destined to be the first witness to our Lord's Resurrection; moving Simon Peter from cowardice to legendary leader; and transforming Paul from persecuting skeptic to powerful messenger of the gospel.

The discovery of God's mercy is always a transforming experience. When we hear of God's power to separate us from our wrongdoing as far as the east is from the west, we receive good news. But discovering God's mercy can also be painful, because experiencing that power involves honesty with God. We must admit our mistakes before God can separate us from them.

God's mercy is a shower of blessing that cleanses, transforms, and refreshes us, and we experience it by turning to God. As we turn to God, we begin to grow as "imitators" of God, and the Beatitude comes alive in us: as we are merciful, we receive mercy. Remember, when Jesus talked about judgment and the life beyond, he singled out mercy—or the lack of it—as the determining factor of our ultimate destiny (Matt. 25:31–46; Luke 16:19–31).

Please note that this is not merit theology—making a claim on God's mercy because of our deeds. We simply must practice mercy as we seek to be like God. And we must continue to allow God's mercy toward us to renew and refresh our hope. When we do this, Christ truly becomes alive in us, alive to provide forgiveness of our sins, healing in our brokenness, direction in our disorientation, joy in our sadness, and one day—one day—our own Resurrection from the dead for eternal life with Him.

This is the gospel by which we are saved—and the gospel by which we live, in the shadow of his great mercy and grace.

THE HEART OF THE MATTER

❋ Have you ever felt that the things you wanted most and the things you thought would set you free have not done so? How did you react to that awareness?

❋ Have you ever visited the "far country?" What drew you back home?

❋ Can you identify with Paul's statement, "By the grace of God, I am what I am"? Why or why not?

TO LIVE
IN JOY

*Hallelujah! Salvation and glory and power belong to
our God. . . . Hallelujah! For our Lord God Almighty
reigns. Let us rejoice and be glad and give him glory!*
Rev. 19:1, 6–7

In these busy times of ours, retreats can offer a much-
needed break. In my own life, they're essential. Since
I'm with people all the time, my life is intertwined with
many lives. And daily "quiet times"—snatches of solitude now
and then—are simply not enough. I run down and I run out!
Occasionally, then, I have to set aside a deliberate time and
place—two or three days—to be alone with myself and God,
to reflect and meditate, to try to get it all together.

On one of those retreats, I was alone in a little house near
the ocean. Just before dark, I decided to take a walk on the
beach. There is something about being alone on the beach
that is renewing for me—the bite of the wind; the powerful,
swooshing sound of the waves; the struggle between day and
night as one fades and the other comes to life. It is always an
invigorating, renewing experience.

On that occasion, I was walking along with my mind in
neutral, trying to be open to whatever might touch my spirit,
when something drew my eyes downward. I almost stepped
on a beautiful butterfly: velvet black with bright yellow
splotches and rich orange spots on the inner tips of its wings.
It was stuck on a seaweed pod, squirming to be free. I took
its wings gently between my fingers, pulled it clear of the
seaweed, and for a few moments marveled at its beauty. This

fragile creature struggled in my fingers, but when I let go it didn't seem to have the strength to fly. I tossed it gently into the air, hoping to launch it on his way, but it plummeted to the sand.

For a moment I felt pain. I identified with such helplessness. Had I held it too long and made its wings too nimble for flight? I crouched over it, and for a second I was one with this little butterfly, wanting to do something to help it fly. But I could work no such miracle.

In that moment of disappointment, I saw our human plight. Made for meaningful life and fulfillment, most of us are stuck in the web of grueling circumstances. Made for flight, we never rise above the plodding task of getting by as best we can. Something clicked inside me—I'm sure it was the Holy Spirit calling my soul to attention. I became ecstatic; I wanted to sing, to leap, to dance, and to shout. More powerful, and just as real as the roaring waves, a flood of words swept over me.

❋ I have come that [you] may have life, and have it to the full. (John 10:10)
❋ Because I live, you also will live. (John 14:19)
❋ Now this is eternal life: that they may know you, the only true God, and Jesus Christ, whom you have sent. (John 17:3)
❋ God has given us eternal life, and this life is in his Son. He who has the Son has life; he who does not have the Son of God does not have life. (1 John 5:11–12)
❋ Therefore, if anyone is in Christ, he is a new creation; the old has gone, the new has come! (2 Cor. 5:17)

The high tide of that flood of words came with the affirmation from the Book of Revelation:

> Then I saw a new heaven and a new earth, for the first heaven and the first earth had passed away. . . . And I heard a loud voice from the throne saying, "Now the dwelling of God is with men . . . the old order of things has passed away . . . *I am making everything new!*" (Rev. 21:1, 3–5, italics added).

With my heel I drew a deep circle in the sand around my butterfly friend so that I could find it when I came back up the beach. I walked away, pondering life. What does it look like, this life God gives us in Jesus Christ?

It looks like *acceptance* experienced by a despised tax collector. It looks like *forgiveness* experienced by a woman who had sold her body and was about to be stoned by those who didn't understand such forgiveness. It looks like *new meaning* for a person estranged from her community, who comes to the well at midday to find a mysterious young Jew who tells her about the refreshing waters of eternal life. It looks like *healing* for a man possessed by forces that drive him to dwell among the tombs, but has his mind put at ease as his disease is eradicated. It looks like *comfort* and *hope* for two women who are helplessly crying because their beloved brother is in the tomb. It looks like hungry men *sharing* some loaves and fishes on a hillside, like human need of all kinds being met, the lame leaping for joy, the blind receiving sight, the deaf hearing, captives released, *the dead brought to life again.*

It looks like *a man going all the way to a cross,* sacrificing himself in affirmation of all people, and then reappearing on the third day as a stranger who is recognized in the simple act of breaking and sharing bread.

I like the way Eugene Peterson paraphrases Revelation 21:3 in his translation, *The Message:* "I heard a voice thunder from the Throne: 'Look! Look! God has moved into the neighborhood, making his home with men and women! They're his people, he's their God.'"

Do you get it? How can we miss it? But we have. Every day—*every day*—is a now day of Resurrection. Easter is not an annual experience. The living Christ is not to be experienced only on occasion. His presence is to be the dominant reality continually shaping our lives.

THE HINT HALF GUESSED

As humans, we sometimes feel that we're merely guessing at the meaning of the mysteries of our faith, especially Jesus' life, death, and Resurrection. In our culture of instant gratification, we want quick, easy answers. But it is not the way of the sacred to overwhelm us with instant revelation; God gives only hints. And it is easy to miss the hints when we're struggling through the dilemmas of everyday life. Incarnation, God coming to us in Jesus, is a mystery, but it's still real and powerful. Even a half receiving of this gift offers more meaning than any other promise of fulfillment for our lives. Have you reflected on the meaning of God's real, living presence in Jesus? Have you received any glimpses, any divine hints, into this eternal mystery?

WHY WE STILL PREACH THE CROSS

Remember how Milton struggled in trying to write about the cross? We, too, can be at a loss for words. We can ask ourselves time and again, "Can't you do something about that dreadful cross?" The answer is *yes.* We can let it remind us of the beauty that lies within it, the powerful truth it holds that applies to our daily lives. Recall First Corinthians 1:18: "For the message of the cross is foolishness to those who are perishing, but to us who are being saved it is the power of God." The fact that Jesus went to the cross for our sins and yet still lives is the shaping dynamic of the Christian life. In reading more about Jesus this week, has your perception of the cross changed? In what ways?

HE COMES AS HE CAME

Remember Jesus riding on a donkey, exhibiting humility as well as strength. Remember him as he wept over the city of Jerusalem, his heart full of compassion, even as he pronounced judgment at the temple. He comes, even today, as he came in the flesh then: showing us new peace and power, exhibiting kindness and compassion, and judging those who do not take his way seriously. Is this consistent with your own personal view of Jesus? As you've gone through the week, have you considered in what ways you are like your Savior—and in what ways you are not? Take a moment to ask him now.

A LOVE LIKE NO OTHER

As humans, our most profound need is to be loved. God offers us a deeply fulfilling, richly satisfying love that we literally cannot find anywhere else. Recall that the way we feel about ourselves has a lot to do with the way we believe the most important people in our lives view us. As Christians, with Jesus our central character, we can walk in confidence knowing that he loves us enough to give his very life. People in our lives may be fickle, but God is not. God loves us unconditionally, and there is nothing we can do to earn or justify that love; it just is. When we are able to accept that, we can become the secure, whole people God intended us to be all along. As you have pondered the questions of this study, have you come across any areas of doubt of God's great love for you? If so, take them to God in prayer, and ask God to show you just how precious you are to him as his adopted child.

The Stone Was Rolled Away

It's hard to imagine the day that the stone was rolled away from the tomb of Jesus, showing that he was no longer inside. What joy! What a surprise! Remember, though, that it was not just a one-time occurrence. We, too, can experience the joy and surprise as we allow Jesus to roll away our stones of sorrow, despair, and death. And when those stones are gone, hope can flow in. Remember that before the Resurrection, hope was dependent on the episodic breaking in of God upon human history. But now, thanks to Jesus, we can sustain that hope every day of our lives. Hope has been given the substance of life itself. In recent days, as you have focused on all that Jesus is, has your level of hope increased? Have you been able to rejoice at the now-empty tomb?

The Gospel by Which We Are Saved

Do you recall the vivid imagery of the jaws of death and hell? The good news is that you no longer have to live there. Christ is the infallible Savior who has delivered us. Remember now the story of the young man who left his parents for the far country, finding all sorts of trouble. It was the love of God and the salvation of Jesus that brought him home again. The same presence that wooed him woos us as well. When we receive this mercy, it both transforms and re-creates us. Christ becomes alive in us, alive to provide forgiveness of our sins; healing in our brokenness; direction in our disorientation; joy in our sadness; and one day, Resurrection from the dead for eternal life with him. Is anything standing between you and this great, generous gift? If so, take it to the Lord in prayer.

Week Three

ALIVE IN CHRIST

THE ESSENCE OF
THE GOSPEL

For God, who said, "Let light shine out of darkness,"
made his light shine in our hearts to give us the light of
the knowledge of the glory of God in the face of Christ.
2 Cor. 4:6

T he year was 1958. It was Senior Recognition Day at
Candler School of Theology at Emory University, and
I was graduating. The dean had invited the powerful
preacher Dow Kirkpatrick to address our senior recognition
service. Dow was at his best that day—and that best was great.

He told a story I'm sure I'll ever forget. It came out of the
World Methodist Conference, which met in Oxford in 1951.
The high point of that program was the service of commemo-
ration held at St. Mary's Church, the University Church,
honoring John and Charles Wesley. There was only one man
alive at that time who was the right person to preach on such
an occasion. He was John Scott Lidgett, then more than ninety
years of age. Lidgett's mother had heard John Wesley preach in
person, and had shared those memories with her son.

In 1951, the elderly Lidgett was in good health, but he
didn't have much strength. His doctors decided that if they
could conserve his strength, he might be able to preach that
evening. So they brought him to Oxford on the train and put
him in a hotel to rest. Then they dressed him in his preaching
robe and drove him to the church. The pulpit chair was
carried out to the car; he was lifted into it, then carried back
to the platform, and he didn't stand at all during the service
until time to preach. Then, when it was time for Lidgett to

preach, he spoke for almost thirty minutes—vigorously. Just as he asked the congregation for the closing prayer, he swooned, every ounce of energy having gone from him.

Many people in the congregation undoubtedly thought they were witnessing the passing of a great man. Lidgett was taken out of the church and rode in an ambulance back to his hotel room, where a doctor was waiting. The report is that, about 2 AM, he roused, opened his eyes, and said, "Preaching always did take something out of me."

Well, it does, and it should. Just hearing that powerful story—and the Scripture that accompanied it—confirmed my own calling. For me, that graduation day was one of those Mount Tabor experiences, when God allows us to see a huge portion of his glory, and in the ecstasy of that experience lays his claim upon our lives, and we can never quite forget it.

The Scripture was Second Corinthians 4:6: "For God, who said, 'Let light shine out of darkness,' made his light shine in our hearts to give us the light of the knowledge of the glory of God in the face of Christ." I'm sure I had read the verse before, but it never really hit me. That day it did. It penetrated to the deepest core of my being, enveloped my soul, and has been a part of me ever since.

I don't know another text that gathers up the essence of the gospel as that one does. By essence, I mean what the dictionary says: "That which makes something what it is—the distinctive quality or qualities of something."

That which makes the gospel what it is, is here in this text—and there's only one word for it—incredible! The radiant glory of God shines in the face of Jesus Christ. This is the incredibility of the Incarnation. The radiant glory of God shining in the face of Jesus Christ has shined in our hearts. This is the incredibility of the Christian experience.

The radiant glory of God shining in the face of Jesus Christ which has shined in our hearts is ours to declare. This is the incredibility of the Christian witness. All together, it provides the essence of the gospel and its call upon us.

THE INCARNATION

That incredible gospel is Christianity's unique claim. The radiant glory of God shines in the face of Jesus Christ. God's ultimate revelation is Jesus Christ—we call it the Incarnation. On that night when Jesus was born, in response to the cries of the righteous for an answer to the terrible silence of God, God sent an infant who, at that moment, could do little more than cry. On that night, God stooped to our level, and bending over this violent playpen we call home, gave us truth in the only way we might possibly understand: a baby lying in a manger. On that night, a world which couldn't care less came face to face with a God who couldn't care more.

The author of the Letter to the Hebrews put it this way: "In the past God spoke to our forefathers through the prophets at many times and in various ways, but in these last days he has spoken to us by his Son . . ." (1:1–2).

"ALMOST"

Let me put all this in contrast. Few people in the twentieth century seemed as immortal as Mao Tse-tung. Chairman Mao became the incarnation of a movement, a system of thought, and a revolution that affected 900 million people. He lived to his early eighties and was China's leader for more than three decades. It was difficult for even the most astute observer to imagine a China without Chairman Mao. Yet, he died. Orville Schell wrote shortly after Mao's death: "He conceived of the Chinese revolution, and then helped cause it to happen, and in the process every thought of Chairman Mao became the primary thought of almost every Chinese. The word almost literally became flesh."

Jesus is God's irresistible invitation to salvation and eternal life.

Note the conditional word *almost*—the word almost became flesh. Of course, Chairman Mao will take his place in history with other great shapers of national life, but the limitation is still there. John, writing of Jesus said, "The Word became flesh." No reservation; no conditional definition.

My first trip to China was in 1978, two years after Mao's death. His likeness in picture and statue was still everywhere. The little red book of his quotations was still in all the bookstores. When I was in China the following year, the magnificent mausoleum that had been built for Chairman Mao was closed. The official statement was that it was closed for repairs, but the informal word passed on among the guides was that there was a deliberate effort to diminish Mao's presence in the minds and hearts of the people. And that diminishing work has continued in China to the present day.

In Mao, powerful man that he was, the word *almost* became flesh. But with Jesus, the Word *did* become flesh and dwelt among us. We beheld his glory. This is the incredibility of the Incarnation, that the radiant glory of God shines in the face of Jesus Christ. The witness of this incredible event is present on every page of the Gospels.

At Jesus' birth, angels sing in the skies. At Jesus' baptism, a mysterious voice is heard from heaven. At Jesus' death, darkness covers the earth and earthquakes shake the very rocks apart. At Jesus' Resurrection, angels appear, as does an unrecognized gardener. What's more, there is an empty tomb and a body that can walk through doors. And at Pentecost, mysterious tongues of flame come to rest on the heads of the disciples, accompanied by the roaring of a gale-force wind.

Jesus is central in the gospel because Jesus is God's movement of love toward us. Jesus is God's irresistible invitation to salvation and eternal life. He is God's affirmation that we are not left to make it on our own. We're not forgotten, we're not forsaken, we're not given up to be sojourners in a foreign land with no signals to guide us and no destination to move toward. Incredible!

God has become one with us to make us one with him. If we don't get this in our understanding of the gospel, we don't get the rest. If we don't begin here, there's no place to go. There will be no renewal of the church, no revival of faith among us, and no witnessing to the world until we lodge this truth solidly in our minds and hearts and proclaim it unreservedly. The radiant glory of God that shines in the face of Jesus Christ is the incredibility of the Incarnation.

THE CHRISTIAN EXPERIENCE

The radiant glory of God shining in the face of Jesus Christ, Paul said, has shined in our hearts. This is the incredibility of the Christian experience. We call it conversion, salvation, or being born again.

These days the term *born again* is not in good stead among many, because it has been distorted in its use. But let's not give it away—let's understand and claim it, since Jesus insisted that we must be born again. I believe in being born again. I believe it because Jesus calls us to it, but I believe it also because I have experienced it.

Even though I believe in being born again, I pray that the day will soon come when we won't have to talk about being a born-again Christian. You see, that phrase is redundant. If one is born again, one is a Christian and it is a life-or-death issue, eternal life or eternal death. *How* it happens is not the issue; the fact that it happens is the most important thing in the world. The truth is, there is no Christian tradition without some personal encounter with the living Christ.

There is a story about a husband who was berating his wife for her irresponsible spending. "How many times do I have to tell you," he warned angrily, "that it's economically unsound to spend money before you get it?"

That didn't intimidate her one bit, for she replied, "Oh, I don't know about that. This way, if you don't get the money, at least you have something to show for it."

If you have had a Christian experience, whether you say you've been "born again," have "new life in Christ," or know "the light of the knowledge of God shining in the face of Jesus Christ shining in our hearts"—it doesn't matter how you talk about it, you have something to show for it. You are alive in Christ!

THE CHRISTIAN WITNESS

That leads us to the incredibility of the Christian witness. The light of the knowledge of the glory of God, shining in the face of Jesus Christ, is ours to share. Witness is the vocation of every Christian. This vocation is connected with, defined through, and empowered by the facts of the Incarnation and the Christian experience of which we have been speaking. We'll consider this more in days to come.

Let me close with this reminder: *what we think about Jesus Christ and how we experience him determines the shape of our personal life and destiny.* Not only that, but it also determines the shape of our ministry, both as lay and clergy. What we think about Christ and how we experience him will determine the shape of our personal congregational life. What person or congregation dares withhold from others what they have experienced as a free gift from God?

THE HEART OF THE MATTER

※ In what ways do you reflect the radiant glory of God in your life? Are there areas where you feel a bit "dim"?

※ Have you had a personal "Mount Tabor" experience, when God allowed you to see a huge portion of his glory? If so, describe it. If not, how do you imagine God might reveal himself to you?

※ Are there certain things you think about Jesus that have shaped your life for the better? How might some of your thoughts about Jesus be keeping you from experiencing the light of the knowledge of God shining in the face of Jesus Christ in your heart?

ALIVE IN CHRIST

To them God has chosen to make known
among the Gentiles the glorious riches of this
mystery, which is Christ in you, the hope of glory.
Col. 1:27

On and off for over a dozen years, my morning ritual has included a word to myself. Sometimes I speak it aloud; sometimes I simply register it in my awareness. Sometimes I make it a liturgy, repeating it over and over again in a breathing-in-and-out exercise: "Maxie, the secret is simply this: Christ in you! Yes, Christ in you bringing with him the hope of all glorious things to come." (This is Phillips' translation of Colossians 1:27, addressed to me personally.)

If there is a growing edge in my life—and I pray that there is—it is at this point: I'm seeking and discovering the experience of the indwelling Christ. I have come to believe that this is the key to the Christian experience, certainly the key to authentic Christian piety and spirituality—to be alive in Christ.

It is interesting to me that Paul, in all of his writings, does not tell about his Damascus Road experience in descriptive detail. Luke records that dramatic event in the Acts of the Apostles. But Paul doesn't recount an outward description of being struck down by a blinding light and hearing the voice of Christ. Rather, he talks about the meaning of that event and almost sings about it in exulting joy: "I have been crucified with Christ and I no longer live, but Christ lives in me. The life I live in the body, I live by faith in the Son of God, who loved me and gave himself for me" (Gal. 2:20).

What an unbelievable, breathtaking possibility! It is an extravagant claim. We could pass it off and not pay too much attention to it if this were an isolated instance in Scripture. However, this is the language Paul uses throughout his letters.

"In Christ," "in union with Christ," "Christ in you"—these are recurring words in Paul's vocabulary. Variations of the phrase occur no less than 172 times in the New Testament. Paul's definition of a Christian is a person in Christ: "Therefore, if anyone is in Christ, he is a new creation; the old has gone, the new has come!" (2 Cor. 5:17).

Paul is not the only person to use that language. Do you remember Jesus' allegory of the vine and the branches in the fifteenth chapter of John? He tells us who the Father is and who he is in relation to the Father. And then he tells us who we are in relation to him.

> I am the true vine, and my Father is the gardener. He cuts off every branch in me that bears no fruit, while every branch that does bear fruit he prunes so that it will be even more fruitful. You are already clean because of the word I have spoken to you. Remain in me, and I will remain in you. No branch can bear fruit by itself; it must remain in the vine. Neither can you bear fruit unless you remain in me. I am the vine; you are the branches. If a man remains in me and I in him, he will bear much fruit; apart from me you can do nothing. (John 15:1–5)

Extravagant, but yet, reality. Simple, but not simplistic. Jesus came for one purpose and one purpose alone: to bring himself to us, and while doing so, to bring God. Not only does he justify us by providing full pardon for our sin, but he also indwells us to give us the power to be and do all those things God requires us to be and do. The message of justification by faith is our evangelistic proclamation which must never be diminished. It is crucial. However, it is not complete.

Remember that the Christian experience is more than conversion. We talk about becoming Christian in ways like "accepting Christ," "inviting Christ into our lives," "receiving Christ as Savior," "being born again by allowing Christ to be born in us." Whatever the language, the faith and experience is that, as we confess and repent of our sins, we are forgiven. We are justified and accepted, and we enter into a new relationship with God, who then lives in us through the power of his Spirit as the indwelling Christ.

The idea of being alive in Christ, then, is a common theme in Scripture. Beyond that, it's one of the most exciting possibilities we are offered.

THE SHAPING POWER OF OUR LIVES

If we are to take this seriously, we must understand that the presence of God in Jesus Christ is not just to be experienced on occasion; the indwelling Christ is to become the shaping power of our lives.

Picture that possibility. I have a friend who is a Benedictine monk. The way we live our lives is vastly different, but I feel a real kinship—a oneness of spirit—with Brother Sam. One of the most meaningful memories, to which I return often in my mind, is an evening he and I spent together sharing our Christian journeys. The vivid highlight of that evening was when he shared with me the occasion of his solemn vows, the service when he made his life commitment to the Benedictine community and the monastic life. It was a commitment that included the vows of poverty, chastity, and obedience.

In that service of commitment, Brother Sam prostrated himself, covered in a funeral pall, before the altar of the chapel in the very spot where his coffin will be set when he dies. The bell that tolls at the earthly parting of a brother sounded the solemn gongs of death. Then there was silence—the silence of death. After a few moments, the silence of the gathered community was broken by the singing of the word to the Colossians: "For you died, and your life is now hidden with Christ in God" (3:3). After that powerful word, there was more silence as Brother Sam reflected upon his solemn vow. Then the community broke into singing Psalm 118, which is a part of the Easter liturgy in the Benedictine community: "I will not die but live, and will proclaim what the LORD has done" (v. 17).

After this Resurrection proclamation, the liturgist shouted the word from Ephesians 5:14: "Wake up, O sleeper, rise from the dead, and Christ will shine on you." Then the bells of the abbey began to ring loudly and joyfully; Brother Sam rose; the funeral pall fell off; the abbot brought the white robe of the Benedictine order and placed it upon him; he received the kiss of peace from all the brothers and was welcomed into that community to live a life "hidden with Christ in God."

It is a great liturgy of death and Resurrection, and is a symbolic reenactment of the Christian experience. When Brother Sam and I shared, I relived in vivid memory my own baptism in a rather cold creek in rural Mississippi one September. Paul gave powerful witness to it over and over again: "I have been crucified with Christ and I no longer live, but Christ lives in me."

LIVING OUR LIVES IN CHRIST

To be a Christian is to change. It is to become new. It is not simply a matter of choosing a new lifestyle, though there is a new style. It has to do with being a new person. The new person does not emerge full-blown. Conversion—passing from death to life—may be the miracle of a moment, but the making of a saint is the task of a lifetime. The new process of saint-making is to work out in fact what is already dynamic in principle. In position, in our relation to God in Jesus Christ, we are new persons. Now our condition—the actual life that we live—must be brought into harmony with our new position.

A man once said to Dwight L. Moody, "Sir, I am a self-made man." Moody replied, "You have saved the Lord from a very grave responsibility."

Conversion may be the miracle of a moment, but the making of a saint is the task of a lifetime.

Paul contends that we are new creatures, perfect in Christ Jesus (Col. 1:28); created after the likeness of God in true righteousness and holiness (Eph. 4:24); and renewed according to the image of God who created us (Col. 3:10). Nothing less is the aim of the Christian life, and Paul uses a striking word to describe our new life in Christ, the word in the liturgy of Brother Sam. "For you died, and your life is now hidden with Christ in God" (Col. 3:3).

Can you imagine a more stupendous claim than the idea of living our lives in Christ? That Christ can live in us? This is radical, but I believe it is at the very heart of the Christian faith. And it can have a profound effect, no matter who we are.

I remember when Larry, a man in his mid-thirties, asked to meet with me. He shared the sad news that he had to leave our church; his job was taking him to another city. He was sad because he didn't want to leave our congregation, but there was a radiant joy about him as he reminded me of the commitment to Christ that he had made just a year prior. He even recalled the occasion and the sermon. That commitment led him to tithe his income, which he said was giving him incomparable joy. It led him to living daily with the Scriptures, which had enriched his life and deepened his faith. It led him to praying, which had become a vital reality to him; he talks and listens to God.

We must remember that Christ becoming alive in us doesn't have to be a dramatic experience. Larry was not delivered from drugs or alcohol; he didn't have a sordid past that had completely spoiled his life. Even so, he needed the light of the knowledge of the glory of God.

Larry's was a quiet but definite experience in which he came clearly to the conviction that something was missing in his life. He was without spiritual direction and meaning. There was no assurance of salvation. There was no joy in his life, but then it happened. He learned to live a new life "hidden with Christ in God."

Oh, that we would learn the same.

THE HEART OF THE MATTER

❋ What does the phrase "hidden with Christ in God" mean to you?

❋ Do you know anyone you would consider alive in Christ? What characteristics make you think so?

❋ When you gained new life, what parts of your self were you able to bury with the old? Take a moment now to thank God for that experience.

CONSTANTLY ABIDING

As the Father has loved me, so have I loved you.
Now remain in my love. If you obey my commands, you
will remain in my love. . . . I have told you this so that my
joy may be in you and that your joy may be complete.
John 15:9–11

A s I grow older, and hopefully wiser, I am more convinced that despite the limitations of my early life, the soil in which my roots originally grew was fertile. The richness of love in our home was more powerful than material poverty. The warm concern, gentle care, and self-sacrificing of my parents for their five children gave us a heritage money can't buy.

Though limited in some ways, the faith we shared in our little country church had an expansive simplicity to which I often return. On a visit not long before my parents died, I celebrated this faith with them as we worshiped in the same church where I took my initial stumbling steps in Christian living. Nothing seemed to have changed—the spontaneity, the informality, the earthiness—except maybe the sermon. The simple ritual consisted of congregational singing, a prayer by someone called upon in the congregation, announcements, sermon, altar call, and dismissal.

The music's lack of sophistication was more than made up for in enthusiasm, total congregational participation, and joy. We sang as though we meant it. The songs were not preselected. Worshippers had the opportunity to call out their favorite numbers. I flipped through my book, and there it was: I hadn't thought of it or sung it for years—but it was one of my favorite gospel songs. I called out the number: 168, "Constantly Abiding." The chorus of that song rang out and burrowed its way into my soul.

> Constantly abiding, Jesus is mine;
> Constantly abiding, rapture divine;
> He never leaves me lonely, whispers, O, so kind—
> "I will never leave thee," Jesus is mine.

Some may call it sweet piety, but it is really good theology. Claiming that Jesus is mine may sound simplistic and self-centered. I prefer another phrase. Instead of "Jesus is mine," we can proclaim, "I am his." Either way, the thought remains: it's all about constantly abiding.

THE SPIRIT WHO LIVES IN YOU

At its simplest level, this is what the gospel is all about: the life that comes to us as we allow the presence of Jesus to find expression through us. Think again of John 15:4, which promises us that if we abide in Christ, he will abide in us. Simple, but not simplistic! Jesus came for one purpose: to bring himself to us, and in bringing himself, to bring God. He came to give us the power to be and do all those things God requires us to be and do.

Now, there is a difference between *following Jesus* and being *in Christ*. Without a doubt, we should see Jesus as a model and seek to follow him, to be like him, to do what he would do. Nor is there any doubt that we are judged by Jesus. In his presence, putting our lives alongside his, we are reminded of what is possible for our lives.

Jesus was human—don't forget that. But look at the new dimension he brings to our humanity. We can't capture his spirit and still excuse our sin and failure by claiming that we are *only human*. We look at Christ—and to take Christianity seriously is to really look at him—and hear his call to our unachieved personhood. And a Christ like that can do something for us if we let him.

> *Constantly abiding means allowing*
> *both the guiding nature and the creative*
> *force of Jesus to be active in our lives.*

On a practical level, constantly abiding means allowing both the guiding nature and the creative force of Jesus to be active in our lives. There is a marvelous word about that in Romans 8:14: "Those who are led by the Spirit of God are sons of God."

Throughout the New Testament, especially in the writings of John and Paul, the Holy Spirit, the Spirit of God, and the Spirit of Christ are used interchangeably and are often indistinguishable. Paul's word, then, follows a passage in which it is impossible to distinguish Christ dwelling within from the Holy Spirit. Consider this:

> You, however, are controlled not by the sinful nature but by the Spirit, if the Spirit of God lives in you. And if anyone does not have the Spirit of Christ, he does not belong to Christ. But if Christ is in you, your body is dead because of sin, yet your spirit is alive because of righteousness. And if the Spirit of him who raised Jesus from the dead is living in you, he who raised Christ from the dead will also give life to your mortal bodies through his Spirit, who lives in you. (Rom. 8:9–11)

This is the language of the Trinity, not easy to explain, so we sing it as "God in three persons, blessed Trinity." So we talk about Father, Son, and Holy Spirit.

In John 14:18, Jesus tells his disciples, "I will not leave you as orphans; I will come to you." He then makes it clear that his Spirit, the Spirit of God, will be an abiding—and guiding—presence in their lives. Most of us can recall occasions when we knew for certain that we were being guided by a presence bigger than our selves. But how often do we live in anxiety, uncertain about the direction we should take, immobilized by choices, impotent in the presence of opportunity because we are indecisive? We need guidance and we can't grab hold of it.

There are great decisions in life—vocation, marriage, career movement, crisis situations—when our need for direction is vividly pronounced. But what plagues us most and drains us of so much energy are the decisions we face every day, when we have to choose which way to go. To be sure, we need guidance at the major intersections of our lives, but we need it also at the little crossings and turnings that make up the bulk of our lives. It's time to renew our thinking about guidance, to see it not as an intermittent need, but as an ongoing dynamic which shapes our very being and inspires decisions both large and small.

The guidance of the indwelling Christ is both consistent and continual. Of course there will be times when we seek explicit direction in particular situations, but we do not come "cold turkey" to a crisis. If we want to truly be delivered from feeling frantic when facing major decisions, we need to cultivate an ongoing awareness of the indwelling Christ through prayer and other spiritual disciplines. We have the inner sense of Christ's presence, so when we call upon that presence, direction is often so clear that the right decision comes easily and naturally.

THE OLD IS GONE

There is more to this business of abiding. In addition to providing guidance, the Spirit of Life allows us to be constantly re-created. "If anyone is in Christ," Paul reminds us in Second Corinthians 5:17, "he is a new creation; the old has gone, the new has come!" This offer of life is central to the New Testament; John firmly nails it down describing the purpose of Jesus' coming as the abolition of death and the possibility of abundant life for all persons. Again, death is not nonexistence, and life is not simply existence. *Death* is existence without God. *Life* is life *in God*. The claim of the New Testament is that the presence of God with humanity is a reality in Jesus. But it goes much further than that—this presence of God in Jesus can be experienced by each and every one of us.

I completely missed this truth for a long time. For years after my conversion, even while I was preaching the gospel, I was missing *life*. I preached grace without living this reality: I am incapable of saving myself. Nothing I do can earn my salvation. The New Testament teaches that we begin our fellowship with God by grace. The Holy Spirit, by grace, draws me to Christ as my only hope. The Holy Spirit, by grace, renews me, transforming, forgiving, and re-creating me as a new person in Christ. This is the new birth—all by grace!

We easily forget that not only do we come into the Christian life by grace, we can live this new life *only by grace*. We can try struggling and straining at righteousness, mustering all our strength and putting forth all our efforts to be Christlike. We can try to whip ourselves into the image of Jesus, setting up performance standards and disciplines that we think will conform to his likeness. But it never works when our efforts are driven by our egos.

As do-it-yourself people, one of our most difficult lessons to learn is how to live by the Spirit. Most of our Christian activity is the result of our own design and effort, not Spirit energy. So we keep on failing. We keep on straining and struggling, wearing ourselves out, dying of heart failure because we don't recognize and exercise the indwelling Christ. Our competence in doing this work, Paul says, comes only from God. "He has made us competent as ministers of a new covenant—not of the letter but of the Spirit; for the letter kills, but the Spirit gives life" (2 Cor. 3:5–6).

I like to call the practice of walking in that competence "grace-full" living. Grace-full living is not based on rules and regulations we can't obey, but on a personal relationship. The closer we walk with Christ—the more we abide—the more the Spirit within us produces life.

In my own life, I have found the discipline of affirming the living Christ to be absolutely essential; my freedom and joy depend on it. We must continually remind ourselves that *Jesus is alive today.* He is a *now* reality, and this reality must become personal. Jesus is alive in me! This is what Paul was trying to teach the Colossians: ". . . Christ in you, the hope of glory" (Col. 1:27).

To truly abide, we must also enter into a healthy dependence upon Christ. My greatest challenge in life is not knowing what to do. In most situations, I am well aware of what I ought to do. My problem is putting that knowledge into action. What I need is *power.* So it is not enough to recognize the indwelling Christ, I must exercise him; that is, I must depend upon and allow him to work through me.

As Christians, we must also learn to live in the now and "hang loose." It may sound flip, but it's actually quite profound. Jesus had a specific word about this:

> Therefore I tell you, do not worry about your life, what you will eat or drink; or about your body, what you will wear. Is not life more important than food, and the body more important than clothes? . . . See how the lilies of the field grow. They do not labor or spin. . . . Therefore do not worry about tomorrow, for

tomorrow will worry about itself. Each day has enough trouble
of its own. (Matt. 6:25–34)

When we realize this truth, that there is nothing we can do
without Christ, then there is nowhere else to go but to him. We
claim his forgiveness when we sin or fail. We remember that our
relationship with him does not depend upon our success, but
upon his grace and forgiveness. We are not under the law, where
everything depends upon our performance. We are under
grace, where everything depends upon his love. When we
accept this, we can relax. We can live in the now and hang loose.

Just one more thing: constantly abiding also means acting
boldly in the confidence of Christ's strength. Too many of us
pray for God's will in our lives without any intention of
following the guidance we receive. It is interesting to know, but
actually doing it—that's the rub! The power of the indwelling
Christ is exercised as we act. Continuing to abide, then, means
continuing to walk by faith, relying on God, and being aware
of the constant presence of the Spirit in our daily lives. That's
where we find grace—and the grace-full life begins.

THE HEART OF THE MATTER

* What does abiding in Christ mean to you? In what ways do
  you practice abiding in him, and in what ways do you not?

* Is worry a constant challenge for you? If so, what are some
  steps you can take to overcome it?

* In what ways can we tap into the re-creating force of the
  Spirit in our lives?

HUMBLE AND AVAILABLE

Blessed are the merciful, for they will be shown mercy.
Blessed are the pure in heart, for they will see God.
Matt. 5:7–8

One of the most effective and colorful congressmen ever was a crusty old gentleman from Texas named Sam Rayburn. He served Congress for more than fifty years and, during the last ten of those years, he was speaker of the house. But the real greatness of Sam Rayburn was not in the public positions he held; it was in his common touch.

One day Rayburn heard that the teenage daughter of a Washington reporter had died. Early the next morning, he went over to the reporter's house and knocked on the door. "I just came by to see what I could do to help," he said.

The reporter was obviously touched. "Well, thank you, Mr. Speaker, but I don't think there is anything you can do. We're handling all the arrangements."

Rayburn said to him, "Let me ask you—have you had your coffee yet this morning?" When the reporter said that he had not, Rayburn said, "Well, I'll make it for you."

Without giving the fellow time to object, Rayburn went into the house and began to make coffee in the kitchen. The reporter was taken aback. "Mr. Speaker," he said, "I thought you were having breakfast at the White House with the President this morning."

Mr. Rayburn responded, "Well, I was, but I called the President and told him I had a friend who was having some trouble, and that I wouldn't be in today."

That's a great story, isn't it? More than anything else, it demonstrates a much-needed dimension of the Christian walk, another essential dimension of being a person alive in Christ: generosity of self. And that plays out by being willing and able to serve others wherever needed.

Yesterday, we talked about constantly abiding and being alive in Christ. If that means anything, it means that we are *in* love. As John wrote:

> Dear friends, let us love one another, for love comes from God. Everyone who loves has been born of God and knows God. Whoever does not love does not know God, because God is love. This is how God showed his love among us: He sent his one and only Son into the world that we might live through him. This is love: not that we loved God, but that he loved us and sent his Son as an atoning sacrifice for our sins. Dear friends, since God so loved us, we also ought to love one another. No one has ever seen God; but if we love one another, God lives in us and his love is made complete in us. (1 John 4:7–12)

In essence, John is saying that God sent Jesus into the world to be the ultimate expression of himself, an expression of love. We are to love in that same way, but we can't do that if we're so focused on ourselves—so caught up in our own pride—that we miss the cries of the people around us. Pride is one of the greatest barriers in our relationship with God. Humility, on the other hand, is essential for that relationship with God to unfold. As writer William Law says, pride means death and humility means life. "Love has no more of pride, than light has of darkness; it stands and bears all its fruits from a depth, and root of humility."

LIFE IN ALL ITS FULLNESS

Another relevant story tells of a reporter visiting a small community of Roman Catholic lay workers. The workers, located in northern California, took in and cared for babies who were dying of AIDS. The reporter was talking with a woman who was holding a pathetically small baby girl who was obviously very ill. When the reporter asked the woman about the baby, she said, "Her mother was a prostitute, a heroin addict, and she didn't want a baby. The baby was born addicted to heroin and infected with AIDS." Then she added, "The baby will probably die soon."

"Then why do you do this?" asked the reporter. "I mean, why did you bring her up here to your community if she is going to die very shortly?" The woman responded without hesitation, "So she will know life in all its fullness."

The reporter was obviously taken aback by this. He was incredulous. With a tone of cynicism in his voice, he said, "How can this pitiful baby know life in its fullness?"

And the caring shepherd of this baby said, "She will know that there are people in this world who love her."

> *Becoming channels of love is rarely a convenient affair, but the person alive in Christ responds, "Here I am. Send me!"*

That is what everybody needs to know, isn't it? And those of us who are on the Christian walk must be the channels of that love.

Becoming channels of love, however, is rarely a convenient affair. God is not in the habit of asking us to pick the best time in our schedules to be Christ's love to others. But that's where humility comes in. The person alive in Christ—the person truly walking in meekness—is the one who responds, "Here I am. Send me!" whenever the Lord calls.

Don't misunderstand—I'm not saying that the person willing and able to serve is called to be a doormat. Instead, by following the guidance of the Spirit, that person can know when and whom to serve. It is not God's will to wear us out, and there will always be more needs than we can personally meet. But there are times, if we choose to ignore that gentle tug in the direction the Lord would have us go, that we will miss a great blessing. And so will the person we are called to serve.

GOD, HAVE MERCY

As we continue to grow in our walk with Christ, the ongoing challenge is that we resist becoming smug. Freed from some addiction, having defeated some harmful and shameful sin, we may get comfortable and even cocky, forgetting that what once tripped us up can trip us up again. Problems arise when we stop recognizing and cultivating our awareness of the indwelling Christ. But that's not all. Smugness like this can also keep us from being there for others, especially if we consider ourselves better than them because we've managed to come through to the other side. We must continue to bear fruit, rather than resting on our laurels.

Again, the key is remaining in Christ, and continuing to understand that without the grace of God, we'd be in a great mess ourselves. In the parable of the Pharisee and the tax collector found in Luke 18:9–14, Jesus spoke of two men who went to the temple to pray.

The first man, the Pharisee, made the mistake of comparing himself with others, rather than with God's standard of righteousness. He thanked God that he was not like other people. Instead of being humble-minded, he was filled with pride. His self-assurance and self-satisfaction were so blatant that he missed God's mercy. How often are we like the Pharisee, not claiming the gospel of love but comparing ourselves to others? We manipulate life into an acceptable pattern that we can control.

Then there was the tax collector, fully aware of his own failings. He could only stand at a distance. "He would not even look up to heaven, but beat his breast and said, 'God, have mercy on me, a sinner'" (v. 13). Which one, according to Jesus, do you think went home righteous before God? He said, "For everyone who exalts himself will be humbled, and he who humbles himself will be exalted" (v. 14).

The tax collector's hesitancy is certainly understandable. As we come into the presence of Christ, there is always some reservation, a quivering inside. Many times we—like the tax collector—cower because of deep feelings of unworthiness. Imagine how Peter and his companions felt when Jesus directed the group to a source of abundant fish after their all-night effort had yielded nothing. Jesus proved his power in the arena of nature and in the work where Peter was a master. Peter was overwhelmed by a sense of divine power and love, which—no surprise—made him feel so small and unworthy that he had to say, "Go away from me, Lord; I am a sinful man" (Luke 5:8).

I've also had times when I felt I couldn't bear to be in Jesus' presence. I remember a prayer meeting in a hotel room in Beijing in 1978. The Bamboo Curtain was being pulled back just slightly, but most Chinese Christians were still practicing their faith and worshiping underground. In fact, it was dangerous for Christians in that country to meet with Americans. Three Christian couples braved exposure, meeting with a small group of American Christians, of which I was a member. These couples had suffered for their faith—husbands and wives separated for long years, as they were being re-educated for the Communist kingdom. Two of them had been tortured almost to death.

As we prayed together, it was obvious that these people were in a relationship with Jesus far deeper than I had ever imagined possible. Christ was present in that room in such a real way that I felt I couldn't bear it. My own limited life of faith and limited experience with Jesus were made glaringly real. I wanted to cry out like Simon Peter, "Go away from me, Lord; I am a sinful man!"

There have been other experiences. Recently I had a conversation with a young couple who were graduating from seminary. They talked of their return to Bangladesh as missionaries with their three children. I knew the setting into which they were headed, the hardship and danger. But they couldn't wait—their excitement was contagious. They were on the edge of their seats with excitement as they shared their understanding of God's call, and their faces were radiant. I felt I was on a kind of Mount of Transfiguration with this young couple and Jesus. Instead of wanting to build tabernacles to stay there, though, I had an urge to run away. There was something in their commitment, in their willingness to risk everything—including family—for the sake of the kingdom that made me uneasy—that challenged my own discipleship. I knew I was in the presence of Jesus, and I quivered inside. Deep feelings of unworthiness began to rise within me.

It doesn't hurt us to be reminded of our weakness, does it? Though God has given us power, strength, and courage, we must always remember the source. We may believe we have a choice about whether we walk in humility, but for the person alive in Christ, *not doing so* is not really an option. The more we see of God's greatness, the more we realize who we are, in contrast, and the more we want to focus on God's plans rather than our own.

THE HEART OF THE MATTER

※ Are there any obstacles that prevent you from being more humble or available in your own life? If so, what are they, and how can they be overcome?

※ Why is it so important for Christians to model humility to the world?

※ Recall a time when you chose to humble yourself rather than seek a reward. What happened next?

THE SHAPING POWER OF
THE INDWELLING CHRIST

For we are God's workmanship,
created in Christ Jesus to do good works,
which God prepared in advance for us to do.
Eph. 2:10

Back in 1990, my wife, Jerry, gave her brother Randy a bone marrow transplant. His malignancy was so pervasive that the doctors said a transplant was the only hope.

Through that experience, all sorts of amazing and beautiful things happened. At first, though, the doctors were brutally honest. It was going to be tough for Randy; he was going to be brought to the door of death as his marrow was destroyed and his immune system reduced to zero before he received the transplant. Even after that, if the transplant worked, he would still be flirting with death for a long time. He would be vulnerable to all the germs, since he would have no immunity to them. Yet, his only hope was the transplant.

There was excitement and rejoicing when we discovered Jerry was a perfect match for the transplant. Though it was a painful procedure for Jerry, few folks can know the joy she has known, to literally give life to someone who was dying.

I will never forget February 1, 1990, the day when the doctors made the transplant. Jerry was in the hospital room down the hall from Randy. As she was coming out from the anesthesia, her marrow was being fed into Randy's system. When the last drop of the marrow had gone into his system, the nurse said, "That's it, Randy, this is your new birthday. You've been given a new life."

Randy and Jerry gained a special oneness through it all, based on the fact that her life had been able to create life in him. It was delightful to hear them talk about her marrow in him. He would jokingly blame her for his bad moods, anger, or emotional outbursts. Randy lived about two years after that, before the cancer finally got him, but those two years were glorious.

To discover Christian wholeness, it is absolutely essential for us to claim that every person is a miracle of existence.

This experience reminds me of the "marrow" of Christ in us: his Spirit. Today, we'll consider that marrow—the indwelling Christ—first as an affirming presence in our lives.

Blessed indeed is the person who does not, or has not, felt the desperate need to be affirmed and accepted by others. I've never known such a person. We spend a great deal of our time and energy attempting to win acceptance. We pretend and put on masks, perform, and seek to prove ourselves worthy. With chameleon-like cunning, we present ourselves as we think others would approve. The time comes, however, when we know the charade must end, and we have to take off our masks.

To discover Christian wholeness, it is absolutely essential for us to claim that every person is a miracle of existence—including us. Yes, a miracle of existence. Jesus said so plainly: "Are not five sparrows sold for two pennies? Yet not one of them is forgotten by God. Indeed, the very hairs of your head are all numbered. Don't be afraid; you are worth more than many sparrows" (Luke 12:6–7). The marvelously liberating message of Christianity is that *you are important.*

Unlike the pop psychology of today, the Christian faith affirms the fact that we gain our importance through relationship to God, not through relationships to other people. It is that relationship to God, in which we are declared to be precious and ultimately important, that can make our affirmation complete. I don't intend to minimize the importance of interpersonal relationships; rather, I want to emphasize the fact that the spirit aspect of our being requires Spirit affirmation.

Are you familiar with a movement called Emmaus? It was launched in the United States by The Upper Room. At the heart of this movement is a seventy-two-hour experience of people living together in community, hearing numerous talks on the grace of God, seeking to appropriate the meaning of that core message of Christianity. This seventy-two-hour Walk to Emmaus closes with the participants having the opportunity to share what they have personally experienced during the retreat and how they intend to incorporate that experience into the whole of their lives.

My daughter, Kim, had a profound experience of self-discovery there. For the first time, she was able to see herself as God had seen her all along: not just as someone's daughter, wife, or mother, but simply God's beloved child. Here's how she described it:

> What a remarkable experience of love—God's love transmitted through the love of others—for me. *Me*—the unique, unrepeatable miracle of God that I finally understood myself to be (even though I had been told I was that by my parents for longer than I could remember). *Kim*—not Maxie's daughter, not John's wife, not Nathan's or Maggie's or Hannah's mother, but *Kim*. It was as though a bright cloud had descended on me and I heard God's voice saying, "this is my beloved child." I knew who I was even if everyone else saw just Kim. . . .

Kim finally realized that—as we had been saying her entire life—she was *a unique, unrepeatable miracle of God.* It was, in her own words, a "watershed weekend;" suddenly, she knew who she was. Praise God—for Kim, yes—but for the possibility that belongs to all of us.

At Emmaus events through the years, many people have shared the overwhelming awareness of God's love and acceptance. This beautiful realization is witnessed over and over again, yet each time it's fresh and unique—it arises from the miracle of existence of each person. Sooner or later, we will all be faced with the question of whether we believe it—or not.

Hear this, friend: the path to self-acceptance is not through conformity to the world's ideas of who you ought to be; it is grounded in God's unqualified *yes* to you in Jesus Christ. There is a hole in God's heart that only you can fill. You are already loved as much as you can be. Let me say that plainly: anything that needs to be changed, he can deal with, and if not in this life, then in the Resurrection of the dead.

The unfortunate thing is that it's not enough to experience the love and acceptance of God on one occasion. Ongoing affirmation comes as we accept the fact that God knows us thoroughly and loves us totally. Knowing that we are pardoned, accepted, and affirmed by God is the ongoing dynamic that makes our acceptance possible.

A FORGIVING AND HEALING PRESENCE

Let's look now to the fact that the indwelling Christ is a forgiving and healing presence.

There is a close relationship between the forgiving and healing ministry of Jesus. Mark 2:1–12 tells a story that makes this intimate link. The man in the story, the recipient of Jesus' forgiveness and healing, was a paralytic. The picture is at once pathetic yet hopeful, tragic yet heroic. We are introduced to a victim, an immobilized man carried about on a stretcher. Yet his courageous and hopeful friends wouldn't cease believing that there was help. They were bold in their pursuit of healing—bursting through the ceiling of the house where Jesus was teaching in order to get their sick comrade into Jesus' presence.

What happened next astounded those present, as it may astound us if we give it thought. Jesus, seeing the faith of the man and the four fellows who brought him, announced to the paralytic, "Son, your sins are forgiven" (Mark 2:5). The men must have wondered what was going on. They didn't bring him to Jesus to have his sins absolved; instead, they were focused on the poor fellow's inability to walk. The truth is, they must also have been deeply puzzled and shocked—as were others in the crowd—at the blasphemy of such an announcement. "Who can forgive sins but God alone?" (v. 7).

The interesting thing is that no one doubted what was going on; they questioned who was doing it. Knowing that, Jesus completed his act of mercy and affirmed his self-awareness, making his mission clear: he healed the paralytic. Mark records that Jesus explained his reason for the healing:

> He said to them, "Why are you thinking these things? Which is easier: to say to the paralytic, 'Your sins are forgiven,' or to say, 'Get up, take your mat and walk'? But that you may know that the Son of Man has authority on earth to forgive sins. . . ." He said to the paralytic, "I tell you, get up, take your mat and go home." (vv. 8–11)

The fellow sprang to his feet, picked up his bed and walked away, leaving no doubt about Jesus' power both to forgive and heal.

We might have our doubts about Jesus connecting spiritual and physical disease in a cause-effect fashion, but there's no room to question the connection between forgiveness and healing. Of course, our spiritual health is linked to our physical and mental well-being—as the frontiers of modern medicine are just beginning to reveal—that's why we talk about the indwelling Christ as a healing presence.

James K. Wagner has written a rather definitive book on how to have an intentional healing ministry in the church. He titled it *Blessed to Be a Blessing*. Just before the book was published, Jim *happened* to see a painting by my wife and was captivated by it—as many have been. He asked that it be used as the cover for his book on healing. I understand why he asked: the painting is an impressionistic design of color and movement, dominantly blue from deep shades to translucent light. The person in the painting, faintly outlined, is not obvious at a glance, but is distinct and focal once really seen. The person stands in the swirl of color and movement surrounded by light and life that is beyond, yet you know that there is a power that is energizing and giving the person life.

Jerry called her painting "Grace," and wrote this about it for the book:

> In this painting, I have sought to express my experience of God's love as stated in the hymn "I Sought the Lord." One day I was overwhelmed by the realization that while I sought the Lord, all along he was seeking me.

> I sought the Lord, and afterward I knew
> He moved my soul to seek Him, seeking me;
> It was not I that found, O Savior true;
> No, I was found of Thee.
> Thou didst reach forth Thy hand and mine enfold;
> I walked and sank not on the storm-vexed sea;
> 'Twas not so much that I on Thee took hold,
> As Thou, dear Lord, on me.

I find, I walk, I love, but oh, the whole
Of love is but my answer, Lord, to Thee!
For Thou wert long beforehand with my soul,
Always Thou lovedst me.

Though Jerry wasn't thinking of healing when she did the painting, she easily understood the connection: the ministry of healing is a manifestation of the grace and power of God's love in our lives. And the painting captured the moment of her response to God's love, which is always a healing experience.

It is true: our response to God's love is always a forgiving and healing experience, and the indwelling Christ keeps that love alive in our lives. That is what grace is all about.

THE HEART OF THE MATTER

❋ Has Jesus been an affirming presence in your life? Has he been a healing one? Describe your experience of the indwelling Christ.

❋ Think of a time in your life when you pursued something with all your energy, like the friends of the paralytic sought Christ for their comrade's healing. What motivated your search? How might your energies be focused more on seeking Jesus?

❋ Why do you think Jesus so clearly connected physical healing and forgiveness?

WHAT CHRIST HAS BEEN AND DONE FOR US

*If a man remains in me and I in
him, he will bear much fruit;
apart from me you can do nothing.*
John 15:5

In John 15, Jesus gives us a powerful symbol for participating in the work of God. The image is that of a grapevine, and it's worth a closer look. The vine grows along the ground or attaches its tendrils to another tree or a frame. From the vine, little branches shoot out, intertwining as they climb. Then, from these branches, the clusters of grapes come forth. A cultivated grapevine may grow very long and high, with many bunches of fruit hanging down.

The grapevine had long been a symbol for Israel, God's people. On the temple in Jerusalem, a huge grapevine was carved into the stone of the entrance. Its trunk rose higher than a person, and its branches spread out further above, adorned with rich gold leaves and bunches of gilded grapes. Moreover, during the brief time of Israel's revolt against Rome, the coins minted bore the grapevine as the symbol of the nation. The grapevine served as an image of hope that the people could be something fruitful for their God.

In reality, however, that grapevine became a reminder of failure. The Hebrew prophets often employed this figure of speech in terms of judgment. Consider Isaiah 5:1–10; there, Israel becomes the vine that had not produced the fruit God expected. Instead of choice produce, wild grapes had sprung forth, worthless for either wine or food. God's people, by their own efforts, could not fulfill their task in the world.

Jesus, however, employed the symbol in a new way. The conversation in chapter 15 of John's Gospel on the night before the crucifixion could have taken place near the Temple, under the light of the Passover moon, with its beam shining upon the engraved vine. Jesus was using the symbol they knew so well to call them to a life they had not known before.

Alive in Christ, we are called to be instruments of blessing for those Jesus said would be blessed.

It is sobering to realize that even mighty works in the name of Christ will come to nothing if they are not grounded in this essential order: not I, but Christ; not me for God, but God for and through me. When we make this connection, then even the smallest actions by the most limited of people become great contributions to the kingdom.

Consider this challenge: being alive in Christ means that *what Christ has been and done for us, we must be and do for others.* And I don't know a more definitive word to describe Jesus than compassion. A Christ-centered life is a life of compassion.

DOING CHESED

The fourteenth-century mystic Walter Hilton taught that the spiritual life is based on the twin virtues of meekness and charity. I believe those virtues express themselves in compassion. When we are meek and when we love others, compassion pours out of us naturally.

I didn't formally study Hebrew in divinity school, but my Old Testament professor, Dr. Boone Bowen, introduced me to the richness of that language. His favorite word—which he contended was descriptive of God and was to characterize all of God's people—was *chesed*. My memory rings with the deep, bass resonance of Dr. Bowen's sounding of that Hebrew word. But more, my mind is filled with the right meaning of it as he interpreted it for his students. *Chesed* is sometimes translated as "compassion," sometimes as "mercy," sometimes as "pity." Dr. Bowen kept reminding us of the inadequacy of one-word translations of *chesed* in English, Greek, or Latin. What is missing in every one-word translation is the dimension of action that the Hebrew language implies. The Hebrew talks of "doing *chesed* with someone." The word is often connected with *mishpat*, the Hebrew word we translate "right" or "justice." So Micah 6:8 reads, "What does the Lord require of you except to do *chesed* (compassion) and to love *mishpat* (justice). . . ." Today's NIV translation of that verse is a good one: "And what does the LORD require of you? To act justly and to love mercy and to walk humbly with your God."

Chesed is more than a sentiment of love and pity. It demands a "volitional attitude." That is what distinguishes biblical love from current usage of the word. Biblical love includes justice and even judgment. That is the reason I identify compassion as an outward expression of the twin virtues of Christian spirituality: meekness and love.

I want now to identify two explicit aspects of compassion which have special relevance to our being and doing for others what Christ has been and done for us: sharing the suffering of others and acting to bring justice to the world.

SOLIDARITY WITH THE POOR

As Matthew Fox has so well said, "Compassion is not knowing *about* the suffering and pain of others. It is, in some way, knowing that pain, entering into it, sharing it, and tasting it in so far as possible." We are not simply called to know that others suffer, or to assess the painful situations in which they may be; we are to feel the other's feelings. And not only feel the other's feelings, but act on behalf of that person, too.

This is at least part of what it means to be *in solidarity with* the poor and oppressed of the world. But that is so difficult, even for those who feel deeply the call to be so identified. I am working on that in my own life and am constantly driven to confession of and deep penitence for my failure. I have found, though, that there are three ports of entry in experiencing solidarity which are proving meaningful to me. The first is *direct action*. Where possible, I must act. The Epistle of James says it clearly:

> Suppose a brother or sister is without clothes and daily food. If one of you says to him, "Go, I wish you well; keep warm and well fed," but does nothing about his physical needs, what good is it? In the same way, faith by itself, if it is not accompanied by action, is dead. . . . You see that a person is justified by what he does and not by faith alone. (2:15–17, 24)

The second port of entry into solidarity with the poor and oppressed is *the stewardship of my money and other resources*. I control the way I spend my money and I make the decision as to how I will use the resources that are mine.

The third expression of solidarity with the poor and oppressed is *prayer, especially intercession*—seeking to identify with and reach out to the hurting of the world. In a mysterious way that we can never understand, prayer allows us to not only identify with, but also take upon ourselves the suffering of others. So rather than being private, intercession is intensely social.

Prayer, then, can be an expression of our greatest love. It can also be a gateway to solidarity. Instead of keeping pain away from us, loving prayer leads us into the suffering of God and of others. The deeper our love of God, the more we will suffer. The more we suffer, the more we will pray.

Our suffering and the suffering of others is embraced by the compassionate Christ, in a way that we may never fully understand; our intercession, through identity with suffering, becomes a channel of Christ's liberating power.

INSTRUMENTS OF BLESSING

There's another aspect of compassion that characterizes our being Christ to others. It is inherently social, leading to justice-making action in the public and political areas of life.

Alive in Christ, we are called to be instruments of blessing for those who Jesus said would be blessed. His Beatitudes form the charter for the kingdom in which we dwell, living in him. These Beatitudes outline the core values that are to be incorporated into our lives, and for which we must contend on behalf of others. The poor in spirit and in substance are blessed; they know their need for God. Comfort is promised to those who have learned to cry for the world. The meek are the ones to whom the earth belongs, and they will eventually possess it. Those who hunger for justice and who show mercy will find meaning and will receive mercy. The pure in heart, not the manipulators and controllers, will see God. As for the peacemakers, they will be blessed and will be called God's own children. For the grand finale, Jesus blesses those who suffer unjustly for the cause of compassionate justice. To them he promises the kingdom.

Being Christ to others means we are instruments of blessing for those who Jesus said would be blessed, and this calls often for political action and social witness that expresses outrage against systems and institutions that take no account of the needs of the poor and oppressed. We need to consider this call in a very specific way:

- As Christ has been a forgiving presence in our lives, we must be a forgiving presence in the lives of others.
- As Christ has been an affirming presence in our lives, we must be an affirming presence in the lives of others.
- As Christ has comforted us and given us hope, we must comfort and give hope to others.
- As Christ ministered to the "least of these" and gave his life as a ransom for many, we must be his presence to the poor, marginalized, and sexually broken; to the immigrant strangers in our midst, prisoners, homeless, the forgotten, and the forsaken.
- As Christ has been present with us in the valley of the shadow of death, in the agony of personal tragedy and loss, so we must be Christ's presence for others when they are in the valley, and when hope has gone from their lives.

Jesus Christ always lived what he preached, and that meant compassion for all. But here's one more thing to think about: Christ's compassion played out not just in his actions, but also in the way he did things. In Mark 7:31–37, there's a story about how the crowds brought a deaf man with a speech impediment to Jesus for healing. And here we get another perspective on the Messiah. Verse 33 says that he took the man aside from the multitude. That implies far more than it says. Author and philosopher D. Elton Trueblood refers to this act of taking the man away from the crowd as an example of the "courtesy of Jesus." It is at least that, but far more. Jesus was not willing to embarrass the man. Already, no doubt, he was victimized by low self-esteem, by the embarrassment that comes from stammering speech, and by living in a world of silence. Jesus was aware of his suffering. He would not contribute further to making this man a spectacle of pitiful humanity. So he took him aside. The feelings of the deaf man came first.

Jesus ministers to us in the same way. His ministry is personal. He deals with each one of us, one by one. He meets us at the point of our deepest need, perhaps at a point where we are embarrassed, feeling with us our estrangement and separation, our sense of despair and futility. Christ is for the world, but he is also for *me*. The gospel becomes vibrantly alive in our hearts only as we claim this fact of Jesus' ministry. If we can insert our own name in the extravagant affirmation, John 3:16, then we are on the way: "For God so loved _____ that he gave his one and only Son."

As the understanding of that extravagant love sinks deeper and deeper into our hearts, the easier it is to pass it on.

THE HEART OF THE MATTER

❈ On a scale of one to ten (ten being the highest), how compassionate would you say you are? Why do you think so?

❈ What does it mean to you to "be Christ to others"? Is it difficult for you to do so? Why or why not?

❈ Think now of a time that someone else showed the love of Christ to you. How did that affect you?

DYING AND RISING
WITH CHRIST

When Christ, who is your life, appears,
then you also will appear with him in glory.
Col. 3:4

U ndoubtedly, modern science has been full of
accomplishments. But one of the most revolutionary is the mapping of genes. Our DNA—that
awesome, complex, and individual set of genetic instructions
used in the development and functioning of all human
cells—is unrepeatable in another human being. And the
wonder goes beyond that.

The same DNA permits a caterpillar to become a pupa and
the pupa to become a butterfly. But here's a fascinating fact:
at the pupa stage, the caterpillar degenerates into somewhat
of a DNA soup. It loses its structure and has to hang around
believing that something good can come of the mess.

Wonder why? Because a butterfly is not just a caterpillar
with wings on it.

The evolution from caterpillar to butterfly has long been
a suggestive metaphor for any kind of transformation. And it
is certainly a challenging symbol for the new life that is ours
in Christ. With that, however, we have to remember that a
butterfly is not just a caterpillar with wings on it. And we are
not the same as we once were, either.

As Christians, we are new persons in Christ; death and
Resurrection are part of the ongoing rhythm of our lives.
Paul contends that nothing less than a new creature *perfect
in Christ Jesus* (Col. 1:28), "created to be like God in true

righteousness and holiness" (Eph. 4:24), renewed according to the image of him who created him (Col. 3:10), is the aim of the Christian life.

A number of other phrases describe this transformation into new life, especially in the second and third chapters of Colossians. You have *died* with Christ and have been *"buried* with him in baptism." You were also *"raised* with him through your faith in the power of God. God *made you alive with Christ"* (2:12–13, italics mine); "you have been raised with Christ" (3:1).

Note the emphatic underscoring of accomplished reality. It is a settled fact that we are dead with Christ. And there is no question about it: we are also risen with him. We have died to all Christ died to; we are raised to all he was raised to. We now have to live out in practice what has already happened in fact.

We see how emphatically Paul states the case when he refers to the future event of Resurrection not as the Resurrection of the dead, but as the Resurrection of life in which Christians already participate, hidden with Christ in God: "When Christ, who is your life, appears, then you also will appear with him in glory" (Col. 3:4). Paul's common phrases "in Christ" and "with Christ"—which describe the new person—almost merge. The new life *with* Christ, which is received by faith and acted out in baptism, is demonstrated in conduct as we live *in* Christ.

The Christian is a new person united with Christ. The two overwhelming events through which Jesus passed into the power of endless life were death and Resurrection. Those who are united with him must reproduce in their personal spiritual histories these two events. To be *in* and *with* Christ is to be identified with him in death and Resurrection.

How we look at the cross—at Christ on the cross—is a huge factor, perhaps the biggest factor in determining how we live.

TAKING UP THE CROSS

When Jerry and I experienced the Passion Play in Oberammergau, Germany, I remembered a story from an earlier performance of this once-each-decade event. An American businessman was backstage following a performance visiting with Anton Lang, the actor who played the role of Christ. Seeing the cross Lang had carried in the drama, the businessman seized the photo opportunity. Handing the camera to his wife, he instructed her to take his picture when he lifted the cross to his shoulder. But to his surprise and chagrin, he could hardly budge it from the floor.

"I don't understand," he said to Lang. "I thought it would be hollow. Why do you carry such a heavy cross?"

Lang's reply explains why this play draws people from all over the world to that little Bavarian village every decade. "If I did not feel the weight of his cross, I could not play the part."

We must also, however, feel the Resurrection. Not only do we share in the death of Christ, we share in his Resurrection. "Now if we died with Christ, we believe that we will also live with him" (Rom. 6:8). The new life into which we enter by conversion is nothing else than the life of Christ himself, Paul insists. He speaks of "the life of Jesus" being carried around in our bodies (2 Cor. 4:10). The "law of the Spirit" which overcomes "the law of sin and death" brings the life which is in Christ Jesus (Rom. 8:1–2).

This new life is not different from the old life only in degree; it is a new kind, a new quality of life. Paul makes the radical claim that this new life is nothing less than a new creation (2 Cor. 5:17). Sharing in Christ's Resurrection means being raised to newness of life.

This means at least two things. One, death has no power over us. The risen and exalted Lord conquered death. We do not wait for eternal life; it is ours now. Risen with Christ, we have the glorious privilege of beginning now the life with Christ which will continue eternally.

Sometimes we tend to discredit thoughts about life after death as mere sentiment. Not so—it is the heart of our faith that God will finish what he has begun, and nothing is finished in this world until God is finished with it. John boldly claims that God will not be finished until he brings into perfect existence "a new heaven and a new earth" (Rev. 21:1). Death has no power over us because in Christ, we have begun that new life which transcends death and is being perfected by God.

Sharing Christ's risen life means a second thing: the power which raised Jesus from the dead is also our power. So this is our challenge and our thrilling opportunity: to participate in the working power of God in the past brought into the present. This is the paramount miracle: that God's immeasurable power in Christ is available now to redeem us from sin, energize our wills, heal the sick, drive out demons, renew our spirits, and reconcile our relationships.

Is this our vision of reality? Or have we reduced our faith to an intellectual conception, a set of dogmas, a religious system to which we give assent and which we practice by rote with no impact or power in our daily lives? The power which raised Jesus from the dead is available to us. There are those who are claiming that power, receiving it for the transformation of their lives.

Our Christian faith journey begins with our acceptance of the incredible fact of our unconditional acceptance by God. Nothing we do can earn or prove our worth. Our value in God's sight has been affirmed once and for all by the gift of Jesus Christ in death on our behalf. We continue on our Christian journey as forgiven and affirmed people, as we allow our lives to be shaped by the indwelling Christ who keeps affirming our worth and impelling us to be Christ to others, demonstrating the rhythm of death and Resurrection.

THE ESSENCE OF THE GOSPEL

The radiant glory of God shines in the face of Jesus Christ—this is the incredibility of the Incarnation. The radiant glory of God shining in the face of Jesus Christ has shined in our hearts—this is the incredibility of the Christian experience. The radiant glory of God shining in the face of Jesus Christ which has shined in our hearts is ours to declare—this is the incredibility of the Christian witness. All together, remember, these three truths define the essence of the gospel and its call upon us. Has this study given you a deeper understanding of who Christ is, what he has done for us, and how the radiant glory of God can be ours, too? How have those revelations changed you? Recall the story about Mao Tse-tung, and how "the word almost literally became flesh." With Jesus, however, the Word truly did become flesh. Jesus is central to the gospel because he is God's invitation to salvation and eternal life.

ALIVE IN CHRIST

Recall that Jesus came for one purpose, and one purpose alone: to bring himself to us, and while doing so, to bring God as well. Not only does Christ justify us by providing full pardon for our sins, but he also indwells us to give us the power to be and do all those things God requires us to be and do. As you have taken part in this study, have you seen new evidence of Christ being alive in you, empowering you to do the things God has called you to? In what ways? What can you do to further fan the flames of that indwelling fire?

Remember that your life is now "hidden with Christ in God." Yes, it is an extravagant claim, but it is backed up by Scripture.

CONSTANTLY ABIDING

Keep in mind the difference between simply following Jesus and *being in Christ*. We have the opportunity to dwell there, to constantly abide, and the benefits are many. For one thing, the guidance of the indwelling Christ is consistent and ongoing. Jesus is always there, leading us in the way that is best for us. But constantly abiding also means that we are continuously being renewed. As Paul reminds us in Second Corinthians 5:17, "he is a new creation; the old has gone, the new has come!" The offer of life is not just a biblical story; rather, it's ours for the taking today. The closer we walk with Jesus—the more we abide—the more the Spirit within us produces life. So how is your own walk these days? Is there evidence that you have been "constantly abiding"?

HUMBLE AND AVAILABLE

Remember the touching stories of Speaker of the House Sam Rayburn, who gave up breakfast with the president so he could be there for a reporter, and the woman who cared for an AIDS-infected, terminally ill baby so that the child could know that she was loved. Though our circumstances may not always be as dramatic, the person alive in Christ—the one truly walking in meekness rather than pride—is the one who responds, "Here I am. Send me!" whenever the Lord calls. Keep in mind, however, that God has not called us to be door-mats for others, and this is another great reason to remain tuned in to the work of the Spirit in our lives. God has great things for us to do, as long as we remain humble and willing to do them. What has this week's study taught you about the level of humility in your own life?

THE SHAPING POWER OF THE INDWELLING CHRIST

God has so much to offer! Christ in us is both an affirming and a healing presence. Through him, we can know that we have been given new life, that his "marrow" matches our own. But we can also know that we can be healed and forgiven, as well. Recall the close relationship that Jesus demonstrated between forgiving and healing through the story of the paralytic. It is the same today. As you have continued this study, have you experienced new levels of healing, forgiveness, or affirmation? Also, recall that in order to discover Christian wholeness, we must claim that every person is a miracle of existence—including us. Have you thanked God for the miracle of your existence lately?

WHAT CHRIST HAS BEEN AND DONE FOR US

Never forget that being alive in Christ means that what Christ has been and done for us, we must be and do for others. The definitive word here is *compassion*. A Christ-centered life, then, is a life of compassion. That takes not only knowing about the pain and suffering of others, but actually sharing it. The way of compassion is not always an easy road, but it is the one to which we are called all the same. Direct action is one method of identifying with the oppressed, and intercessory prayer is another. The deeper our love of God, the more we will suffer. The more we suffer, the more we will pray. So, how have you been doing at being Christ to others during this study? Are there any areas in particular in which God has pricked your heart? If so, what have you done about it?

Week Four

FIT FOR KINGDOM LIVING

CHRIST FREES US AND FITS US

*And if the Spirit of him who raised Jesus from the dead
is living in you, he who raised Christ from the dead will
also give life to your mortal bodies through his Spirit. . . .*
Rom. 8:11

Among Christians in Africa, the New Testament
word for *redemption* translates as "God took our
heads out." It's a rather awkward phrase, but when
you trace it back to the nineteenth century, when slave
trading was practiced, the meaning becomes powerful.
White men invaded African villages and carried men,
women, and children off into slavery. Each slave had an iron
collar buckled around his or her neck, and the collar was
attached to a chain. The chained slaves would be driven to
the coastlines and shipped to England and the United States.

From time to time, as the chain of slaves would make its
way to the coast, a relative, loved one, or friend would recognize someone who had been captured as a slave and would
offer a ransom for the captors to remove the collar and free
the person. Thus the word for redemption: "God took our
heads out."

No matter how we state it, though, no matter the image
we use, the word *redemption* means that God's action—the
sending of Jesus Christ—sets us free from the bondage of sin,
guilt, and certain death.

The New Testament offers all sorts of images for Christ
freeing us. One of the most dramatic was used by Paul. He
wrote to the Colossians, "For he has rescued us from the
dominion of darkness and brought us into the kingdom of

the Son he loves, in whom we have redemption, the forgiveness of sins" (Col. 1:13–14).

Here is the picture of redemption in a person: a young woman, thirty years old, finished her theological studies at Asbury Seminary. Before she got there, however, she had a life-changing encounter. After graduating from college and being on a fast career track, she found herself on a fast life track, as well. And that fast track ended in alcohol and cocaine addiction. She woke up one day in a hospital—and learned she'd been there for seven days.

The Lord came to her there. Three months of treatment—and three months of spiritual therapy with a caring minister in a Christian church that reached out to recovering folks —marked the beginning of a life of faithfully following Jesus. When she spoke in chapel a few months before graduation, she was radiant, excited about the life of ministry that lay ahead of her. She told her story and then simply said, "I don't know how it happened, only that it did happen, so I can sing about it: I once was lost but now I'm found, was blind but now I see."

This radiant woman is living proof that the full measure of the blessing of Christ means that he comes to free us. But what about you? What are the areas in which you haven't yet found freedom? What is holding you back from receiving it?

Do you feel burdened by guilt? Do you feel heaviness or pain in your heart because there is a severed relationship that needs reconciliation? Do you feel helpless because you are held in the tenacious grip of a debilitating habit? Is your energy drained because you live too close to the line of moral compromise, preoccupied with sexual lust or addiction to pornography? In your heart of hearts, do you know that you are more than racially prejudiced and that your feelings verge on hatred? Does your pride often put you in the position of thinking more highly of yourself than you ought to, looking down your nose at others?

We could go on and on. You may want to stop reading now and probe your own heart. Remember that as you do, God will meet you wherever you are. The point I am underscoring, however, is that we all need deliverance. And the good news is that Christ delivers. He comes to free us—but that's not all.

CHRIST COMES TO FIT US

Christ comes not only to free us, but also to fit us for kingdom living.

Paul begins the eighth chapter of his Epistle to the Romans with the word "therefore." It's a seemingly insignificant word, but pay attention to it—always—when you are reading Scripture. Go back to what precedes the word, because only in knowing what has been said before will you know the full meaning of what is about to be said. In this case, Paul has been talking about his own plight, his enslavement to sin, and his inability to break free of the chains that have bound him. He has talked about the death of Jesus Christ as God's gift of love for our forgiveness and freedom from condemnation.

In Romans 7:19–20, Paul agonizingly opens his heart. "For what I do is not the good I want to do; no, the evil I do not want to do—this I keep on doing. Now if I do what I do not want to do, it is no longer I who do it, but it is sin living in me that does it." Paul goes on to say that the struggle that is going on in his soul is really a civil war, and that he is being brought under captivity to the law of sin. He groans and moans: "What a wretched man I am!" And then he raises that anguishing question: "Who will rescue me from this body of death?" (v. 24). He answers that question immediately: "Thanks be to God—through Jesus Christ our

Lord!" (v. 25). Then he opens chapter 8 with that glorious word: "Therefore there is now no condemnation for those who are in Christ Jesus."

Do you see the chasm of difference between Paul's condition that he expresses so dramatically in chapter 7—"What a wretched man I am!"—and the beginning of chapter 8, "Therefore there is now no condemnation for those who are in Christ Jesus"?

> *We can't give our sins to Jesus;*
> *We give ourselves to Jesus*
> *and he takes away our sins.*

How do you leap over that chasm? You don't! Here is a profound, redeeming truth: we don't give our sins to Christ. Perhaps someone has told you to do that. "Just give your sins to Jesus." But that isn't it—that's impossible. We can't give our sins to Jesus; if we could, we would all be saved. We give ourselves to Jesus and he takes away our sins. He fits us for kingdom living.

There is a story about a man who was tired and weak all the time, constantly drained. Finally, he decided to visit his doctor. "Doctor," he said, "I feel totally exhausted. I don't seem to have any energy. I have a chronic headache. I feel worn out all the time. What's the best thing I can do?"

The doctor knew about the man's wild and fast-paced lifestyle. "What's the best thing you can do? You can go home after work every day, eat a nutritious meal, get a good night's rest, and stop running around and carousing all night—that's the best thing you can do."

The man pondered for a moment, then asked, "What's the next-best thing I can do?"

Too often we choose the next-best thing because we're not willing to be who God called us to be. We are not willing for Christ to fit us for the kingdom. But listen, friends—holiness is not an option for God's people. There ought to be something about us Christians that distinguishes us in our ethical understanding, in our moral lives, in how we relate to others, and in the way we look at and regard the poor and the oppressed.

Christ will make that difference in us. If we will yield to him, he will fit us for the kingdom.

"DO YOU WANT TO BE HOLY?"

I remember a time in my own life when this idea became significant to me. It was the early 1960s, and I was a young Methodist preacher in Mississippi. I was the organizing pastor of a congregation that had known amazing growth and success.

The fellowship of that congregation, however, was splintered by my involvement in the civil rights movement. I didn't think there was anything radical about my taking part, but many folks in the church could not understand my commitment and participation. I couldn't understand their lack of understanding. To me, at least, the gospel seemed clear.

Eventually, the pressure, stress, and tension wore me out. I was physically, emotionally, and spiritually exhausted and ready to throw in the towel. Then I went to a week-long retreat—a Christian ashram—led by the world-famous missionary evangelist E. Stanley Jones. I will never forget going to the altar one evening to have Brother Stanley lay hands on me and pray for me. He knew my story, and as I knelt, he asked, "Do you want to be whole? Do you want to be holy?"

It was a shocking question. That was a single, sanctifying experience in my life, changing forever the direction of my ministry. In that moment, I realized that I am as holy as I want to be. And through the years since, I have constantly asked myself: *Do I want to be holy? Am I willing to yield?*

Christ still has the power to show up wherever we are and to offer us whatever we need. Sometimes that means freeing us and sometimes it means fitting us. Remember, though, that in the process of fitting us for his kingdom, God will put his ways into our hearts as well as write them on our minds. This is, after all, the eternal mystery of grace. Eventually we find that we want to do what pleases God.

For many years I was confused about the word of Paul to the Philippians: "Continue to work out your salvation with fear and trembling, for it is God who works in you to will and to act according to his good purpose" (Phil. 2:12–13). In our English language, the words are contradictory. How can we work out our salvation and, at the same time, allow God to work within us to will and to act out his good purpose? But then I learned that the Greek word Paul uses for "work out" in verse 12 has the idea of bringing something to completion. He is saying, then, "Don't stop halfway." Don't accept grace as a way to just *get in on* the Christian life; accept it as the way to *stay in* with freedom and joy.

One last thing: this holy lifestyle requires determination, and it must be noted that having good intentions about the way you want to live is not the same as living intentionally. Shakespeare was right when he said, "The road to hell is paved with good intentions." Living intentionally—deciding to be a person alive in Christ and actually carrying through with it—means that we deliberately, self-consciously resolve on a certain course for our lives. It means following in the way of Jesus, who said of his life, "I have authority to lay it down and authority to take it up again" (John 10:18). It means being tuned in to the Spirit who is at work in the world, and becoming self-conscious instruments of the Spirit's ministry to people. It means translating our good intentions into flesh and blood—and allowing Jesus to continue to both free us and fit us.

THE HEART OF THE MATTER

❋ If you didn't actually stop to probe your heart regarding the questions in today's lesson, please do so now. Pray for God's revelation, rather than simply going by your own insights.

❋ How do you understand the process by which Christ "fits us" for kingdom living? In what ways can we help—or hinder—that process?

❋ How has Christ been "fitting" you in your own life?

CLAIMING THE PROMISE

*I tell you the truth, anyone who has faith in me will do
what I have been doing. He will do even greater things
than these, because I am going to the Father.*
John 14:12

The pages of the Old and the New Testaments are punctuated with promises—all sorts of promises, including God's very offer of life. The New Testament, however, is especially rich in this area; many of the promises come from Jesus himself.

- Because I live, you also will live. (John 14:19)
- Never will I leave you; never will I forsake you. (Heb. 13:5)
- I have come that they may have life, and have it to the full. (John 10:10)
- Come to me, all you who are weary and burdened, and I will give you rest. (Matt. 11:28)
- But you will receive power when the Holy Spirit comes on you. (Acts 1:8)

And then, one of the most fantastic promises of all in John 14:12: "I tell you the truth, anyone who has faith in me will do what I have been doing. He will do even greater things than these, because I am going to the Father."

Isn't that a breathtaking statement? If this is even remotely possible, then mustn't we admit that we have never taken Jesus seriously? The least we have to confess is that we have certainly been satisfied with far less than he has in mind for us as his followers.

Do you believe it? Don't answer too quickly. Do you believe it enough to start claiming this promise?

CONSIDER THE SOURCE

The message of John 14:12 becomes even more dramatic when we consider the source. It was Jesus himself—the man who came to save the world, the man who forgave and loved, the man who washed his disciples' feet. He was also the man who made the lame walk and the blind see; the man who calmed the storm and held little children on his lap and blessed them. He ate with sinners and flung his life in the face of the rampant prejudice of his day by conversing with the Samaritan woman at the well. He finished all the work God gave him to do, and is now seated at the right hand of the Father, crowned with glory and honor. Can you believe it? That's the man— Jesus—who said to you and me, "You will do even greater things than these, because I am going to the Father."

Charles Schulz once drew a *Peanuts* cartoon with Snoopy, that hound of heaven, saying of Woodstock, that would-be bird of paradise, "Woodstock is going to be a great eagle." Then in the next frame, Snoopy says, "He is going to soar thousands of feet above the ground." Woodstock takes off into the air, and as Snoopy looks on, he sees the bird upside down, whirling around crazily. So Snoopy has second thoughts. In the third frame, he says, "Well, maybe hundreds of feet above the ground. . . ." But the words hardly escape his mouth before Woodstock plummets to the ground and lies there on his back, looking dazed. Snoopy concludes, "Maybe he will be one of those eagles who just walks around."

Isn't it amazing how quickly we settle for less than is promised and far less than is possible? Our problem is that we trust Jesus with some things, but we need to trust him with all things.

MORE THAN YOU THINK YOU ARE

It is important to be reminded that *you are more than you think you are.* I think that's at least a part of what Jesus is saying in today's Scripture.

I read recently of an elderly bachelor and an old maid who started dating. Each had lived alone for many years, but gradually the old gentleman recognized a real fondness and a definite attachment to his friend. He was shy, though, and afraid to tell her his feelings. Finally one day he mustered up the courage to say, "Let's get married!" Surprised, she threw up her hands and shouted, "It's a wonderful idea—but who in the world would have us?"

It's so easy to sink into that kind of self-concept, isn't it? When I'm feeling down on myself, when depression threatens to turn the sky of my life into dark clouds of gloom; or when I sense I'm becoming preoccupied with failure, I try to remember the Eighth Psalm. Do you know it?

> When I consider your heavens,
>   the work of your fingers,
> the moon and the stars,
>   which you have set in place,
> what is man that you are mindful of him,
>   the son of man that you care for him?
> You made him a little lower than the heavenly beings
>   and crowned him with glory and honor. (Ps. 8:3–5)

If I can put this word of the psalmist together with what Jesus said, then I can know that *I am more than I think I am.*

You may be thinking, "How can I believe that I am more than I think I am?" Listen: you are important to God. In fact, you are a unique, unrepeatable miracle of God. Not to believe this is a sin of disbelief that causes much dysfunction, emotional illness, and spiritual impotence. You are important to God. You have that on the authority of God's Word. It's in the book! Don't you remember? Jesus said it himself. Not even one sparrow falls to the earth without the Father noticing it, and you are of more value than many sparrows. He went even further than that, saying that even the hairs on your head are numbered. That's the witness of Scripture—*you are important to God.* Let me express it one other way. God loves each of us as though we are the only person in the world to love. If you were the only person in the world, God still would have sent his Son to save you.

Some time ago, Jerry attended a women's retreat led by a Roman Catholic nun, Sister Susan. A few days after returning from the retreat, Jerry received a letter from Sister Susan which concluded with this prayer, "Oh God, help me to believe the truth about myself, no matter how beautiful it is."

What a prayer! Does it shock you? "Oh God, help me to believe the truth about myself, no matter how beautiful it is." Praying that prayer will help you claim the promise of Jesus: you are more than you think you are.

SOMETHING WE CAN BE AND DO

There is another affirmation that we must consider: *there is something we can be and do, but will never be and do apart from Jesus Christ.* I believe this, too, is part of what Jesus is saying in his promise about us doing greater works.

Let me share a story. Two of the most dynamic and powerful Christians I know are Abel and Frieda Hendricks of South Africa. Abel is a Methodist preacher and Frieda is a Christian educator. Abel was the two-time president of the

Methodist Church in Southern Africa and recipient of the 1980 World Methodist Peace Award. He and Frieda received the 1986 Upper Room Citation. They are among the most dedicated Christians I have ever known.

> *You are important to God.*
> *In fact, you are a unique,*
> *unrepeatable miracle of God.*

Abel went to jail a number of times for his opposition to apartheid and for his commitment to solidarity with the poor and the racially oppressed of South Africa, a nation whose political system denied almost every basic human right to the vast majority of the population. Abel was identified by the government as "Cape Coloured," which was one step above the status of blacks in South Africa's rigid social structure.

To offer a morsel of appeasement, the South African government devised a system that would involve the Asians and Coloureds in separate branches of parliament, intentionally seeking to keep the majority black race in helpless oppression. Abel could have played a role in the new system, but his commitment to the tremendous majority who continued to be oppressed led him to oppose it.

Abel had written a pastoral letter to the Methodist people asking them to boycott the new elections as an expression of solidarity with the poor and as a witness against apartheid. In the midst of the struggle, white leaders came to Abel and urged him to rescind his letter.

The Hendrickses were poor; they had no security, so the white government leaders thought they could persuade Abel by appealing to his self-interests. He was not many years away from retirement, had no property of his own, and had a very uncertain future. They offered him a retirement home, fully paid for, if he would simply be quiet.

I'm sure Abel's smile—illuminating a humility that resonated with confidence and power—was one of the most disarming the officials had ever seen. He withstood the temptation. "In my Father's house are many mansions," he said. "I dare not risk losing my house in heaven for anything you might offer me on earth."

On one occasion, after Abel had just been released from jail, I had the chance to speak with him over the phone. I was seeking to encourage and strengthen him, but instead he encouraged and strengthened me. He quoted Paul, and never have the words had such power: "It is not I who lives, but Christ who lives in me . . . I can do all things through his strength."

Where does that kind of power come from? Abel had discovered the source and had claimed the promise of Jesus, "He will do even greater things than these, because I am going to the Father."

THE HEART OF THE MATTER

❈ When you hear that you will do greater things than Jesus, how does that make you feel? Why do you think that is? What is your deepest desire in that area?

❈ Have you ever gone through the Bible in search of the promises God has made to you? If not, consider doing so now, and jotting down a few that you find. You might also consider memorizing these Scriptures, so you'll have them immediately on hand in your times of need.

❈ Are there any areas where it's hard for you to completely trust Jesus? What are they? Why do you think obstacles are present there?

THE SUREST
PATH OF ALL

When he had received the drink, Jesus said, "It is finished."
With that, he bowed his head and gave up his spirit.
John 19:30

The apostle Paul had a one-track mind. He wrote to the Corinthians, "For I resolved to know nothing while I was with you except Jesus Christ and him crucified" (1 Cor. 2:2). Galatians 2:20 is his one-sentence autobiography: "I have been crucified with Christ and I no longer live, but Christ lives in me." Paul's commitment to Christ shaped every decision he made and determined every step he took. But what did it really mean for him to be "crucified with Christ?"

Paul and the other writers of Scripture were convinced that if we are going to see Jesus, we have to see him on the cross—vulnerable and weak. If we are going to be his disciples, we must seek to live in solidarity with him, to share in the fellowship of his suffering. Paul understood this clearly:

> But whatever was to my profit I now consider loss for the sake of Christ. What is more, I consider everything a loss compared to the surpassing greatness of knowing Christ Jesus my Lord, for whose sake I have lost all things. I consider them rubbish, that I may gain Christ and be found in him, not having a righteousness of my own that comes from the law, but that which is through faith in Christ—the righteousness that comes from God and is by faith. I want to know Christ and the power of his resurrection and the fellowship of sharing in his sufferings, becoming like him in his death, and so, somehow, to attain to the resurrection from the dead. (Phil. 3:7–11)

Paul simply had one passion: to know Christ. He realized that knowing Christ involved the cross for himself.

The concept of sharing Christ's suffering became such a radical part of Paul's life that he never ceased talking about it. He wrote to the Colossians, "Now I rejoice in what was suffered for you, and I fill up in my flesh what is still lacking in regard to Christ's afflictions, for the sake of his body, which is the church" (Col. 1:24). The idea that we might share Christ's suffering is strange and somewhat confusing. Some may charge Paul with thinking that somehow Christ's suffering was insufficient for human sin and that he (Paul) had to do something about it—but that's not the issue at all.

There is nothing deficient in Christ's offering of himself as a reconciling act. Paul expressed what he sought to live out as the deepest desire of his life: to join in the *fellowship* of Christ's suffering. He called for the pattern of Christ's own saving work to be incorporated into the life of every Christian. Paul hoped that we would reproduce that kind of passion, that willingness to suffer, to give ourselves in a cross-bearing style of life: a *life of mourning*.

Being crucified with Christ, then, was an experiential fact for Paul. We must guard against the temptation that has plagued the church from the beginning—the temptation to take Paul's crucifixion with Christ as merely symbolic.

GLORY IN OUR TROUBLES

In Romans 5:3–5, we find a strange word: we are to rejoice in our sufferings. Some versions say "glory in our troubles." This is a new idea; we don't usually glory in our troubles. Instead we moan and groan, we surrender to self-pity, and we wallow in the dust of our own weakness.

Paul's advice to the Roman Christians is dramatically different. In one of his greatest lyrical passages, he almost sings the intimate joy of his confidence in God. Remember that Paul was writing to the Christians in Rome—a place where it wasn't easy to be a Christian. In Rome, Christians were burned at the stake to provide light for the emperor's sporting events. They were fed to hungry beasts to entertain the clamoring mobs. It was more than difficult to be a Christian in Rome. Paul knew this, so he rose to this great height of Christian affirmation:

> We also rejoice in our sufferings, because we know that suffering produces perseverance; perseverance, character; and character, hope. And hope does not disappoint us, because God has poured out his love into our hearts by the Holy Spirit, whom he has given us.

How differently do we face the same situation! One may be driven to despair, the other spurred to triumphant action. One may see the situation as the end of hope; to the other it may be seen as a challenge to greatness.

We face situations differently according to the difference within us. If we've allowed ourselves to become weak when circumstances challenge us, if we whine and grovel under affliction, then when crisis comes, we can do nothing but despair. On the other hand, if we insist on meeting life with our heads up, determined to face and conquer obstacles, we can meet every situation with hope for victory.

NOT ALONE IN THE FIGHT

Let's nail this down now: the Christian faith makes no promise to deliver us from difficult situations—Jesus himself was not delivered. It is precisely because he had no relief, no deliverance, no escape from the inevitable cross, that we look to him for guidance. We feel that he was one of us, that he suffered as we suffer, that the antagonistic circumstances of life did not bypass him. So, this strange man upon his cross keeps driving us back again and again to the struggles that are a part of the very fabric of life.

Can you imagine how the followers of Jesus must have felt on the day of his crucifixion? Not only was there physical darkness because the sun veiled its face, but there was spiritual darkness of the bleakest order. Hopes and dreams were shattered.

But something happened to change things. That which at first seemed to be tragedy became the greatest triumph yet known to humanity. Out of the final depth of human wickedness has come the redeeming power of God for all people—the cross.

The cross assures us we are not alone against darkness— God is with us. God cares so much, his love is so deep, his concern is so compassionate that, in Christ, he will die for us.

The universe is not hollow at the center; the world that surrounds us is not an immense spiritual emptiness. At the heart of the universe and enveloping all of life is the God who cares for us, loves us, and longs for fellowship with us—this is what the cross says to us. If God can turn that tragedy into triumph, think what he can do with your life and mine—if we will let him.

That's the challenge. When it comes to the inevitable experience of suffering, we make two primary responses: *rebellion* and *resignation*. Both have some merit. For instance, we are to rebel if rebellion means struggle. This is especially true in our praying. One stance of prayer is *wrestling*. Paul says that when we don't know how we ought to pray, God's spirit "intercedes for us with groans that words cannot express" (Rom. 8:26). He also wrote to the Ephesians, "For our struggle is not against flesh and blood, but against the rulers, against the authorities, against the powers of this dark world and against the spiritual forces of evil in the heavenly realms" (Eph. 6:12).

So we rebel and we wrestle. In prayer, especially, we struggle to understand as we join with God to fight against evil and sin and sickness and suffering. But rebellion as our only, or primary, response to suffering will lead to resentment and bitterness.

The cross assures us we are not alone against darkness—God is with us.

Resignation is another common response. If resignation is the passive giving in to whatever is, it will destroy our spirits. But if resignation is the active yielding of ourselves to Christ, the willingness for him to set the pace and lead the way, the positive joining of our strength with his in surrender to his will, then resignation becomes a creative force.

A movement between rebellion and resignation, the rhythm of which is set by acceptance, will make suffering, struggle, and pain creative. By *acceptance* I do not mean that God causes or initiates pain and suffering. God allows it and uses it for our good and God's glory. So we accept suffering as a part of life where God has given us freedom and called us to be responsible, in a world where unexplainable evil is obviously present.

Under these conditions, we offer our suffering to Christ, and we begin to believe that God will not waste any of our suffering and struggle.

CONFORMED TO CHRIST

Martin Luther could not have expressed his thoughts about Christianity more clearly: "He who is not *crucianus,* if I may coin a word, is not *Christianus;* in other words, he who

does not bear his cross is no Christian, for he is not like his
Master, Jesus Christ."

Jesus' death on the cross and his call to deny ourselves,
take up his cross daily, and follow him are the heart of the
Christian faith, spirituality, and discipleship. Luther talked
about this idea in terms of being conformed to Christ:

> The cross teaches us to believe in hope even when there is no
> hope. The wisdom of the cross is deeply hidden in a profound
> mystery. In fact, there is no other way to heaven than taking up
> the cross of Christ. On account of this we must beware that the
> active life with its good works, and the contemplative life with its
> speculations, do not lead us astray. Both are most attractive and
> yield peace of mind, but for that very reason they hide real
> dangers, unless they are tempered by the cross and disturbed by
> adversaries. The cross is the surest path of all. Blessed is the man
> who understands this truth. It is a matter of necessity that we be
> destroyed and rendered formless, so that Christ may be formed
> within us, and Christ alone be in us. . . . Real mortifications do
> not happen in lonely places away from the society of other
> human beings. No! They happen in the home, the market
> place, in secular life. . . ."Being conformed to Christ" is not
> within our powers to achieve. It is God's gift, not our own work.

Luther's reflection was a response to Romans 8:28–30:

> And we know that in all things God works for the good of those
> who love him, who have been called according to his purpose.
> For those God foreknew he also predestined to be conformed
> to the likeness of his Son, that he might be the firstborn among
> many brothers. And those he predestined, he also called; those
> he called, he also justified; those he justified, he also glorified.

Luther does not limit his warning. In both our contempla-
tive and active lives, we can be led astray. Both lifestyles are

inviting, yielding peace of mind. Yet, implicit in both is the danger of betraying our Christian vocation. Peace can be seductive and numb us to the need for a dynamic relationship and dependence on God. The cross is essential. Keeping the cross at the center of our awareness always—just like Paul—forces us to assess the depth of our discipleship and the degree of our surrender to Christ.

THE HEART OF THE MATTER

※ How do you think perseverance in suffering leads to character, and how do you think character leads to hope?

※ Have you experienced rebellion and/or resignation in your relationship with God? Describe your experience.

※ What does "sharing in Christ's sufferings" mean to you?

THE HANDS AND FEET OF JESUS

If any of you lacks wisdom, he should ask God,
who gives generously to all without finding fault,
and it will be given to him.
James 1:5

Throughout history a few people, like Adam and Moses, have experienced Almighty God firsthand. Others, like Mary, Martha, John, and Matthew, knew Jesus as he walked the earth. But the rest—from the time of the Bible to today—have found their most significant encounters through the Holy Spirit. Make no mistake; these encounters are no less important. The Bible teaches that the three persons of the Trinity—God, Jesus, and the Holy Spirit—are different, yet in essence the same.

Let's imagine, then, the Day of Pentecost, a time when the early followers of Jesus experienced the Holy Spirit for the first time. Jesus had already been crucified, resurrected, spent forty days on earth, and then ascended back to heaven. His promise to them then, as told in Acts 1:8, was that they would receive power when the Holy Spirit came upon them, and that they would be witnesses "to the ends of the earth."

Notice that there was a succession of events: Jesus told his disciples to wait for the Holy Spirit first, and *then* they would receive power and be witnesses. So wait they did. The group continued to meet together for worship and prayer, and about ten days later, it happened:

Suddenly a sound like the blowing of a violent wind came from heaven and filled the whole house where they were sitting.

> They saw what seemed to be tongues of fire that separated and
> came to rest on each of them. All of them were filled with the
> Holy Spirit and began to speak in other tongues as the Spirit
> enabled them. (Acts 2:2–4)

A crowd quickly gathered to see what was happening, and after
a newly emboldened Peter began to speak, three thousand
people repented and were baptized. And the "church" began
to spread.

The problem, however, was that these new Christians
needed more than just forgiveness. They needed instruction
on how to live their lives in this new way. They needed, above
all, to be followers, *disciples* of Jesus.

WHAT WE DON'T WANT TO HEAR

When we consider the small group that experienced
Pentecost, James, the brother of Jesus, is not usually the first
person who comes to mind. He was one of two men named
James who was present that day, and he wasn't the one who
had been a part of Jesus' inner circle. No, this brother of Jesus
did not even believe Jesus was the Messiah until after the
Resurrection. And yet, in those days, a new life was born. And
with the power of the Holy Spirit leading him, James went on
to disciple the churches of the day—and every reader of the
Bible since—with his wisdom, challenging insights, and
forceful teachings. In the first chapter of his book, he reminds
us to consider it "pure joy" when we face trials. (v. 2). He
instructs us to be "quick to listen, slow to speak and slow to
become angry" (v. 19), and says that anyone who cannot keep
a tight rein on his tongue, "deceives himself and his religion is
worthless" (v. 26).

The thing about discipleship is that it often involves hearing
things we don't want to hear. But when spoken in love—and

guided by the power of the Spirit—those words can mean all the difference in our lives. And as we mature in our own relationship with God, we are called to disciple others with the help of that same power. As Jesus said, "Therefore go and make disciples of all nations, baptizing them in the name of the Father and of the Son and of the Holy Spirit, and teaching them to obey everything I have commanded you. And surely I am with you always, to the very end of the age" (Matt. 28:19–20).

> *Discipleship often involves hearing things we don't want to hear, but those words can mean all the difference.*

In a very real sense, each of us within the Christian community is to be a priest who ministers to others. We are to be an affirming, loving, and forgiving people—openly accepting of each other. When James wrote that we are to "pray one for another," he knew, I'm sure, that it is impossible to honestly pray for another person without coming to love, accept, and understand them.

Behavioral scientists tell us that most people today are plagued by feelings of loneliness and alienation. Even in urban centers, where neighbors are crowded in close around us, we live under an oppressive cloud of isolation. Never before has there been a time when our need for community was greater. We desperately want and need to share our deepest feelings with each other *and be listened to.*

Discipleship offers this enriching opportunity. Being open with one another about our faults and our feelings, and being humble enough to learn from others a little further down the path can be a powerful redemptive factor in physical and relational healing. To be a disciple is to be a learner, a follower. The word has the same root meaning as *pupil*. An apostle, on the other hand, is a doer—one who is sent to act out what he has learned. To be a Christian is to be a disciple *and* an apostle of Jesus Christ—this is being and doing. We take our shape from Jesus as disciples; we live out our wholeness as apostles. As much today as in the time of James, Jesus is our way to be and to do.

TESTIMONY, DEEDS, AND ENCOURAGEMENT

When George Morris and Eddie Fox wrote the book *Faith-Sharing* in 1996, they noted that approximately 77 percent of the persons who become Christian disciples do so because of the testimony, deeds, and encouragement of someone they trust. The authors remind us that there are three crucial issues revealed in this statistic.

> Effective faith-sharing involves a proper balance of word, deed, and encouragement. Word here is understood as proclamation and/or testimony. Deed is understood as faithful Christian lifestyle and service. Encouragement is understood as active initiative on the part of the faith-sharer. The Christian must take the initiative and do as Jesus commanded—"Go." Christians must go to the people, love the people, share word and life with the people, listen to the people, and offer Christ to the people.

This suggests a crucial issue for the local church. If 77 percent of the persons who become Christian disciples do so because of the testimony, deeds, and encouragement of someone they trust, then person-to-person faith-sharing—both evangelism of non-Christians and discipleship of Christians—must be the highest priority, and we must train our people in this ministry. Christians must be equipped not only with the personal knowledge of Jesus Christ and a knowledge of the gospel; they must also know how to relate to another person in such a way that trust develops.

That's really what discipleship is about, isn't it? Trust. And trust is built only through relationship. As Christians, we draw strength and courage from one another. In sharing, we learn from each other. This is emphasized in the words of John Wesley, who said that a caring fellowship exists when "one loving heart sets another heart on fire."

When I hear the words "heart on fire," I think of a woman named Pauline Hord. What a remarkable person! And what a unique blending of prayer, personal piety, servant ministry, social concern, and a life poured out for others.

One of Pauline's passions was literacy and prison ministry. Our state, Tennessee, has a tremendous literacy problem. Thousands of people in our home city of Memphis can't read and write well enough to function in an adequate way in society. Pauline was working with the public schools, training teachers in a new literacy method. She was giving three days a week, four or five hours a day, to teaching this new method of literacy in model programs. But also, once a week, she was driving more than a hundred miles each way to Parchman State Prison down in Mississippi to teach prisoners how to read and write. Along with this, she ministered to them in a more encompassing way as she shared her love and faith, and witnessed to the power of the gospel. And let's just say she was a "senior" senior at the time.

Back then, President George H. W. Bush had started a program in the United States called "Points of Light." He called for citizens to exercise positive and creative influence and service in the areas where they lived. (Sounds a lot like discipleship, doesn't it?) In the different cities and communities of America, people were recognized for being "points of light." I nominated Pauline Hord for that honor, and she was written up in our daily newspaper.

Well, President Bush came to Memphis. He wanted to honor the seven most outstanding "points of light" in our city—the people who had done the most for the sake of humankind. And Pauline Hord was one of those selected. The president invited these seven to have lunch with him when he came for his visit to Memphis.

But President Bush made a mistake: he scheduled the luncheon on a Tuesday. That was the day Pauline spent at Parchman Prison in Mississippi, teaching prisoners to read and write and witnessing to them of the love of Christ. She would not give that up to have lunch with the president.

Pauline knew that being a disciple meant commitment. For her, being the hands and feet of Jesus was more important than anything—including a meal with the President of the United States.

But what about us? How are we doing with discipling others? How are we doing with allowing them to disciple us? According to Jesus, the cost of discipleship is losing our lives in order that we might find them. Now, he did not call us to self-deprecation, but rather to self-fulfillment. Jesus knew, as modern psychologists are beginning to learn, that life is found only by getting outside ourselves.

In his marvelous book *Self-Renewal,* John W. Gardner puts it in proper perspective. He says:

> In the process of growing up the young person frees himself from utter dependence on others. As the process of maturing continues he must also free himself from the prison of self pre-occupation. To do so he need not surrender his individuality. But he must place it in the voluntary service of larger objectives.

What better objective than serving Christ?

Remember that serving Jesus means that we are to be his disciples, his learners and followers. And that may take us into areas of our cities, towns, and countrysides where we don't want to go. It may put us with people with whom we are not comfortable. It may call us to tasks we would not choose ourselves.

I have been warmed by the well-known story of a war correspondent who paused long enough to watch a nun as she unwrapped a wounded soldier's leg. Gangrene had set in, and the stench from the pus and blood was so repulsive that he turned away as he mumbled beneath his breath, "I wouldn't do that for a million dollars." She glanced up and replied, "Neither would I."

Because of who she was, she did not have to add—"But I do it for Jesus' sake, and out of love for him."

What are we willing to do out of love? Who will we lead, and who will we follow?

THE HEART OF THE MATTER

* When you hear the word *discipleship,* what comes to mind? Is the term positive, negative, or a mixture of both?

* Does your family of faith have structured discipleship programs? And if so, have you considered being involved? Why or why not?

* How can discipling others help us grow?

COMMUNION THROUGH CONVERSATION

Our Father in heaven, hallowed be your name,
your kingdom come, your will be done
on earth as it is in heaven.
Matt. 6:9–10

When our grandson Nathan was five months old, it became obvious that he had a vision problem; he couldn't focus his eyes. A pediatric ophthalmologist pronounced the grave word that Nathan had an underdeveloped optic nerve that was not medically correctable. The doctor used these words to indicate the condition: "The nerve is thin and white and about 50 percent normal size." He indicated that Nathan could face other vision problems as he grew and developed, as well.

As grandparents, Jerry and I were very concerned. We shared this struggle with our congregation in Memphis, and they journeyed through the trauma with us. They sustained our family in their loving prayers as countless people across the land sought God on Nathan's behalf.

When Nathan was nine months old, he and his family moved from Columbus, Ohio, to Hartford, Connecticut. Instead of following their original plan of waiting until Nathan was one year old to get another examination, his parents took him to the pediatric ophthalmologist in Hartford. This visit was nothing short of miraculous.

Nathan's new doctor couldn't believe the previous diagnosis. Instead of Nathan's optic nerve appearing "thin and white and about 50 percent normal size," the doctor said it looked "pink and healthy, and smaller than normal."

My daughter, Kim, couldn't believe what she was hearing. She knew, however, that God was at work, and prayer had been a huge dynamic in releasing and experiencing God's grace.

To be sure, there is mystery. Not all people for whom we pray are healed. What we need to claim is simply this: redemptive and wholeness-giving things happen when we pray that do not happen if we don't pray.

Prayer gives God an opportunity to meet our needs. Rather than some mandatory idea of *checking in*, it offers us the chance to commune on a regular basis with the one who made us, showing yet another example of God's extravagant heart in relationship with us.

HEARING, LISTENING, RESPONDING

Before we go any further, it's important to note that Christian prayer is not telling God what to do. Rather, it is conscious communication with God, sharing our needs with our Creator and making our requests known. But there is mystery here, too. Prayer involves struggle and surrender.

When we pray, we do not presume to tell God what to do, but we do not hesitate to share our needs. We leave it to the wisdom of God to decide precisely what is to be done about them. And we do not stop believing that the very sharing of those needs plays a dynamic role in God's response.

Though we believe that God knows best and is ordering all things for the best, we must not cease working toward the best that God has for us. The stoic may submit to fate and not work for the fulfillment of the good, but not the Christian. When a friend or family member is suffering through an illness, we do everything possible to demonstrate our loving care in the situation. We employ the best treatments of modern medicine as well as psychological support to enhance healing.

Shouldn't it be the same for prayer? If it is right to work for a certain end, isn't it just as right to pray for that purpose? The theologian John Baillie states it succinctly: "Clearly we must not pray for any end towards which it is wrong to labour, but likewise we must not labour toward any end for which it is wrong to pray."

If it is right to work for a certain end, isn't it just as right to pray for that purpose?

Clearly we must also understand that God wants to give good gifts to us, and that one of those gifts is to be in relationship with him. Communication with God really is possible. That seems so simple and so obvious, but is it?

Believing that I could actually talk with God and that God would *hear* and *listen* and *respond* to me has been one of the greatest difficulties in my life. This is an enormous assumption that needs to be fixed firmly in our minds. What it means is that I, among all the millions of people in the world, can have personal interaction with the Father.

God is like a shepherd who misses even one lost sheep from the flock; like a homemaker who sweeps a house clean to find one lost coin; like the father who grieves for one prodigal son who has left home. As Matthew 18:14 reminds us, "Your Father in heaven is not willing that any of these little ones should be lost."

Take a few minutes right now to think about that. God cares for each one of us as individuals. Is it hard for you to accept that? Do you believe it? Have you been praying as though you believe it?

One of the characteristics of a caring father is the desire to communicate with his children. He may communicate directly, by talking and spending time with them; or indirectly, by withholding the wisdom of his experience to encourage his children to think and judge for themselves. If God is like a father, then communication, direct or indirect, must be at the heart of our relationship.

The eleventh chapter of Luke tells us so much about prayer. In the parable of the friend at midnight, Jesus says to his disciples:

> Suppose one of you has a friend, and he goes to him at midnight and says, "Friend, lend me three loaves of bread, because a friend of mine on a journey has come to me, and I have nothing to set before him." Then the one inside answers, "Don't bother me. The door is already locked, and my children are with me in bed. I can't get up and give you anything." I tell you, though he will not get up and give him the bread because he is his friend, yet because of the man's boldness he will get up and give him as much as he needs. (vv. 5–8)

Please be aware that Jesus is not saying that the reluctant neighbor is a symbol or a metaphor for God. In this parable, Jesus is not teaching about the nature of God—he's teaching about the nature of our praying. Unfortunately, we often get confused on that point. That's the very reason we must keep our focus clear. God is the one whom we address as "Abba, Father." Jesus is saying that sincerity, persistence, and the voicing of our deepest needs, in keeping with God's will, is what prayer is all about.

We need that word. Many of us would be embarrassed to knock on a neighbor's door at midnight. But the parable reminds us that we can call on God at any time. Many of us would be reluctant to admit that we haven't been prepared for the very small emergency posed by the arrival of just one unexpected guest. Many of us hesitate to pray when we know we are at fault and have not done everything we should have done to remedy a situation. But this parable instructs us to ask God's help no matter what we have done or what we have failed to do. Many of us quickly take one *no* or even a *maybe* as a final answer to any request. But the parable tells us to persist, to keep on asking and seeking and knowing until we receive what God wants to give us.

Jesus brings it to a close with this: "So I say to you: Ask and it will be given to you; seek and you will find; knock and the door will be opened to you. For everyone who asks receives; he who seeks finds; and to him who knocks, the door will be opened" (Luke 11:9–10). Prayers that voice our deepest need in keeping with God's will are answered.

PRIVILEGE VS. DUTY

We need to consider another dimension of prayer. It's one of those *what if* questions that demands more action and life-response than it does reason or argument. "What if there are some things God either cannot or will not do until people pray?"

This question may seem shocking to you. At one time, it was to me, as well. It is common to think and affirm that God acts through persons. Deeds of mercy, acts of reconciliation, expressions of loving-kindness, deliberate righteous activity, peacemaking performances—all are seen as God's work through people. God's will is accomplished through us, we often say. On earth, God's work must be our own. So why is it such a long leap in our minds to think that God is as dependent upon our praying as he is upon our acting?

I have used the word *dependent* advisedly. I know it raises all sorts of theological red flags in many minds. To say that

God is dependent upon us creatures for anything is probably presumptuous to say the least, and blasphemous, to say the most. Yet, I use the word deliberately and ask you to consider the question openly. What if there are some things God either cannot or will not do until people pray?

Regardless of your response, we must remember that prayer is a privilege, not a duty. When considering it as a privilege, we begin to understand that it offers us creative freedom rather than bondage. We've been taught that we ought to pray, and when we don't, we feel guilty. But like love and friendship, music, books, art, laughter, and play, prayer is a great opportunity. Not to pray is an act of self-robbery.

We are free to pray. The privilege is open to all of us. The privilege is communion with God, feeling God's presence, and being aware of God's guidance.

Always remember this: prayer is relationship. It is being with God. It is meeting. It is a personal relationship in which you and God move from a *hello* of politeness to an embrace of love. It is communion. All other dimensions of prayer must take second place to this.

Relationship is a personal matter. In prayer, we are relating specifically to God who claims our total allegiance, calling us to love with all our heart, soul, and might: "Hear, O Israel: The LORD our God, the LORD is one. Love the LORD your God with all your heart and with all your soul and with all your strength" (Deut. 6:4–5).

A relationship becomes meaningful and real the moment you begin to single out a person from the crowd. Prayer becomes real when it is no longer a relationship in the third person but in the first and second persons, when God becomes more than the remote "Almighty," and becomes the singular and unique "Thou" or "You." The psalmist had discovered this intimacy: "O God, you are *my* God" (Ps. 63:1, italics mine).

When we discover a personal relationship with God, prayer goes beyond being a shop where we go to bargain and barter for the gifts of God. It becomes the home of the Father with whom we live, where all the treasures of God's love and concern are ours for the receiving.

THE HEART OF THE MATTER

❀ How would you describe your prayer life?

❀ Describe a time that God directly answered a prayer. How did that make you feel?

❀ What steps could you take to make your prayer times even more personal and relevant to your life?

PLANTED BY THE WATER

*. . . in all your ways acknowledge him,
and he will make your paths straight.*
Prov. 3:6

In his book *Invitation to Pilgrimage,* John Baillie wrote, "I am sure the bit of road that most requires to be illuminated is the point where it forks."

He's right. There is no place on our life journey where we need more light than at a crucial fork in the road, where we have to make a decision about which direction we are going to go. Thankfully, however, there's a promise related to that, too: God's Word, according to Psalm 119, is a lamp to our feet and a light for our paths (v. 105).

We do have a right to ask, seek, and know the will of God. But here's the catch: once we know it, nothing but obedience will do. The saints sought to arrive at the place in their relationship with Jesus that their one longing was to live and walk in a way that would please God and bring glory to God's name. St. Francis de Sales insisted that attaining this goal is possible:

> It is a great error of certain souls otherwise good and pious that they believe they cannot retain interior repose in the midst of business and perplexities. Surely there is no commotion greater than that of a vessel in the midst of the sea; yet those on board to not give up the thought of resting or sleeping, and the compass remains always in its place, turning towards the pole. Here is the point: We must be careful to keep the compass of our will in order, that it may never turn elsewhere than to the pole of the divine pleasure.

But how do we know God's will? How do we keep the compass of our will in order? The first and primary condition is complete surrender to obedience, which fits us to receive instruction and guidance about God's will for us.

There are three seeds which, when planted in the soil of obedience and humility, produce the fruit of God's will in our lives: (1) Scripture study; (2) Christian conferencing, or deliberately and honestly sharing with godly persons for both instruction and discernment; and (3) divine conviction brought by the Holy Spirit.

EVERYTHING WE NEED

I believe that God has a general will for all of God's people, which we can, to a marked degree, learn from the Bible. The apostle Paul makes it clear in his Second Letter to Timothy: "All Scripture is God-breathed and is useful for teaching, rebuking, correcting and training in righteousness, so that the man of God may be thoroughly equipped for every good work" (2 Tim. 3:16–17).

Christians believe that the Bible is God's Word. The Bible contains everything we need for salvation; for growth and discipleship; and for teaching, correction, and training in righteousness. Scripture has everything we need to be equipped for every good work.

In the divine school of obedience, then, there is only one textbook. We see it even in the life of Jesus. Though he communicated directly with the Father, he still depended on Scripture. He used it to teach and to convince others. He also needed it and used it for his own spiritual life and guidance.

Throughout his public life, Jesus lived by the Word of God. He conquered Satan with the sword of the Spirit, saying, "It is written." The consciousness with which Jesus opened his public preaching of the gospel was shaped by Scripture: "The

Spirit of the Lord is on me" . . . "so that the Scripture would be fulfilled . . ." (Luke 4:18; John 19:36). Jesus' understanding of Scripture illumined his suffering and allowed him to give himself to the cross. When he met with his disciples after his death and Resurrection, he taught them "what was said in all the Scriptures concerning himself" (Luke 24:27). In Scripture, Jesus found God's plan. He gave himself to fulfill it, and he used God's Word for his continual teaching.

WHERE TWO OR THREE ARE GATHERED

The second resource for knowing God's will is Christian conferencing. Jesus promised that where two or three are gathered in his name, he will be present also (Matt. 18:20). Conferencing with other godly persons who love Jesus and who want God's will for their lives and for ours is a dependable way to seek God's will.

I based one of the most dramatic moves of my life on accepting God's will as a result of Christian conferencing. My primary calling is clear: to be a pastor/preacher. Before this move, I was exercising my vocation with great joy, fruitful response, deep meaning, and continual spiritual growth as senior minister of a large congregation. People were being converted, healed, and coming to maturity in Christ. Our church's outreach ministries to the "least of these" and to non-Christians were expanding. My wife and I could not have been happier. We had served that congregation for twelve years and intended to stay until retirement.

Then came the call to the presidency of Asbury Theological Seminary. For months I would not consider the possibility, refusing even to talk with the search committee. The Holy Spirit impressed upon Jerry that I should at least consider what seemed to be a clear call through the committee. So we did— but without clarity on my part. In desperation, really, I began a conferencing process with godly people whom I loved and trusted, some that I had shared my Christian walk with for twenty-five years. I knew they loved God. I was certain they loved me and wanted God's best for me.

Through them, I discerned God's will. And once I made the decision to accept the seminary presidency, I had little doubt that I was in the center of God's will. Over and over again, my calling to that ministry was confirmed.

PLANTED IN OUR SPIRITS

As we said earlier, God has a general will for all believers that we can, to a large degree, learn from the Bible. There is, however, a special application of God's will concerning each of us personally. One of the ways we discern and test this is through Christian conferencing. We must not, however, forget one of the most powerful possibilities—the guidance that comes through the Holy Spirit. On many occasions, the Holy Spirit plants solidly in our minds and feelings certain convictions about God's will.

It was the Holy Spirit that quickened Jerry's heart and led her to convince me to consider talking with the presidential search committee of Asbury Seminary. Had she not responded to that impression of the Spirit, we might have missed God's call.

The Holy Spirit's work comes in different ways: through an intuition, the source of which we may not be able to identify; through an idea that comes seemingly from nowhere; through the word of a friend or a chance encounter; or through a surge of strength to our wills that calls us to act in a certain way in a particular circumstance.

These possibilities happen in the context of our sincerely wanting to be in God's will, when we are willingly submissive to his guidance. It is an amazing potential: that the Holy

Spirit will guide us. We have it on the promise of Jesus. When he was preparing his followers for his death, he promised them the Holy Spirit. Of the Holy Spirit he said, "When he, the Spirit of Truth, comes, he will guide you into all truth" (John 16:13). We can count on convictions that will come, impressed upon us by the Holy Spirit.

> *Knowing—and doing—God's will helps us become like trees planted by the water, producing fruit in season.*

We dare not fail to be open, and certainly we must not ignore and/or quench the Spirit. Yet, it is altogether in keeping with God's direction that we test even these convictions with Scripture and Christian conferencing.

PLANTED BY THE WATER

Remember, however, that once we discern God's will for our lives, we really have no choice but to obey. We become responsible for what we know. Knowing—and doing—God's will helps us become like trees planted by the water, producing fruit in season.

Have you ever noticed how many stories the Bible offers about trees and fruit? Jesus used the metaphor of trees and fruit for one of his most challenging teachings: "No good tree bears bad fruit, nor does a bad tree bear good fruit. Each tree is recognized by its own fruit. People do not pick figs from thornbushes, or grapes from briers" (Luke 6:43–44).

One of Jesus' harshest acts came one day when he was hungry and sought fruit from a fig tree. Finding nothing but leaves when it should have had figs, Jesus cursed it: "May you never bear fruit again!" (Matt. 21:19).

There is also that very first psalm:

Blessed is the man
who does not walk in the counsel of the wicked
or stand in the way of sinners
or sit in the seat of mockers.
But his delight is in the law of the LORD,
and on his law he meditates day and night.
He is like a tree planted by streams of water,
which yields its fruit in season
and whose leaf does not wither.
Whatever he does prospers.
Not so the wicked!
They are like chaff
that the wind blows away.
Therefore the wicked will not stand in the judgment,
nor sinners in the assembly of the righteous.
For the LORD watches over the way of the righteous,
but the way of the wicked will perish.

The psalmist presents a graphic parallel. The godly person, again, is like a tree planted by the water, which produces fruit in its season. The picture of the wicked, the ungodly, is in stark contrast. The psalmist changes the metaphor. They are "like chaff that the wind blows away."

The prophet Jeremiah paints a similar picture:

This is what the LORD says: "Cursed is the one who trusts in man, who depends on flesh for his strength and whose heart turns away from the LORD. He will be like a bush in the wastelands; he will not see prosperity when it comes. He will dwell in the parched places of the desert, in a salt land where no one lives. But blessed is the man who trusts in the LORD, whose confidence is in him. He will be like a tree planted by the water that sends out its roots by the stream. It does not fear when heat comes; its leaves are always green. It has no worries in a year of drought and never fails to bear fruit." (Jer. 17:5–8)

The message is clear through both the psalm and the prophet. There are two choices: we either trust in ourselves or we trust in God. Those who trust in themselves will be like chaff that "the wind blows away," like "a bush in the waste-lands." But those well-watered souls who trust in God—who seek and do the will of the Father—continue to be satisfied by the source.

The good news is that God's will for our lives is better than our human minds can ask or imagine. I see an unintentional description of this in a tribute to W. Robertson Nicholl, who for many years was the editor of *British Weekly*. George Jackson said, "He flung down a bunch of keys for me, and has set me to opening doors for myself on every side of me."

This is what God does. Even when we are walking closely with him, even when we are alive in Christ, he does not open all the doors. He flings down a bunch of keys and lets us find them and use them to unlock the doors for ourselves. In him we do not find a retreat from the pressures of life; we do not go into some monastery, closing the door behind us; but rather, life with God enables us to live with determination even amid the perplexities that once confounded us.

Paul was honest in his perplexity. "I do not understand what I do," he confessed. "For what I want to do I do not do, but what I hate I do" (Rom. 7:15). Conscious of his inadequacies and failures, he became increasingly aware that the only answer was a constant contact with the source of life: God. He found that source—the water by which he planted his tree—in Jesus Christ. And yet he lived out his life as a Christian amid the stress and strain of a pagan world. Paul's limitation in face of the perils he confronted only emphasized his frailty.

Although Paul's life was always difficult, the reality of Jesus' constant presence gave him determination and enabled him to say, "We are hard pressed on every side, but not crushed;

perplexed, but not in despair; persecuted, but not abandoned; struck down, but not destroyed" (2 Cor. 4:8–9).

Paul had found the true service of God in his life. His faith in God—and his dependence on God's leading—gave the confidence that no person can conjure up on his or her own. The same service of God is available for our lives. God casts a bunch of keys down before us; they are waiting to be used to unlock any door of life through which we might enter. Which one will you choose?

THE HEART OF THE MATTER

❋ In what ways has God offered you guidance?

❋ Do you relate more to the tree planted by the water or the bush in the wastelands? Why?

❋ Is there anything God has revealed to you about your life that you have yet to take hold of? What's standing in your way?

CHOOSING TO
BE WHOLE

*Create in me a pure heart, O God, and renew a steadfast spirit
within me. Restore to me the joy of your salvation
and grant me a willing spirit, to sustain me.*
Ps. 51:10, 12

Have you ever looked up the definition of *integrity*?
One definition is "the state of being complete or
undivided." It's a challenge I have experienced in
my own life.

For a long time, even in the early years of my ministry, I
was a one-man war. I used my deprived background as a
rationalization to excuse my dividedness. If I wasn't
successful, I had an excuse for my failure—even God
wouldn't expect much out of a poor kid from Perry County,
Mississippi! I didn't use this excuse often, but when I did, it
served as an ace in the hole. With it, I could explain away an
occasional bad grade in college or seminary; my background
was inadequate. I had a dreadful fear of failure, and this
rationalization was always there to fall back on.

I cultivated the estrangement of my various selves, yet
there was within me a surging desire to be whole. There was
something within me that demanded that I acquire—or
recover—integrity. To use the modern idiom, I knew that I
had to get it all together.

All the while, though, I fed myself a prescription from
my "Christian survival kit." It was the remedy we call *self-
condemnation*, and it was one of the primary prescriptions of
my brand of Christianity at that time. Self was to be put

down, negated, and brought under subjection—not to be fulfilled, unified, and made whole.

Instead of curing me, self-condemnation only made matters worse. Then something happened. A psychologist friend introduced me to the work of Abraham Maslow. This was the real treatment I desperately needed.

In the past, psychologists believed that we could best understand psychological health by first understanding psychological illness. Maslow provided an alternative viewpoint. Instead of studying sick people, he studied healthy ones—those who had achieved a high degree of self-satisfaction or fulfillment. These were the "healthy champions," the models of what people could be. That made a lot of sense to me.

I noted that Jesus was one of the people who, according to Maslow, demonstrated self-actualization. I started looking at Jesus in that light. I learned what Jesus was all about. He didn't come to tear me up and scatter the pieces. He came to help me get it all together. His purpose was to help me to find my true self and to celebrate it. That made all the difference. I began to understand the reality of choosing to be whole, not just once, but daily. I became able to look at God's grace and goodness in a new way.

Think of Psalm 51, for example. We may think David is trying to rationalize his actions or seeking to evade responsibility when he says, "Surely I was sinful at birth, sinful from the time my mother conceived me" (Ps. 51:5). This misses the point altogether. If David thinks for a moment that he has an excuse, that thought soon leaves him as he faces the spectacle he has made of himself. Standing before the mirror of his soul, he sees himself in every repugnant detail. He paints a picture of himself so repulsive that he is afraid God will completely recoil from him if he looks upon him before the process of cleansing makes him presentable again. This psalm is the urgent plea from David's heart in seeking a fresh start.

When we look in the mirror of our own souls, we don't all see the same reflection, for we are not the same people. Yet each of us has a soul-reflection. Some of us never look at it, but we need to.

Look now in the mirror of your soul. What do you see? Pride, deception, sexual lust, self-righteousness, wasted talent, callousness toward the needs of others, idolatry (making a god out of your money, security, or self-image), cheating, lying, neurotic fear, failure to develop the gifts God has given you, or exaggerated ego that puts others down and puffs self up?

The good news is, no matter what's there, God offers forgiveness for it, as well as the choice to have it become part of our past rather than part of our present or our future. The new life that God promises is not just some throwaway idea that was only relevant in biblical times; it is every bit as applicable today.

Unfortunately, many professing Christians still don't walk in true freedom, understanding that they can be fit for kingdom living. Is it because we think God has only partly forgiven us? If we have a tough time loving and accepting God, it may be because our attention is still upon our sin, rather than on him. We spend our energy wrestling with our guilt. But true conviction has to come to us at the core of our being, and when it does, it overcomes all other temporary feelings or reversals into guilt and self-condemnation: *Christ has forgiven me. My sin is no longer the issue. I am being made new. I will not be uptight over my sins. I will choose to stand tall in God's forgiveness and allow him to mold me after his likeness.*

In those times, then, when we find our days—or our selves—to be meaningless, when we feel complacent, we must remember that there really is more to life than we have known thus far. The choices that bombard us on a daily basis—everything from a new deodorant to a new Jaguar—won't provide us freedom. But God—through Christ—does. He frees us from meaninglessness by providing a sense of purpose, a sense of mission, a sense of responsibility, a feeling of self-worth, a basis for relationships, and a reason for being. He's just that good.

CHRIST FREES US AND FITS US

The full measure of Christ means that he comes to both free us and fit us for kingdom living. Incredible news, isn't it? Keep in mind Paul's word to the Colossians: "For he has rescued us from the dominion of darkness and brought us into the kingdom of the Son he loves, in whom we have redemption, the forgiveness of sins" (Col. 1:13–14). As for the "fitting" part, recall that the answer is not giving our sins to Jesus. Rather, the key is giving *ourselves* to Jesus and allowing him to take the sins away. In the process, however, we are as holy as we want to be. This week, have you asked yourself: do you want to be holy? Are you willing to yield?

CLAIMING THE PROMISE

Do you recall the grand promise? It's certainly one worth committing to memory: "I tell you the truth, anyone who has faith in me will do what I have been doing. He will do even greater things than these, because I am going to the Father" (John 14:12). Don't forget, though, that it's easy to settle for less than is promised and far less than is possible. Yes, you can do even greater things. For that to happen, however, you must remember that *you are more than you think you are,* and that *there are things that you can be and do, but will never be and do apart from Jesus Christ.* Has this study had an effect on your faith in any area? If so, how?

THE SUREST PATH OF ALL

Think now of Paul's one-sentence autobiography: "I have been crucified with Christ and I no longer live, but Christ lives in me" (Gal. 2:20). Paul's commitment to Christ shaped every decision he made and determined every step he took. How close are we to saying the same? Identifying with Jesus, according to Paul, means identifying with Jesus' suffering. As Christians, we can't simply sidestep challenges just because of the one we serve. But there is good news: suffering produces perseverance, perseverance, character; and character, hope. And knowing this, we can face any situation with our heads held high. In what ways could Jesus be with you in a time of suffering?

THE HANDS AND FEET OF JESUS

The gift of the Holy Spirit, which fell on the early followers of Jesus at Pentecost, changed their lives forever. It still carries the same power today. As we mature in our own relationship with God, we are called to disciple others with the help of the Holy Spirit's power. It matters not whether we've got it all together; God simply works through willing vessels. At the same time, no matter how mature we become, God still expects us to be disciplined, too. Is there anyone in your life that you currently disciple (either formally or informally)? Is there anyone who disciples you? If your answer to either of these questions is no, consider asking God to open your eyes to the people around you. Certainly there are both people who need your wisdom and people who have wisdom of their own to give you.

COMMUNION THROUGH CONVERSATION

Prayer is not about telling God what to do; it's about giving him the chance to meet our needs. Remember that God really does want to give good gifts to us, and that one of those gifts is to be in relationship with us. He is like the shepherd who misses even one lost sheep from the flock, and as such, it is his desire that we come to him with our concerns, our problems, our fears, and our joys so that he might share this life with us. In that vein, have you been considering your prayer life a privilege or a duty? Have you established a regular practice of coming before the Father? If not, what is keeping you from it, and how can you overcome those challenges?

PLANTED BY THE WATER

Yes, we can know the will of God for our lives. We can know it through the Scriptures, through the wise counsel of godly people, and even through the Holy Spirit. But once we hear that direction, we must be obedient to it if we are to walk in the fullness of Christ. Recall now the many examples of trees being planted by the water, gaining their strength directly from the source. Recall, too, that those who choose to live their lives without connection to (and guidance from) God are like a bush in the wastelands. How could/would your life be different if you sought consistent guidance from God?

Week Five

THE HOME OF GRACE

THE DWELLING
PLACE OF WONDER

And God placed all things under his feet and appointed him
to be head over everything for the church. . . .
Eph. 1:22

American dramatist Robert Sherwood once described
theater as "the dwelling place of wonder." That is
well said—but I believe the definition is more apt for
the church than it is for the stage.

Think about it: the church is the dwelling place of
wonder. The idea resonates with Paul's word in Ephesians.
When God raised Jesus from the dead, he:

> . . . seated him at his right hand in the heavenly realms, far
> above all rule and authority, power and dominion, and every
> title that can be given, not only in the present age but also in
> the one to come. And God placed all things under his feet and
> appointed him to be head over everything for the church,
> which is his body, the fullness of him who fills everything in
> every way. (Eph. 1:20–23)

Ephesians has been called the "Epistle of the Ascension,"
and that's exactly what it is; it is here that we meet the
exalted Christ of power.

In the modern church, we make too little of the
Ascension of Christ. The early Christians were post-
Resurrection, post-Ascension Christians. They knew the
gospel story. They knew the Jesus who was once a baby in his
mother's arms—but not that now. They knew the Jesus who
was once a carpenter, teacher, companion, and friend—but

not that now. They knew one whose healing love mercifully blessed all he touched, saw, heard, and spoke to; that healing love is not limited by time and space now. The self-giving, suffering servant who hung on a cross, pouring out his life and love on our behalf does not still hang there. God raised him from the dead!

But there is more: this Jesus ascended, and in doing so, brought the curtain up to reveal a new act in the drama. Pentecost happened. The Spirit of this ascended one poured out on his followers, and the church was born. He remains "far above all rule and authority, power and dominion." His name is exalted above "every title that can be given, not only in the present age but also in the one to come" (Eph.1:21). Everything has been put under his feet. He is the head, the authority. He has been given dominion. And the church is his body—the fullness of him who fills everything in every way.

Do you stir with excitement when you think of that, as I do? The church is the dwelling place of the wonder of Christ. We—the church—are his body.

THE WONDER OF THE GOSPEL

So, what is it that is so wondrous about being Christ's body? It begins with the wonder of the gospel. John Wesley defined the visible church as a congregation of faithful people, "in which the pure word of God is preached." For Wesley, the Scriptures were "the only and sufficient rule both of Christian faith and practice."

In his pamphlet entitled "The Character of a Methodist," Wesley said: "As to all opinions which do not strike at the root of Christianity, we think and let think." One of the distinguishing characteristics of Methodism throughout history is that it has been inclusive in spirit. The Methodist

Church has been ecumenical and open to other denominations. One example of this openness is that it does not require
rebaptism when persons from other Christian denominations
present themselves for membership.

This inclusiveness, however, does not mean that
Methodists are unconcerned about doctrine and theology.
One of the grave problems of contemporary United
Methodism—as well as other mainline churches—is that it
has substituted ideology for theology.

One ideology that is currently damning us is that of
pluralism and diversity. Don't misunderstand me: I do value
cultural pluralism and diversity (and I believe my life in the
ministry witnesses to that fact). However, I believe that when
we make *theological pluralism* an ideology, when we act as
though diversity is redemptive in itself and make it an ultimate value over orthodox Christian doctrine, we undermine
both the gospel and the church. Jesus Christ, and his uniqueness as God's ultimate revelation, is central to the gospel. And
the church must be the dwelling place of that gospel.

For the past couple of decades, the discovered remains of
the sunken *Titanic* have received a lot of media attention.
Along the way, we have learned a great deal about that tragedy.
For example, when the crew of the *Titanic* knew it was in difficulty, an *SOS* radio signal went out. The ship *California* was
only ten miles away, but it could not respond because its radio
was turned off. Though the *Carpathia* was further away, its
radio was on—and that vessel arrived in time to save lives.

Our "radio signal" in the church is the gospel, and the
centrality of Christ is the heart of the gospel. What we think
about Christ will determine how we approach mission and
evangelism. What we think Christ can do for people's lives will
determine how we plan for ministry.

THE WONDER OF GRACE

If the church is the dwelling place of the gospel, then it also must be a dwelling place for grace. Wesley referred to the fellowship of the church as "one loving heart setting another heart on fire." The quality of our fellowship must be so grace-filled that people experience redemptive power in relationships. My favorite way of thinking about that is to picture the church as a home of grace. If the church is a home of grace—if grace is what defines the family of God—then the church must be a home for all.

Over the years, former U.S. President Jimmy Carter has been in the news for a variety of reasons. He has negotiated peace conversations, monitored elections, spoken out on issues like poverty and immigration, and led the cause for a Palestinian state. But almost every time I've seen him on TV or read about him, I recall a story that was printed in *Newsweek* many years ago.

If the church is a home of grace, then the church must be a home for all.

The article was about Hubert Humphrey's memorial service. Hundreds of people came from all over the world to say good-bye to their old friend and colleague. But one guest was shunned and ignored by virtually everyone there. That person was former President Richard Nixon. Not long before, Nixon had endured the shame and infamy of Watergate. Humphrey's service brought Nixon back to Washington for the first time since he resigned from the presidency.

Before the service, people were avoiding Nixon like the plague—no one would talk to him or even acknowledge him.

Then, a very special thing happened, perhaps the only thing that could have broken the ice. Jimmy Carter, who was president at that time, came into the room and was about to be seated. When he saw President Nixon standing against the wall, all by himself, Carter walked over to him as though he were going to greet a family member. Nixon stuck out his hand to the president, but to the surprise of everyone there, the two of them embraced, and Carter said, "Welcome home, Mr. President! Welcome back home again!"

Commenting on the scene, *Newsweek* reported, "If there was a turning point in Nixon's long ordeal in the wilderness, it was at that moment in that gesture of love and compassion."

Isn't that what the church is all about? It's that home of grace where we, too, can be greeted with an embrace and feel that we belong.

WELCOME TO OUR HOME OF GRACE!

What if congregations began posting huge signs that read "Welcome to our home of grace"? Do you think people might show up who hadn't before? How would people respond to your church if the people could say—and really mean—the following?

- Welcome home, you who are weary and heavy laden; welcome home!
- Welcome home, you who are sinking under the onslaught of life; welcome home!
- Welcome home, single mothers, forsaken by selfish men; welcome home!
- Welcome home, young people who love rock music, whose body piercings say more about seeking and desire to belong than protest and rebellion; welcome home!

✳ Welcome home, sexually broken, and you who are confused in your identity; welcome home!

✳ Welcome home, you who are poor, both the working poor and those who have given up altogether; welcome home!

✳ Welcome home, you who have spent your life seeking success but have yet to find significance; welcome home!

✳ Welcome home, you millions of baby boomers who are coming to retirement age but don't know what to do with yourselves; welcome home!

✳ Welcome home, immigrants—legal and illegal— who desperately need safety and a place to belong; welcome home!

✳ Welcome home, you who do not feel at home anywhere; welcome home!

The church is meant to be the home of grace, a home for all. If it is not a home for all, it is not a home at all.

If this is a hard concept to swallow, we must ask ourselves if, at any point, we've lost our confidence in the gospel. The wonder of it all is that the gospel is still a saving, reconciling, healing power.

Though we may think we're doing a good job of letting our lights shine before others and offering a welcoming presence, consider this: large national samples of unchurched people have indicated that most have never been invited to church by a Christian. Not only that, but most unchurched people have said that they've never been told by a Christian what it means to believe in Christ, and never been invited to embrace Jesus as their Lord and Savior.

Has the church really strayed so far from its Wesleyan roots?

John Wesley's central objective—upon which the Methodist movement was founded—was to "widen" and "deepen" what he called "the work of God." George Hunter reminds us that "the work of God" here does not refer to everything we do in obedience to God. Wesley used the term to mean "the conversion of sinners from sin to holiness." He never substantially deviated from that evangelical meaning of the term. Wesley had confidence in the gospel and the claims that the gospel makes about the cross as the heart of its good news. The good news is that through Christ, God has done for us what we could not do for ourselves. Our responsibility, now as much as ever, is to be Christ to others, to extend that sense of wonder, that hand of welcome, and that message of grace.

THE HEART OF THE MATTER

❈ Be honest: how do you feel about the idea of the church as the home for all?

❈ Is it difficult for you to share with others what God has done in your life or to invite them to church? Why do you think that is?

❈ How did you end up in your current congregation? Did you first come because you believed it could be a home of wonder or grace? If someone invited you, take a moment to thank God for that person now.

> *Now you are the body of Christ,*
> *and each one of you is a part of it.*
> 1 Cor. 12:27

Will Campbell has been a prophetic challenger of the church for decades. He's a sort of renegade Baptist preacher who calls himself a "steeple dropout," a preacher without a pulpit, and he ministers to people in some of the most interesting and fascinating ways. He has been a civil rights activist, a prison reform advocate, and even a priest to members of the Ku Klux Klan. He was the minister to the University of Mississippi at the height of the civil rights movement back in the 1960s, and he worked with the National Council of Churches following his time at Ole Miss. But he became disillusioned with the way the National Council did ministry, feeling that they were far more sociological than they were theological, so he became a "minister-at-large."

When I was with The Upper Room, Will Campbell lived close by on a small farm in Mt. Juliet, Tennessee. He was lecturing all over the nation and had written a number of books. In my opinion, his best book is *Brother to a Dragonfly;* it is at once a sensitive biography and a compelling novel.

In the book, Campbell shares a confrontation with an agnostic friend named P. D. East, the editor of a radical little newspaper in Petal, Mississippi. I got to know East during my student days at the University of Southern Mississippi. He had an interesting discourse in which he compared the church to an Easter chicken, and Campbell shared the story in his book.

You know, Preacher Will, that Church of yours and Mr. Jesus is like an Easter chicken my little Karen got one time. Man, it was a pretty thing. Dyed a deep purple. Bought it at the grocery store. . . . But pretty soon that baby chicken started feathering out. You know, sprouting little pinfeathers. Wings and tail and all that. And you know what? Them new feathers weren't purple. No siree bob, that damn chicken wasn't really purple at all. That damn chicken was a Rhode Island Red. And when all them little red feathers started growing out from under that purple it was one hell of a sight. All of a sudden Karen couldn't stand that chicken anymore. . . . Well, we took that half-purple and half-red thing out to her Grandma's house and threw it in the chicken yard with all the other chickens. It was still different, you understand. That little chicken. And the other chickens knew it was different. And they resisted it. . . . Pecked it, chased it all over the yard. Wouldn't have anything to do with it. Wouldn't even let it get on the roost with them. And that little chicken knew it was different too. It didn't bother any of the others. Wouldn't fight back or anything. Just stayed by itself. Really suffered too. But little by little, day by day, that chicken came around. Pretty soon, even before all the purple grew off it, while it was still just a little bit different, that damn thing was behaving just about like the rest of them chickens. Man, it would fight back, peck the hell out of the ones littler than it was, knock them down to catch a bug if it got to it in time. Yes siree bob, the chicken world turned that Easter chicken around. And now you can't tell one chicken from another. They're all just alike. The Easter chicken is just one more chicken. There ain't a damn thing different about it.

Campbell knew that East wanted to argue, so he didn't want to disappoint him: "Well, P. D., the Easter chicken is still useful. It lays eggs, doesn't it?" That's exactly what P. D. wanted him to say.

Yeah, Preacher Will. It lays eggs. But they all lay eggs. Who needs a Easter chicken for that? And the Rotary Club serves coffee. And the Four-H Club says prayers. The Red Cross takes up offerings for hurricane victims. Mental health does counseling, and the Boy Scouts have youth programs.

I share the story to put the question about the nature of the church in perspective. Unfortunately, Campbell's friend is right. Too many congregations are like an Easter chicken, painted up a little bit on the outside, but the same as other chickens when the color's gone—a gathering of people who do not have that distinctive mark of Jesus upon them.

THE BODY

This week, we've already considered that the church can be the dwelling place of wonder, the dwelling place of the gospel, and the dwelling place of grace. We don't have to stretch our thinking, then, to conclude that the church can—and should—also be the dwelling place of Christ. As Christ is the Incarnation of God, so the church is to be the continuation of Christ's presence in the world.

One of the most prominent images of the church in the New Testament, then, is the body of Christ. Donald English tells a quaint but poignant story that speaks to this image. In Birmingham, England, there is a store called Louis'. It's a great chain store in one of the main streets, and it wanted to expand. In the way of the expansion was a little chapel of the Quakers, a Friends Meeting House. Louis' sent a letter to the leaders of the Friends Meeting House, saying:

Dear Sirs:
We wish to extend our premises. We see that your building is right in the way. We wish therefore to buy your building and demolish it so that we might expand our store. We will pay you any price you care to name. If you will name a price we will settle the matter as quickly as possible. Yours, Sincerely

They got a letter back by reply which said:

> Dear Sirs:
> We in the Friends Meeting House note the desire of Louis' to extend. We observe that our building is right in your way. We would point out, however, that we have been on our site longer than you've been on yours, and we are so determined to stay where we are that we will happily buy Louis'. If therefore you would like to name a suitable price we will settle the matter as quickly as possible. Signed, Cadbury

Here's the clincher, if it has not dawned on you. The Cadburys are great chocolatiers in England; they own an enormous business with outlets all across the country. The Cadburys are also Quakers. They could very well have bought Louis' many times over.

We are a letter of Christ; his seal is upon us.

The point is that it is not the size of the building that counts, but who signs the letter. One thinks of Paul's word to the church of Corinth: "You show that you are a letter from Christ . . . written not with ink but with the Spirit of the Living God . . ." (2 Cor. 3:3).

The church is never in a defensive position as long as we remember who we are, and *whose* we are: the body of Christ through whom he intends to become head over everything. Christ himself signs the letter of the church. It is Christ with whom every power in the universe must reckon. We who make up the church are not operating out of human wisdom and strength alone; we are a new creation, a fellowship of Resurrection life. We are a letter of Christ; his seal is upon us.

The church is Christ's body—the fullness of him who fills everything in every way.

BEING CHRIST IN THE WORLD

The image of the church as the body of Christ speaks primarily of serving. To be the body of Christ is to be his presence in the world. Let's ponder what that means.

Being Christ in the world means that we must see through the eyes of Christ. Through Christ's eyes, there is no East or West, no black or white, no slave or free, no male or female. All are one in Christ. Through Christ's eyes, every person is of worth, and the church must respond in loving concern for each one. We must not be selective in our outreach, seeking only those who are like us. In Christ's eyes, every person is a person for whom Christ died.

Not only must we see through Christ's eyes, we must also speak with the voice of Christ. And we must speak to people in every situation and every condition. It is not a matter of social gospel or personal gospel; it's a matter of the good news of Jesus Christ. War and peace, inflation and the national deficit, how the government spends the taxes we pay, where and how people live, abortion, pornography, adultery, immigration—whatever is of concern to human beings is a concern to the gospel. The gospel has something to say for our human plight, and we can't forbid it from addressing any area of human life. Nothing is off limits to Christ.

The church, then, must speak fearlessly and compassionately the word of God's good news to every person, wherever he or she may be. But that's not all; the church must also heal with hands of Christ. The ministry of the church is the ministry of redemption and healing.

I served Christ Church in Memphis, Tennessee, for twelve years before becoming president of Asbury Theological

Seminary. During my last weeks at Christ Church, we received a lot of mail—Jerry and I were overwhelmed with the outpouring of love. But the letters that moved me most deeply were those that witnessed to the transformation that had come through the ministry of the church. Over and over again, people said in one way or another, "the church has been Christ to me."

Consider, for example, a young man who had fought a battle with his sexuality and was being healed. He was finding the power to leave a lifestyle behind; in fact, he was planning to get married and was disappointed that I would not be the pastor performing his wedding. Four sentences in his letter captured the depth of his gratitude.

> Thank you. You knew all about me and you loved me. Thank this congregation. They didn't know, but had they known, I believe they would have loved me just the same. Christ is present here.

I thanked God then that the congregation had come through, and as a result, so had this man. The church had been the body of Christ to him, rather than just some painted-up, no-different-from-anyone-else Easter chicken. That's about as beautiful as it gets.

THE HEART OF THE MATTER

❋ What does it mean to you to be a part of the body of Christ?

❋ In what ways has the church represented the body of Christ to you?

❋ If you were to be honest, how do you do at seeing others through the eyes of Christ? Why do you think that is?

WHAT DEFINES
CHRISTIAN COMMUNITY?

Dear friends, let us love one another,
for love comes from God.
1 John 4:7

The poet Robert Frost once wrote, "Home is the place where, when you have to go there, they have to take you in." Christian congregations are often called *families of faith,* suggesting that the church is that family's home. That's a good picture of the church—a home of grace, the only institution I know where the requirement for joining is that you are not worthy to be a member.

Remember that the message of the Bible is not that we are perfect, or that we should be perfect in the way we normally define that word. The point instead is that God is gracious. Even though we have faults, we have been assigned a place in God's family and a room in God's home. All we have to do is be humble enough to admit our need for such a thing—and be willing to extend to others the same grace that we hope they will extend to us.

Make no mistake: God planned for us to live in communities and environments of grace. We all need grace. All of us enter relationships with others with a mixed bag of strengths and weaknesses. Some folks engender immediate trust; others give us reason to disregard them and write them off. But God created us for community, meaning that we need to trust God and others.

In such a community and environment, we not only deliberately pay attention to and seek to care for others, but we also begin to trust people who are different from us. You can see this dynamic in action at any Alcoholics Anonymous meeting. In that setting, you'll find people from many different ethnic groups: Hispanics, African Americans, Asians, Caucasians. There will be rich and poor folks, men and women, young and old. All have one thing in common: they are battling an addiction. The primary dynamic of the meeting is humility and trust, expressed in statements like, "Hi, I'm Tom, and I'm an alcoholic." That beginning point of humility and trust breaks the grip of alcoholism. If grace can happen in an arena like AA, it can certainly happen with the church, as well.

Although our Christian faith and experience must be personal, they cannot be private. A personal experience of Christ kept private soon dies, because there is no such thing as solitary Christianity. Whether or not this has been your experience, there is no true Christianity apart from the church. The more private we seek to make our faith, the more distorted it becomes. Jesus' life and ministry were never matters of private religious feelings that he kept to himself; he lived his life for others.

God Addiction

What, then, does it take to become a true Christian community? First, I believe, is a complete obsession with God. If we are not completely obsessed with God, we fall short of what should define us.

It's okay if you don't like the way I express that. But if you are going to disagree, first consider what I mean. The driving power of our life is our response to the greatest commandment sounded by Jesus: "Love the Lord your God with all your heart and with all your soul and with all your mind and with all your strength" (Mark 12:30). God should be so real to us that we pulsate with the unshakable conviction that *in God we live and move and have our being;* that *in God lies all truth, love, goodness, and beauty.*

There are different kinds of knowing. It interests me that in both the Old and the New Testament, words for sexual intercourse are translated as *knowing.* Adam *knew* Eve, and she conceived. Joseph *did not know* Mary, yet she conceived a child of the Holy Spirit. The Bible presents that kind of knowing as the deepest human bond—the joining together of male and female.

Then there's the word of Paul to the Ephesians, the prayer that they could "know this love that surpasses knowledge" and "be filled to the measure of all the fullness of God" (Eph. 3:19). Yes, there are different kinds of knowing, just as there are different kinds of congregations, and different kinds of places where people think and talk about God. The hope, however, is that no matter what kind of congregation, denomination, or cultural composition, your church would be a community defined by a complete obsession with God.

In a challenging *Christianity Today* article entitled "Saint Nasty," Mark Galli called the obsession of the saints "God addictions." The most revealing expression of this addiction is the prophet Jeremiah. Like so many others, he was so God-driven that he couldn't break his fixation even when he wanted to. Listen to a verse from Jeremiah chapter 20:

> But if I say, "I will not mention him or speak any more in his name," his word is in my heart like a fire, a fire shut up in my bones. I am weary of holding it in; indeed, I cannot. (v. 9)

SOUR SAINTS AIN'T NO SAINTS AT ALL

In addition to being obsessed with God, I believe the Christian community should be defined as one that is happy and holy. Wesley talked about being holy and happy.

Authentic and strength-giving holiness does not begin with—
nor is it preoccupied with—rules and regulations; rather, it
begins with God. Holiness that centers on rigid rules and
regulations turns us into "sour saints," self-assessing and
constantly stressed out in seeking to keep the law. Sour saints
ain't no saints at all.

*We become holy as God shows us moral
and spiritual things in startling clarity,
and gives us the strength to do his will.*

For holiness to be happy, it must be connected with the Holy
Spirit. We don't become holy by "main strength and awkward-
ness," to use a Mississippi phrase. We become holy by the power
of the Holy Spirit. With heart and soul and mind consumed
with God, our joy lies in doing God's will. We become holy as
God shows us moral and spiritual things in startling clarity, and
gives us the strength to do his will. We not only become holy, we
also become happy. Show me a person who is holy but not
happy, and I'll show you a person whose holiness is at least a bit
distorted. Let's look to Paul's word to the Colossians:

> Let the word of Christ dwell in you richly as you teach and
> admonish one another with all wisdom, and as you sing
> psalms, hymns and spiritual songs with gratitude in your hearts
> to God. (3:16)

That's the description of a joyful and holy community: the
word of Christ dwells within it richly; it is a happy community,
one that sings with gratitude.

Holiness should be contagious. I was talking with Ron
Crandall, a professor at Asbury Seminary, about this, and he

reminded me of C. S. Lewis's phrase, "the good infection." Lewis used this phrase in his book *Mere Christianity* to describe the Holy Spirit as the third Person of the Trinity, generated out of eternal love, for God is not static. "The union between the Father and the Son is such a live and concrete thing that this union itself is also a Person."

Acknowledging that he might be thought irreverent, Lewis contended that the most important difference between Christianity and all other religions is that the life of God is in the Trinity—and is a kind of dance. In other relationships, the spirit, spelled with a lowercase *s,* does not actually become a "person." But in the divine dance of love, the Spirit is truly a Person who is one with and yet other than the Father and the Son. Lewis then writes:

> And now, what does it all matter? It matters more than anything else in the world. The whole dance, or drama, or pattern of this three-personal life is to be played out in each one of us; or (putting it the other way round) each one of us has got to enter that pattern, take his place in that dance. There is no other way to the happiness for which we were made. Good things as well as bad, you know, are caught by a kind of infection. If you want to get warm you must stand near the fire: if you want to be wet you must get into the water. If you want joy, power, peace, eternal life, you must get close to, or even into, the thing that has them. They are not a sort of prize which God could, if He chose, just hand out to anyone. They are a great fountain of energy and beauty spurting up at the very centre of reality. If you are close to it, the spray will wet you: if you are not, you will remain dry.

A NEW PATTERN

The New Testament makes it abundantly clear—as do the early church fathers—that the early Christians saw themselves as part of a new creation. By coming together, they were shaping a new pattern for the human community, a pattern of love and sharing which reflected the very life of the Trinity.

Paul described the essence of the new community, the church, in his call to bear one another's burdens and so fulfill the law of Christ. In his book *Christian Wholeness,* my friend Tom Langford expressed it this way:

> Our strength, as Christians, comes from our relation to God and to the people of God. We are directly related to God, and in that relationship we find our ability to move to action and to live for others. Indirectly we receive the strength of God through sharing in Christian community. This is a sharing which empowers, guides, corrects, and renews our ability to be and to serve.
>
> Emphasis upon Christian strength is often neglected for fear of abuse, and the strength given by community is often neglected because it is so meagerly realized in contemporary experience. Yet the church is the Body of Christ; it is the special embodiment of the Holy Spirit. The church is the community graciously given by God to persons who need and who intensely seek community. Into our solitary, isolated style of living there comes a concrete community of persons who are willing to bear one another's burdens, enhance one another's living, to be together in joy and in sorrow, in hope and in hurt, at ordinary moments and in critical junctures of human experience.
>
> In the context of the church, strength comes from lives which are bound together. The chief binding is not that of a desperate clinging to one another in a dangerous and frightening world. . . . The deeper truth, however, is that persons in Christian community are bound together by a common love, by a common worship, and by a common mission. The church is the community of persons who are in community with Jesus Christ. It is a community of persons precisely because there is a common center for their lives.

THE HEART OF THE MATTER

❈ On a scale of one to ten (ten being the highest), how "addicted" would you say you are to God? Why is that?

❈ In what ways could holiness be contagious? What about joy?

❈ Is your congregation bound by common love, common worship and common mission? In what ways can you individually improve—or detract from—the situation?

THE PEOPLE OF GOD

Once you were not a people,
but now you are the people of God.
1 Pet. 2:10

I was converted under the powerful preaching of Brother Wiley Grisson, a preacher at the Eastside Baptist Church in Perry County, Mississippi. Holy Communion was not a big part of the worship life of that congregation; they observed it twice a year. That's the way they talked about it, too—they *observed* it. They would not have been familiar with the word *Eucharist,* our term for Holy Communion. They would not understand—and would certainly be taken aback—to hear me refer to one of their classic gospel songs as a great Eucharistic hymn.

All the same, I remember the joy with which we sang "Come and Dine." Today, when I am in a worship service where people are cold and formal, moving through the liturgy without feeling, not truly acknowledging who we are as Christians, I remember that song and how those people sang.

> Jesus has a table spread
> Where the saints of God are fed
> He invites his chosen people, "Come and dine";
> With his manna he doth feed
> And supplies our every need;
> O 'tis sweet to sup with Jesus all the time!

And how the chorus would ring out:

> "Come and dine," the Master calleth, "Come and dine";
> You may feast at Jesus' table all the time;
> He who fed the multitude, turned the water into wine,
> To the hungry calleth now, "Come and dine."

For those weary, hardworking, poverty-bound country folks, this was the very best image for fellowship: a meal together. They knew joy, despite their circumstances, because they were confident of their salvation. They knew that one day there would be a great banquet spread in heaven; and they knew that Jesus would be the host to welcome them home. The joy of salvation was not squelched, no matter what might be going on in their grinding everyday lives.

PART OF GOD'S HISTORY

Earlier this week, we considered "the body of Christ" as a New Testament image of the church. "The people of God" is also one of the most prominent images in Scripture. Consider 1 Peter 2:9–10:

> But you are a chosen people, a royal priesthood, a holy nation,
> a people belonging to God, that you may declare the praises of
> him who called you out of darkness into his wonderful light.
> Once you were not a people, but now you are the people of
> God; once you had not received mercy, but now you have
> received mercy.

The church, then, is the people of God, called especially to fulfill God's purposes. Notice that Peter applies all of the Old Testament images of "the people of God" to the New Testament church: "a chosen people, a royal priesthood, a holy nation." This image, then, grounds the church in the history of Israel. Having heard the promises of God, and knowing God's discipline and mercy, the church, the "people of God," also knew that it had received a distinct calling. This calling was to "declare the praises of him who called you out of darkness into his wonderful light."

When this image is alive in our congregations, we know we are a part of God's history. When we are firmly grounded in that knowledge, our evangelism, mission, and worship becomes a part of God's working out his purpose in history. The local church becomes a kingdom community.

FELLOWSHIP

One of the most important characteristics of the "people of God" image is fellowship: *we belong*. We belong to Christ, and we belong to each other. That's what the people at Eastside Baptist Church sang about: "Come and dine." We are part of a kingdom people whose roots stretch back to creation, to God's call to Abraham, and our hope stretches forward to a time when all the people of God will be gathered in the kingdom for a heavenly banquet. When this image comes alive in our local congregations, our church will begin to look more like *the church*.

John Wesley emphasized this dimension of fellowship in the way he structured the Methodist movement. He had an exceedingly strong doctrine of the church, and his commitment to the church was unquestioned. He remained a priest in the Church of England, resisting the idea of the Methodist movement becoming a separate body of believers. He urged all the members of the Methodist societies to stay in communion with and to receive the sacraments of the Church of England. His beliefs and his life demonstrated his love and commitment to the established church.

Yet Wesley knew that it took more than hearing the Word and participating in the sacraments for Christian growth and discipleship. A deep fellowship for mutual encouragement, examination, accountability, and service was essential.

There is a dubious story of how actress Tallulah Bankhead went into an Episcopal church that was so "high" liturgically that Roman Catholics were said to attend to see what it was like in their church before all the reform of the second Vatican Council. The procession came in, and it was quite a spectacle, including a crucifer and Bible-bearer, a handsomely robed choir, and a retired bishop who wore a gem-studded chasuble and waved a censer that emitted a cloud of incense. Bankhead, so the story goes, reached over and touched the old gentleman. Getting his attention, she said in her gravelly voice, "Dahling! Your gown is divine, but your purse is on fire."

> *When the fellowship of the church*
> *comes alive by the presence*
> *of the Holy Spirit, it draws people.*
> *That's what evangelism is all about.*

That's *not* the kind of fire we need in the church! We need the fire of Christian fellowship, shaped and empowered by the Holy Spirit—the kind of fellowship Wesley talked about when he talked about one loving heart setting another heart on fire.

Effective evangelism happens when the congregation becomes a living witness, when we move from seeing evangelism as a special program, inspired preaching, or individual Christian testimony to the church and its fellowship being the evangelist. In fact, the research of Wesley scholar Thomas Albin suggests that the early Methodists often witnessed the experience of justifying grace only after they had participated in small group experiences for a period of months or even years. What they knew *about* Christ, as a result of John Wesley's preaching, did not become real for them personally until they had experienced the fellowship, nurture, and accountability of the people of God.

When the fellowship of the church comes alive by the presence of the Holy Spirit, inspiring and empowering people to care for one another, the fellowship is redemptive within itself, and it draws people. That's what evangelism is all about.

COGNITIVE DISSONANCE

Through the years, I have kept a note from a fellow in our congregation in Memphis. He was a part of our singles ministry. I heard him play the flute in a singles talent show and urged our director of music ministries to have him play in the worship service. He had played in one of our Christmas services and I wrote him a note of thanks. This stimulated his note to me:

> Dear Maxie:
> In my adult life I've experienced events that I didn't think possible. My first wife married my best friend, my second wife killed herself, and I've been left with enormous debts. However, I discovered Christ United Methodist and Positive Christian Singles. The unconditional acceptance and true Christian love of PCS Social Singles has changed my life forever. There's no way to describe how, for the first time in my life, I'm truly happy and at peace with God and myself. I may not ever have much money, but there's no one in this church any richer!

My friend experienced a fellowship that was redemptive within itself; it was not simply one person doing evangelism, but the fellowship as a whole, the congregation becoming the evangelist.

Stanford University psychologist Dr. Leon Festinger developed a theory called "cognitive dissonance." As strange as it may sound, it is actually very simple. It refers to our awareness of the big gap between our ideas and our actions. It's about what we believe versus what we do; our goals versus our deeds.

The big problem of the church, I believe, is cognitive dissonance: we know but we don't act. We have head knowledge, but our souls are not burning with the faith that won't let us sit still. We continue to debate the purpose the church. Why so? It is so clear, underscored in every chapter of the New Testament:

- Go into all the world and preach the good news to all creation. (Mark 16:15)
- Whatever you did not do for one of the least of these, you did not do for me. (Matt. 25:45)

Our witness is in word and deed, in our speaking and in our actions. Our witness is also in the quality of our fellowship. I do believe that our personal testimony is important, but the quality of our fellowship within the Christian community is another ingredient in proclaiming the wonderful deeds of him who called us out of darkness into his marvelous light. There must be a quality about our life together that will reach out and invite— and when people come, the fellowship must be redemptive.

Are we ready, then, to work on this together, to "come and dine?" There is much work to be done, and the people of God are the ones most fit for the job.

THE HEART OF THE MATTER

- What has God taught you through the fellowship of other Christians?

- Why might congregational evangelism—the idea of the church itself being the witness—be as important as individual evangelism?

- What does it mean to you to love your neighbor as yourself?

ESSENTIAL CHARACTERISTICS

> *They devoted themselves to the apostles' teaching*
> *and to the fellowship, to the breaking of bread and to*
> *prayer. Everyone was filled with awe, and many*
> *wonders and miraculous signs were done by the apostles.*
> *Acts 2:42–43*

Can you imagine being a member of the first church? From the very beginning, it was miraculous. In a single day, according to Acts 2, some three thousand people gladly received the gospel and were baptized. That marked the mighty beginning of a church that would turn the world upside down. It would be worthwhile, then, for us to take a closer look.

A LEARNING CHURCH

The early church was made up of people who had come to a sure knowledge of salvation through Christ's death and Resurrection and had received the living presence of his Spirit. Those first Christians were sure of who they were, because they were sure of Christ.

Does that raise a question in your mind? Are we sure of who we are? One of the primary tasks of any congregation is to recover a strong sense of identity. This church at Pentecost was made up of people who were thoroughly convinced, soundly converted, and Holy Spirit-filled.

That's not all: another reason to look to the first church for inspiration, encouragement, and guidance is that it was a learning church. In the King James Version, Acts 2:42 says that the church members "continued steadfastly in the apostles' doctrine." The word for *doctrine* is an active rather than passive term. In his book *The Acts of the Apostles,* William Barclay explains this approach to understanding the continually unfolding wisdom of God:

> One of the great perils of the Church is that it offers a static faith which looks back instead of looking forward. The riches of Christ are unsearchable and inexhaustible, therefore we should ever be going forward. (Ever seeking to probe the mystery and find its direction for our present day life). The Christian must journey, not looking to the sunset, but to the sunrise. We should count it a wasted day when we do not learn something new and we have not penetrated more deeply into the wisdom and the grace of God.

A PRAYING CHURCH

The first church was also a praying church. You can't miss that, even at a casual reading of the text: "They devoted themselves to the apostles' teaching and to the fellowship, to the breaking of bread and to prayer" (Acts 2:42).

Not that long ago, I came across Psalm 130 in my devotional reading. For me it is one of the most moving of the psalms, and I especially like verses 5 and 6:

> I wait for the LORD, my soul waits,
> and in his word I put my hope.
> My soul waits for the LORD
> more than watchmen wait for the morning,
> more than watchmen wait for the morning.

I am sure this psalm was often on the people's lips. They were a praying people, as part of the faith life of Israel.

The believers who received Christ at Pentecost may have known those verses, too. They had the vibrant, vital presence of the Spirit, and it invested their prayers with even deeper meaning. They could wait for the Lord as a watchman waits for the morning, because of the sure gift of the Holy Spirit. They took into that early fellowship their strong commitment to prayer, which was now clothed with new power, the power of the living Christ, present through the Holy Spirit. No doubt, the early church was a praying church.

Today, we need to be the same. I am convinced that we are not as effective in our Christian living as we could be, and we do not live in the power of the Holy Spirit because we don't spend enough time on our knees.

A SHARING CHURCH

The early church was also a sharing church. Their sharing is as important as any other aspect. "All the believers were together and had everything in common. Selling their possessions and goods, they gave to anyone as he had need" (Acts 2:44–45). They were a radical people— it was their response to the Holy Spirit working in their lives and making them genuinely concerned for the total community's well being.

Unfortunately, the system didn't work, and the church gave it up before the end of the first century. It failed simply because of sin, not because it wasn't God's way. There is no question about it: the model reflects the heart and mind of Christ. Those early Christians had an intense feeling of responsibility for each other. So great was their commitment to one another that they willingly sold everything they had and distributed the essentials of life according to the need of everyone. And remember, all of that was in response to the living Spirit of Christ taking control of their lives. It was a sharing fellowship.

A CHURCH IN FELLOWSHIP

I once read of a seminary professor whose last years were spent in and out of hospitals, suffering from a debilitating and incurable disease. As he reflected on his ministry, he said that when he began, he thought of himself as the expert, standing upon the bank of the stream of life, shouting instructions to the swimmers down below.

In the second stage of his ministry, if he saw someone going down for the third time, he would plunge into the water, get the person started in the right direction again, and then return to the bank. He was the rescuer.

But during his last years, he saw the human family—his fellow strugglers in the water, their arms around each other, all trying to reach the shore. What a marvelous image of the church: fellow strugglers, arms around each other, committed to the same Lord and to the same purpose in life. With that picture in mind, let's pursue one more essential characteristic modeled by the early church: fellowship.

Almost everything that happened in the early church took place either within the fellowship or grew out of the direction and power received from the fellowship. For the most part, the believers practiced their fellowship in small groups—gathering in homes, breaking bread together, listening to the teaching of an apostle, sharing with one another about their lives, praying for one another, and then returning to the world.

As we noted earlier, John Wesley, the founder of the Methodist movement, knew that it took more than hearing the Word and participating in the sacrament for Christian growth and discipleship. A deep fellowship for mutual encouragement, examination, accountability, and service is essential. Colin Wilbur Williams explains:

> Wesley sought to restore the depth and transforming power of the fellowship present in the early Church. He felt the Church of England did not sufficiently provide for the fellowship of

Christian people, which he sensed to have been the unique characteristic of the early Church. Speaking of the failure of the fellowship of the Church of England, he wrote: "Look east or west, north or south; name what parish you please: is there Christian fellowship there? Rather, are not the bulk of parishioners a mere rope of sand? What Christian connection is there between them? What intercourse in spiritual things? What watching over each other's souls? What bearing of one another's burdens?"

Wesley established class meetings to provide the fellowship essential for Christian growth and discipleship. I do not believe there is anything more essential for growing as a disciple than this kind of experience.

I've seen it in my own life—I could share witness after witness of the power of small-group fellowship, the growth it provides, the changed lives, the attitude shifts, even the vocational moves. We all need a support system; without it, we can't stay alive spiritually, and many people can't survive emotionally or even physically.

> *We all need a support system;*
> *without it, we can't stay alive spiritually.*

Consider this example: a man had been unfaithful to his wife, walked all over her, used her, and went his own selfish way. At the same time, he kept coming back to his wife, asking her to accept him, and promising to be faithful. The story repeated over and over again, until the woman could take it no more. She committed suicide. That woman had a friend in our church who had a similar experience with her own husband. The church member told me the story of her friend's suicide.

As she wept, she confessed, "That has been my temptation. You don't know how many times I have been on the verge of suicide. But I couldn't follow through on my temptation, because of the love and support of Christ through this church." The people in her small group, she said, literally kept her alive.

You see, at the heart of small-group fellowship is the genuine care that all of us desperately need. We study, we pray, we talk with one another at a level deeper than the superficial conversations that make up most our days, and by the work of grace, a community of caring develops. Who doesn't need that?

One of the most exciting things I see happening in the church today is coming from people coming together as "missional" groups. They are committed to discerning God's will as individuals. They want to know the best way to invest themselves vocationally as servants of Christ. They are also committed to finding a corporate expression of ministry in which to live out their call as Christians together.

As an expression of this dynamic, I have seen four young couples in Memphis deliberately relocate from middle-class suburban neighborhoods to a community of the working poor fighting all the battles of poverty: drug infestation, substandard housing, and the diminishing of identity. I have seen small groups, inspired separately but acting corporately, ignite a congregation into taking on a radical ministry of serving designed to transform an entire urban residential community. The primary expression of this ministry is redevelopment, not only of housing needs but also of community structures—all in the name of Jesus Christ. I have seen the radical commitment of four young doctors, who came to Memphis just out of medical school "on mission," result in the establishment of Christ Community Clinic, which has become a national model for delivering health care to the poor.

Memphis is not unique. Anywhere Christians are being faithful in the church, these incredible changes can happen. But they don't just occur naturally—it takes guidance from the Holy Spirit, as well as the support of a loving congregation that understands learning, praying, sharing, and fellowship as much as the people of the early church.

THE HEART OF THE MATTER

✳ When you hear stories about the couples who gave up the comforts of their suburban neighborhoods for the challenges of poverty-stricken communities, how does that make you feel? Inspired? Challenged? Uneasy? Why do you think that is?

✳ Where do you personally find fellowship in the body of Christ?

✳ How is your congregation like/unlike the early church?

THE PRIESTHOOD
OF ALL BELIEVERS

But you are a chosen people, a royal priesthood, a holy nation,
a people belonging to God, that you may declare the praises of
him who called you out of darkness into his wonderful light.
1 Pet. 2:9

E arly one morning, a woman heard the garbage truck arrive, and suddenly remembered that she had not put out her trash the night before. She was barely out of bed; her hair was rolled in those ugly, prickly wire curlers; she had on a shabby bathrobe; and her face was covered with a chalk-like, white cream. She was a sight to behold. She went running out and shouted to the garbage truck driver, "Am I too late for the garbage?"

He took one look at her and said, "No, hop right in!"

This woman definitely looked peculiar, but the King James Version uses the word "peculiar" in a different way—to describe God's chosen people, who have been called out of darkness into God's wonderful light. The word *peculiar* comes from Latin, meaning "of one's private property." So, as Christians, our relationship to God is unique: we are God's own people, God's possession.

Our identity and vocation—as both individual Christians and the corporate church—are tied together and shaped by the nature of God, to whom we belong. In Acts 15, Paul and Barnabas witnessed to what God was miraculously doing among the Gentiles. James sought to interpret their story: "Brothers, listen to me. Simon has described to us how God at first showed his concern by taking from the Gentiles a people for himself" (Acts 15:13–14). The King James Version calls it "a people for his name." The Greek word for *people* is *laos*.

Our identity comes from God and our relationship to God. He has taken "a people for himself," or "a people for his name."

Throughout the history of the church, there has been a lay/clergy dichotomy—a sharp division between those who "do" ministry and those to whom it is "done." There is something ironic about the development of this dynamic, because there is absolutely nothing in the New Testament to suggest the notion. In his book *The Other Six Days*, R. Paul Stevens reminds us that the word *layperson* (*laikoi*) was first used by Clement of Rome at the end of the first century but was never used by an inspired apostle to describe second-class, untrained, and unequipped Christians. Stevens suggests that we ought to eliminate it from our vocabulary. I'm not sure about that, but we need to stay aware of the fact that "laity" in its proper New Testament sense of *laos*—the people of God—is a term of great honor denoting the enormous privilege and mission of the whole people of God. That's what Peter is talking about. Once we were not a people at all—but now, in Christ, we are a "chosen people, a royal priesthood, a holy nation, a people belonging to God."

*The church does not **have** a ministry; it **is** a ministry. It does not **have** a mission; it **is** a mission.*

Here is a rather ironic twist: Stevens tells us that the word *clergy* comes from the Greek word *kléros*, which means "the appointed or endowed" ones. But here's the kicker. In Scripture, this word is not used for the leaders of the people, but rather for the whole people of God (Col. 1:12; Eph. 1:11;

Gal. 3:29). Again, ironically, the church is without laity in the usual sense of the word, but full of clergy in the true sense of the word—all baptized Christians are endowed, commissioned, and appointed by God to continue God's service and mission in the world.

So underscore this in your reflection: the church does not *have* a ministry; it *is* a ministry. It does not *have* a mission; it *is* a mission. There is only one people in the church—God's own people. "Only a layperson" is a phrase that should never be found on our lips. It is irreverent and demeaning and a denial of the truth.

God has adopted, called, empowered, and gifted all Christians to receive the incredible privilege of being co-laborers of God, lovers of one another, and those who share God's love with the world—this is our true identity and the essence of the phrase "the priesthood of all believers."

To gain perspective on this calling, we can observe the areas of the world where the church is experiencing explosive growth. God is bringing revival in China, where thirty-two thousand people pray to receive Christ every day. It's happening in Africa, too; twenty thousand people pray to receive Christ there every day. In Iran—can you believe it—more Muslims have come to know Christ since 1980 than in the previous one thousand years in that nation. We must not give up on the Muslim world.

These revival fires are burning where Christians claim their identity, or where ministers are willing to repent, humble themselves, pray, and seek God's face. These revival fires are burning where people take seriously their call to witness, declaring the praises of him who called them out of darkness into his wonderful light.

The church is growing in those places where Christian believers are open to and dependent upon the Holy Spirit. I have observed it in believers all around the world. They are what I call "practicing supernaturalists." They expect the Holy Spirit to be dynamically present, converting, reconciling, healing, providing, and guiding. It is no wonder that the church is spreading like wildfire in China, Africa, Cuba, and other places around the world, and that stories of miracles abound. Believers fan the fire of the Holy Spirit. Christians in those regions—not just the ordained folks—see themselves as ministers, and they live as such.

Great revival is going on all over the world—and for the most part, the mainline church of America is missing it. Diminishing membership suggests that we have become too secure in our congregations, giving all of our attention to ourselves and forsaking the evangelistic call to go into all the world and preach the gospel. We have become "come-to," rather than "go-to," churches. And the reason for that may be that we don't know who we are and we don't know what our function is.

It is rather easy for Western Christians, especially in the United States, to settle into the comfort and security of congregational life that meets *our* needs. We worship with our friends and with like-minded people, and we have pastors who function primarily as chaplains: baptizing babies, marrying our children, visiting the sick, and directing funeral services. As a result, the church becomes a kind of "spiritual resting place" by default. Maintenance rather than mission claims our attention and energy.

There is another problem as well. *Awakened* Christians—those who have experienced a "second touch" and have been renewed and revived by the Holy Spirit in their faith and Christian walk—grow weary from what they experience as dullness, even deadness, in the church. Sometimes we feel bereft of power, and wonder if God is going to act in our setting. Here, then, is a word for us:

> Like newborn babies, crave pure spiritual milk, so that by it
> you may grow up in your salvation, now that you have tasted
> that the Lord is good. As you come to him, the living Stone—
> rejected by men but chosen by God and precious to him— you
> also, like living stones, are being built into a spiritual house to
> be a holy priesthood, offering spiritual sacrifices acceptable to
> God through Jesus Christ. (1 Pet. 2:2–5)

There is our power—Jesus Christ, the living stone, who builds
us into a spiritual house. His Spirit, indwelling us, is the
constant source of power which keeps us going and growing
as God's people. God is not going to give up on his church.
The Holy Spirit is alive and working.

EMPOWERED BY THE HOLY SPIRIT

One final observation: the church that is responsive to the
gospel and earnestly desires to obey the Great Commission is
charismatic by its very nature. By *charismatic,* I mean that the
church came to birth through the Holy Spirit, thus the church
lives and functions by the Holy Spirit. Theoretically, no one
would disagree with that. But functionally, we do disagree.
Where is the mainline denomination, or the classic evangelical
denomination, that incorporates this conviction as a core principle by which the congregation orders its life? The charismatic
church not only depends on the power of the Holy Spirit for
life and sustenance, but also expects a Spirit-empowered
community of love and mutual caring where forgiveness,
healing, reconciliation, restoration, deliverance, social witness,
and the breakdown of racial, economic, and social barriers are
anticipated as the norm, not the miraculous.

Let's not count out miracles, though. Consider this story
from the book *The God Who Hung on the Cross.* In the Ukraine,
part of the former Soviet Union, thousands of churches had
been destroyed, and of course, the building of new church

facilities had been banned. But after the fall of communism, the government granted a group of believers a swampland in which to construct a new church.

> It took six months, but the Christians packed the marshy bog with fill dirt—wheelbarrow by wheelbarrow. But once they had prepared the site, they could not obtain any bricks to construct their building. So local officials permitted them to tear down a nearby unused nuclear missile silo, a relic of the Cold War.
>
> When the believers started dismantling the silo and carrying the bricks away—again, wheelbarrow by wheelbarrow—one man found a fragile slip of paper, rolled tightly and stuck between two bricks. The others gathered around as he carefully unrolled the old paper and smoothed it flat. "These bricks," he read out loud, straining to decipher the faded ink, "were purchased to build a house of worship. But they were confiscated by the government to build a missile silo. May it please the Lord that these bricks will one day be used to build a house to His glory!"

Those people knew where the power was.

But what about us? Do we know? When was the last time you attempted something so great for God that you knew you would fail unless you were empowered by the Holy Spirit? When was the last time your congregation or ministry looked around, discovered a particular area of concern or need, and attempted to do something about it that on the surface would appear impossible? Maybe you looked at your resources and you looked at the need and you felt it just couldn't be done; there was no way. But you decided to do it anyway, knowing that unless God intervened and provided the supernatural power and resources of the Holy Spirit, you would fail.

You see, we Christians and the church must always be attempting those things that we know we'll fail miserably in unless the Holy Spirit comes with power. It happens—it happens all the time where people are faithful, when they act boldly, when they follow God's will, and when they humbly trust that God will provide.

THE HEART OF THE MATTER

❋ Why do you think Christianity is spreading so much more quickly in other countries than in the United States? What kind of hindrances has our society put in place?

❋ Is your congregation more of a "come-to" or "go-to" church? Why do you think that is? What can you personally do to help it become more "go-to?"

❋ Think now of the last time you experienced something miraculous. Thank God for that miracle once again. (And if you don't believe you ever have experienced a miracle, ask God to show you how he is at work around you.)

Day 35

*Therefore go and make disciples of all nations, baptizing them
in the name of the Father and of the Son and of the Holy Spirit,
and teaching them to obey everything I have commanded you.
And surely I am with you always, to the very end of the age.
Matt. 28:19–20*

My mother and father—whom I affectionately called "Mutt" and "Cobell" in my adult life—are buried at the cemetery near Eastside Baptist Church. On Cobell's tombstone are the last words she spoke to Mutt from her deathbed: "I'll see you." On his tombstone is his response: "I'll be there." It was a great witness to their confidence in eternal life and in heaven as our home.

Last words are important, since they often stem from the very core of our being. Let's turn, then, to some of the last words of Jesus:

> All authority in heaven and on earth has been given to me.
> Therefore go and make disciples of all nations, baptizing them
> in the name of the Father and of the Son and of the Holy
> Spirit, and teaching them to obey everything I have
> commanded you. And surely I am with you always, to the very
> end of the age. (Matt. 28:18–20)

New Testament scholar Otto Michel has said this passage is "the key to understanding the whole of Matthew's gospel" and that these verses are "the summary of the whole gospel." Michel's statement certainly underscores the crucial importance of this word of Jesus. These last words to his disciples represent the marching orders that are to be followed until he returns. There is no more powerful motivational text for Christian mission and evangelistic zeal. Yet in too many cases, this text is not shaping the ministry and mission of our church.

These words, known today as the Great Commission, were spoken by the resurrected Christ, appearing to his disciples. Note that they come after the Resurrection. The gospel is the good news of what God has done to death in raising Jesus from the grave. The heart of the gospel message proclaimed by the apostles was a shout: "Christ is risen!" At Easter, death was conquered and a new ruler was enthroned in the world. "Christ the King!" What happened as a result of that event is absolutely decisive, uniquely authoritative, and universally valid.

"All authority in heaven and on earth has been given to me," Christ claimed. "All nations" are to be made disciples and baptized in the name of God. They are to be taught all that Jesus commanded—and the promise that keeps going is that he will be with us "to the very end of the age."

Somehow, though, the Great Commission is no longer a part of the DNA of the church. Could that be because the church is no longer convinced of the uniqueness of Jesus? If that's the case, then we have no compulsion to share the gospel with the world. Let's imagine, then, a church shaped by the Great Commission—one that truly honors the last words of Jesus.

ONLY DISCIPLES CAN MAKE DISCIPLES

Let's first consider the obvious: only disciples can make disciples. This is an example of what Stephen Covey calls "beginning with the end in mind." The bottom line of the Great Commission is discipleship; that's the "end" we must keep in mind. Otherwise, we will end up with an evangelism void of discipleship, privately engaging but socially irrelevant.

Discipleship means following Jesus to the end that we are transformed into his likeness. Herein lies our problem: the majority of contemporary Christians have no compelling sense that being Christian means understanding and conforming our lives to the teachings of Jesus. As a result, our society is too frequently missing Christians who witness by following their Master in modeling justice, peace, and righteousness. How have we missed the point?

Now, a second observation: a congregation of disciples committed to making disciples will become apostolic in style and passion. In his book *The Once and Future Church,* Loren Mead described three eras in church history. The apostolic era of the church began at Pentecost and was characterized by rapid growth amid hostility and persecution. It ended with the Edict of Milan in 313 AD, when Emperor Constantine "Christianized" the empire. This ushered in a period of seventeen centuries during which the church existed within a culture generally friendly to Christianity. Mead calls this second era "Christendom." Today we have entered another era. Much of the church is once again living in a hostile—or at least indifferent—atmosphere. Mead refers to this as "post-Christendom."

In this postmodern, post-Christendom age, we must become apostolic in our style and passion. In style, we must move from being that previously described "come-to" congregation to being a "go-to" church. Because we've been schooled in the "come-to" church, one credible observer of Christian evangelism claims that 95 percent of all Christians in North America will not lead anyone to Christ in their entire lifetime.

This paradigm shift is not just about style; we must also be apostolic in our passion. For the apostles, Jesus Christ was the good news. This conviction is the only power that will give us the passion to be for our age what the first-century

Christians were for theirs. We must be convinced of—and we must be passionate about—what Christ can do for individuals and for society. Our big task is to put the message of the gospel in context for our culture, because Christ's saving power is universal; it is not culturally bound, but culturally friendly and infinitely adaptable.

This week, we spent a lot of time thinking about the church and our congregations as a dwelling place of wonder, the body of Christ, and the people of God. It isn't enough, however, to just be those things and hope that others outside will somehow stumble upon us. No, we must go into the world, taking with us the message of God's extravagant love.

"Going to" may be the greatest apostolic task of our day. You may know the story:

- Thirty-six million Americans (14 percent of the population) live in poverty. Are we going to them?
- Ninety percent of the United States' population lives in urban settings. Are we going to them?
- Seventy million individuals in the United States are under the age of eighteen. Are we going to them?
- Nearly one million foreign-born people immigrate to this country every year. Are we going to them?
- Thirty-two million people in America speak a language other than English as their primary language. Are we going to them?
- We have more unsaved and unchurched people in our nation than ever before in our history—172 million. Are we going to them?

Next week, in the final few days of this study, we'll look more at how we can be partners in the gospel through our prayers, presence, gifts, and service.

THE DWELLING PLACE OF WONDER

Remember the picture of the church as the dwelling place of wonder, as well as the home of grace. It is meant to be a home for all. Remember, too, the illustration of former U.S. President Jimmy Carter greeting former President Richard Nixon with a bold embrace. Is this concept of grace hard to grasp? Have we lost our confidence in the gospel as a saving, reconciling, healing power? If so, how can we return to Wesley's ideal of the church fellowship as "one loving heart setting another heart on fire?" The quality of our fellowship must be so grace-filled that people experience redemptive power in relationship. If it is not a home for all, it is not a home at all.

THE BODY OF CHRIST

Remember that purple-painted Easter chicken? It looked different than the other chickens on the outside, but turned out to be just like them in the end. So what about the church? Are we just like everyone else? Or do we bear the distinctive mark of Jesus? As the body of Christ, we must remember both who we are and whose we are, and that our calling speaks primarily of service. We must see through the eyes of Christ, speak with the voice of Christ, and heal with the hands of Christ. Then, and only then, will we be able to reach a dying world with the saving grace of the gospel. As you have continued your study this week, have you thought any more about your congregation as the body of Christ? Is that body a healthy one?

WHAT DEFINES CHRISTIAN COMMUNITY?

Make no mistake: God planned for us to live in communities and environments of grace. In that type of environment, we begin to pay more attention to others, and we learn to trust people who aren't like us. That's part of the Christian community, but it's not all. Christian communities must also be places where people are completely obsessed with God. They must be places where the people are both happy and holy. Remember that "sour saints ain't no saints at all"; authentic and strength-giving holiness does not begin with us, and it is not preoccupied with rules and regulations. For holiness to be happy, it must be connected with the Holy Spirit. We become holy only by the power of the Holy Spirit. So how is your congregation? Happy? Holy? Empowered by the Holy Spirit?

THE PEOPLE OF GOD

Recall that one of the most important characteristics of the people of God is fellowship; we belong. We belong to Christ, and we belong to each other. But we can take it a step further. The people of God can move into the place where the congregation as a whole is the witness. When the fellow-ship of the church comes alive by the presence of the Holy Spirit, inspiring and empowering persons to care for one another, the fellowship is redemptive within itself, and that draws people. That's what evangelism is all about. The problem, however, is that the church experiences cognitive dissonance. We know what we're supposed to do, but we still don't act. As you've pondered this idea, have you been compelled to act? How has your view of the congregation—and your place in it—been challenged this week?

ESSENTIAL CHARACTERISTICS

This day's lesson took us back to the early church, a great place for inspiration, encouragement, and guidance. We discovered, first, that these early Christians knew who they were: they were thoroughly convinced, soundly converted, and Holy Spirit-filled. In addition, they were a learning church, consistently sitting under the teachings of the apostles. They were a praying church, and they were a sharing church. They would gather in homes, break bread together, and share with one another what was going on. So how are we doing with all of this in our modern congregations? Remember the importance of true community, including the impact of small-group fellowship, which can offer the genuine care that we all need.

THE PRIESTHOOD OF ALL BELIEVERS

Remember that all baptized Christians are endowed, commissioned, and appointed by God to continue his service and mission in the world. In other words, carrying out the Great Commission—or simply representing Christ—is not just the clergy's job. We are all to be co-laborers with God. Recall that a couple of things are happening in those places where the church is rapidly growing. First of all, the people fully expect the Holy Spirit to be dynamically present; and second, they truly embody the priesthood of all believers. As you've continued through this week's study, how has that truth manifested to you? When you look around your congregation, do you see evidence of each person being involved and expecting the Holy Spirit to show up and help them with the tasks at hand? If not, what can you do to better help that happen?

Week Six

PARTNERS IN THE GOSPEL

PRIVILEGED PARTAKERS
IN THE PROMISE

*. . . I always pray with joy because of your partnership in the
gospel from the first day until now, being confident of this,
that he who began a good work in you will carry it on
to completion until the day of Christ Jesus.*
Phil. 1:4–6

In the 1950s, a tent evangelist came to a northeastern
Pennsylvania town. Among the people who responded to
the evangelist's preaching and accepted Jesus were a
man and woman who had lived together for many years in a
shabby little house on the edge of town. They had a house full
of children, but had never married.

After the evangelist left town, this couple came to the
pastor and asked him to marry them and to receive them as
members of the church. When the pastor did so, one of the
officials of the church was indignant.

"Do you expect us to associate with trash taken in by a fire-
and-brimstone tent preacher? I never thought I would see the
day when a Methodist preacher would marry people like that.
It's a disgrace."

The pastor replied, "The only disgrace is that some
preacher didn't do it sooner. In all the years these people
have lived in this town, we have never invited them to our
church. I'm grateful that a tent evangelist did our job for us."

Isn't this a fitting story for us? In this final week of our study,
we turn our attention to being Christ to others, and being partners in the gospel. What Jesus has been and done for us, we
must do and be for others. There really is no choice in this; our
life in Jesus and our ministry in his name are inseparable. A spirituality that does not lead to active ministry becomes an

indulgent preoccupation with self, and therefore grieves the Holy Spirit and violates the presence of the indwelling Christ.

I think now of Paul's visit to Philippi; the church there was his "joy and crown" (Phil. 4:1). Of all the early churches, it gave Paul the least trouble and the most satisfaction. Paul's letter to the Philippians, then, is one of joy, brimming over with expressions of gratitude, affection, and love.

Philippi was a Roman colony, the leading city of the district of Macedonia. Do you remember how the church was born there? Lydia, a seller of purple silks, was converted, then her entire household responded to the gospel and were baptized with her. A church began in her house. Dramatic events followed: Paul, in the name of Jesus, freed a slave girl from a spirit which made her a source of gain for her owners. As a result of that miracle, Paul and Silas were arrested, flogged, and thrown in jail. But again the Spirit did his work—the jail became the setting for another display of the Holy Spirit's presence and power when the jailer and his household were converted and baptized.

Isn't that a remarkable beginning for a church—the conversion first of a woman and her entire family, then a jailer and his entire family? Think about that: they were probably the most unlikely candidates for church membership that could have been imagined in Philippi. Let me urge you, parenthetically, not to forget that. When was the last time your congregation looked seriously at your community and asked, "What audience are we missing? Who is out there that no church is paying attention to?" Those you think the most unlikely prospects for hearing the gospel may be waiting for you to share it.

Reaching people, however, requires us to be partners in the gospel. Paul gives thanks to the believers in Philippi for their "partnership in the gospel" (Phil. 1:5). This partnership involves three things: privilege, partaking, and promise.

PRIVILEGE

For Christians, it all boils down to this: we belong to Jesus Christ. That is our unique privilege.

Emerson Colaw, a retired bishop of the Methodist Church, tells a story that comes out of his longtime ministry at Hyde Park Community United Methodist Church in Cincinnati. The Taft family (of political fame) was part of that congregation, and the six-year-old daughter of the family was named Mary. During her first week at school, the teacher asked each of the students to introduce themselves and to tell something about their family. When it came little Mary's turn, she stood up and said, "I am Mary Taft. My great-grandfather was the president of the United States. My grandfather was a senator, my father is a congressman, and I am a Girl Scout Brownie."

Isn't that beautiful? We need to celebrate who we are. Our privilege is that we belong to Christ—what a powerful reality! What would happen to your congregation if that reality permeated your corporate awareness?

PARTAKERS

The second word that helps us probe the depths of what it means to be partners in the gospel is *partakers*. Philippians 1:7 says, "For whether I am in chains or defending and confirming the gospel, all of you share in God's grace with me." The New King James version says, "You all are partakers with me of grace."

Consider now your expansive identity and your solidarity with the Christian movement around the world. What would it mean for your church to grasp the reality of what Paul was talking about when he said "partakers with me of grace"— both in his imprisonment and in the defense and confirmation of the gospel?

Paul felt that the Philippians were in solidarity with him in prison. What would it mean for your congregation to be partakers of grace with the ones Jesus termed "the least of these": the hungry, the stranger, the naked, the sick, the prisoner?

Mother Teresa, who was remarkably gifted in demonstrating this dynamic of solidarity—this partaking of grace—put her finger on the deepest need of all human beings, and not just those who were dying in the slums of Calcutta. She said:

> I have come more and more to realize that being unwanted is the worst disease that any human being can experience. Nowadays we have found medicine for leprosy and lepers can be cured. There is medicine for TB and consumptives can be cured. For all kinds of diseases there are medicine and cures. But for being unwanted, except there are willing hands to serve and there is a loving heart, I don't think this terrible disease can be cured.

Willing hands to serve and loving hearts to love—that's what it means to be partakers of grace, and to enter into solidarity with suffering humanity. But not many of us want to be servants like that, do we? We have the notion that Christianity centers in service, but I submit to you that there is a vast difference between the way most of us serve and the willful decision to become a servant after the style of Jesus. Most of us serve by choosing when and where and whom and how we will serve. We stay in charge.

Jesus calls for something entirely different. He calls us to be servants, and when we make this choice, we give up the right to be in charge. Then, amazingly, we experience great freedom. We become available and vulnerable. We lose our fear of being stepped on or manipulated, or taken advantage of—and don't we all experience those fears? In every church where I have served, people have said to me: "Preacher, I don't want to be taken advantage of . . . I don't want to be stepped on." But what joy comes—what energizing of life, what power for ministry—when we act out of the desire to be a servant, rather than the pride-producing choice to serve now and then, and when, where, how, and whom we please.

IN DEFENSE AND CONFIRMATION

Paul says we are partakers of grace with him even in prison. But he also says we are partakers in defense and confirmation of the gospel. I could write many pages on this, but just a word: Methodism is being torn asunder today. Everywhere I turn, people are asking, "Is the church going to split? How long can we survive the tension and strife?"

The unfortunate reality is that nearly every Christian denomination is struggling with a few hot-button moral issues that challenge the very fabric of our faith. But if these fiery issues that make news headlines were to disappear tomorrow, we would still be in trouble as a church.

We would be in trouble because we have forsaken the authority of Scripture; we have diminished the uniqueness of

> *Willing hands to serve and loving hearts to love—that's what it means to be partakers of grace.*

Christ as God's revelation, as God's gift of himself for our salvation; we have made our personal experience the measure of judgment, rather than the faith once and for all delivered to the saints. When everything is relative, you don't have a center, and there is no way to define a circumference. We need to recover Paul's meaning of being partakers *in defense and confirmation of the gospel.*

PROMISE

Listen to this breathtaking promise in the words of Paul in Philippians 1:6. He says he is "confident of this very thing, that he who has begun a good work in you will complete it until the day of Jesus Christ" (NKJV). It is a great day in the life of a pastor and a congregation when they realize the ministry and mission of the church is not dependent upon their human resources. The church is not our idea, anyway. It is God's idea. It is God's kingdom enterprise, and God is in charge.

What a great time this could be in your congregation to turn to a new chapter in your life of faithfulness and service. How that chapter is written will not be dependent upon the gifts and graces of your pastor. The future will be dependent upon:

* How clearly you as a congregation hear God's call;
* How deeply you feel the heartbeat of a hurting world;
* How willingly you will deny self and follow Christ;
* How sacrificially you will give your talents and financial resources as servants of the Servant who is Lord;
* How quickly you will respond to the Holy Spirit's guidance;
* How authentically you will live together as though it were a privilege to be the recipients of grace; and
* How disciplined you are as a praying people, coming boldly to the throne of grace and holding tenaciously to the horns of the altar until God has blessed you with his presence, and you have yielded your will to God's command.

That's where the secret lies. That's the reason you can rejoice in the promise: he who has begun a good work in you will bring it to completion.

I have seen it happen, and I know it will continue. It was dramatically confirmed for me back in January 1990, when Jerry and I visited churches in what was then Czechoslovakia. There were not many Methodist Christians there, but what committed Christians they were. One pastor who came to spend the day with us in a seminar spent more than half his monthly salary to buy the gasoline to drive to the meeting. As I looked around the room, I saw a people who were filled with great hope. It was no wonder—until November 1989, every church in Czechoslovakia was severely restricted by the communist government. Christians could not evangelize. They had to be careful about how they spoke in public. They could post no public notices on their church buildings. No signs or advertisements could be erected outside their churches. They could make no public declarations. They couldn't even ring their church bells.

Then in November 1989—you may remember the story, it was on television and on the front pages of newspapers around the world—a group of students confronted a group of soldiers, and in the magnificent square of Prague, gave the soldiers flowers. That was the catalyst that brought the revolution against the government out in the open and to full blossom. Everybody took to the streets, and the old communist regime knew it was over.

These devoted Christians told us their story: it was decided that on November 27, at noon, everybody would simply walk out of homes, businesses, offices, factories, and fields. Every church bell in Czechoslovakia would be rung at noon. When that day arrived, bells that had been silent for forty-five years began to ring. It was electric—can you imagine the surprise of the pigeons in those bell towers? Everybody knew that something new had come.

Dr. Vilem Schneeberger, one of the pastors, whom I had known during my years as world editor of *The Upper Room,* said that for the first time he was able to put a sign in front of his church in Prague. Do you know what he put on that sign? Just four words: "The Lamb has won!"

What a victory! What a sign of the kingdom. The Lamb had won—not the bear, but the Lamb. Not the tiger, but the Lamb. Not the lion, but the Lamb. He who had begun a good work in them—because of their long years of faithfulness and the faithfulness of the body of Christ around the world—had brought it to completion. The Lamb had won. You can count on the promise: he who has begun a good work in you will bring it to completion. We are to be partakers of that promise, and we are to count it all privilege.

THE HEART OF THE MATTER

❋ Have you ever questioned whether the promises of the Scriptures apply to you personally? If so, take that to the Lord now.

❋ Do you consider it a privilege to be a Christian? Why or why not?

❋ What does it mean to you to be a partaker of grace?

PRAYERS

This is the confidence we have in approaching God:
that if we ask anything according to his will, he hears us.
And if we know that he hears us—whatever we ask—
we know that we have what we asked of him.
1 John 5:14–15

One of my favorite theologians is Charles Schultz, the artist who gave us the wonderful *Peanuts* cartoons. In one installment, the character Lucy storms into the room and demands that Linus change the television channel, threatening him if he doesn't:

"What makes you think you can walk right in here and take over?" Linus asks.

"These five fingers," says Lucy. "Individually, they are nothing, but when I curl them together like this into a single unit, they form a weapon that is terrible to behold."

"Which channel do you want?" asks Linus.

After a moment, he turns away, looks at his own fingers, and says, "Why can't you guys get organized like that?"

Like Linus, most of us need more discipline and organization in our personal lives. How do we withstand the tyranny of the urgent, not allowing the immediate claims on our energy to distort our priorities and sidetrack us from our mission? The ministries we lead and the people we serve need organizational attention as well. To be sure, most of our churches and ministries are organized, but too many are organized for the sake of organization. Maintenance gets far more attention than mission.

As we move into these last days of our journey together, I'd like to reflect on the organizing principle that members of The United Methodist Church use to order their lives. Vows like these are a part of membership in most churches. Even though the vows may be informal, the practices are important expectations. Every person joining a local United Methodist Church takes a vow to uphold the church with prayers, presence, gifts, and service—not a bad way for any denomination to shape its membership. The first vow that we make is to uphold the church with our prayers. It is no accident that it is first.

HOLY HELPLESSNESS

As a pastor who counsels people, I have felt helpless many times. Especially with alcoholics, other addicts, and the mentally ill, I have come to the point of despair, feeling that I had done everything, but had actually done nothing. In those cases, the best we can do—both the least and the most we can do—is pray. Interceding for others is yet another opportunity for us to offer generous grace to those in need.

When I served a church in California, I pastored a couple there for five years. During that time and for at least five years prior to that, the husband was almost completely debilitated by alcoholism. His wife tried everything, seemingly to no avail. She became a member of Al-Anon, a support group for families of alcoholics. She concluded that her husband was helpless, but she continued to love him anyway and began to pray earnestly for him.

Two years after I moved from that community, I received a letter from her sharing the marvelous news that her husband had been sober for nine months. She had waited that long to write to test the reality of his transformation. And last I heard, many years later, my friend is still sober. Neither husband nor wife would hesitate to affirm the role of prayer in his healing process. And he, especially, is quick to say that it is prayer—his and hers—that keeps him sober.

Make no mistake: prayer is essential.

As we have considered all along our study, love is powerful. Compassion is a compelling force. Even so, though our compassion may be deep and our love seemingly limitless, some situations still require more. Occasionally, we will find ourselves feeling helpless. Consider the mother and father willing to give their lives for a dying child, yet unable to restore health. Consider the heartbroken woman whose husband has left or the man just diagnosed with a serious disease.

When we come to that point of helplessness, when we really feel we have nothing else to offer, our intercession (praying on behalf of others) will possess that deep quality which is often called *supplication*. It is simply a feeling for, a wrestling with, and an allowing of the Holy Spirit to pray for us as he does. As Paul said:

> We do not know what we ought to pray for, but the Spirit himself intercedes for us with groans that words cannot express. And he who searches our hearts knows the mind of the Spirit, because the Spirit intercedes for the saints in accordance with God's will. (Rom. 8:26–27)

In our helplessness, we are brought to the place where intercession is both purified and powerful. We come to the place of utter faith in God to do what we cannot do.

SPIRITUAL SOLIDARITY

An interesting thing happens when we pray for others. Our praying doesn't bless only the people for whom we are praying. The more we seek to pray in the name and spirit of Jesus, the more we are driven to experience our own weakness and finitude. We remember Gethsemane and the anguish of Jesus as he embraced his human limits. "Because he himself suffered when he was tempted, he is able to help those who are being tempted" (Heb. 2:18). The writer to the Hebrews makes the case that Jesus' suffering and temptation prepared him to be our priest, our great intercessor.

> And so Jesus also suffered outside the city gate to make the people holy through his own blood. Let us, then, go to him outside the camp, bearing the disgrace he bore. For here we do not have an enduring city, but we are looking for the city that is to come. Through Jesus, therefore, let us continually offer to God a sacrifice of praise—the fruit of lips that confess his name. And do not forget to do good and to share with others, for with such sacrifices God is pleased. (Heb. 13:12–16)

As intercessors, we are to embrace our own weakness as well as the weakness of others. How do we pray for all the poor, the hungry who are dying for lack of food with every tick of the clock? How do we pray for the reign of peace in a world so torn apart by selfish ideology and opposing values?

We intercede by identification. We seek to live in solidarity with the poor, the oppressed, and the suffering of the world. Sometimes we can do that literally, physically entering into the darkness of the sufferer. But most of the time we can't. So our praying becomes a profession of faith. We position ourselves before the God of justice, mercy, and righteousness. We stand with our brother, the suffering Christ. Knowing that in his earthly sojourn of full humanity, Jesus did not meet every need, we anguish with him, as he anguished over Jerusalem. We feel the pain in his heart as he cries out in these words recorded in Matthew 23:37: "O Jerusalem, Jerusalem, you who kill the prophets and stone those sent to you, how often I have longed to gather your children together, as a hen gathers her chicks under her wings, but you were not willing."

Those who practice living prayer often testify that things happen when we pray that would not happen if we didn't pray. People are healed, situations change, conditions are altered, people find direction, revivals come, even the courses of nations are redirected.

> *God has so ordered life and the world that our praying is a vital part of his redemptive plan.*

It appears that God has so ordered life and the world that our praying is a vital part of the redemptive plan for individuals and the entire universe. Through intercessory prayer, God does something that would not otherwise be done. There are numerous facets to intercessory prayer, some that we have experienced, no doubt many that are yet undiscovered. But there is one dimension that is such a part of life that we need to give it attention: intercessory prayer is a ministry of love and care.

In his *Cotton Patch Gospel* version of the New Testament, Clarence Jordan translates Second Corinthians 5:19 in this fashion: "God was in Christ, hugging the world to himself." That's what we do when we pray. We put our arms around another person, a relationship, a situation, our community, even the world—and hug it to ourselves and to God in love. In a mysterious way that we may never understand, something always happens to us, and sometimes in those for whom we pray.

Intercessory prayer also opens our minds to hear what else God wants to tell us about the way we can minister to others. When we pray for another person, we are centered on that person as well as on God. God can then speak to us about the needs of that other person and how we may be instruments of meeting that need. In that way, intercessory prayer can become the launching pad for our service to others. People often say, "Prayer alone is not enough." Frank Laubach, the great practitioner of intercession, reminds us that "prayer that seeks to do God's will is not alone. It will be accompanied by any other approach that God may suggest. It will be accompanied by service, by considerations, by kindnesses of every kind."

We must note that intercessory prayer can also become the power base for our relationships with others. There was a period in my life when I did not take intercessory prayer seriously. During that time, I always felt somewhat frantic and hassled—almost always under pressure for the next appointment or too intense in my relationship with the person with whom I was sharing. Then I began to practice intercessory prayer, always reserving time between appointments to pray for the person with whom I would be counseling next. The practice was revolutionary. I became more relaxed in my relationships, sharper in my perception, and focused in my attention. But more than that, something happened in the people I prayed for, as well. They were more relaxed, more open and honest in their sharing, more receptive to me and what I had to offer, and willing to accept my inability—and often unwillingness—to give advice.

This practice of prayer can be transferred to every area of life. We are empowered to serve others, and we serve with the greatest insight and effectiveness, when we pray for those we seek to serve.

A "War of Amazing Kindness"

Finally, intercessory prayer allows us to invest ourselves in God's design for his kingdom among people and nations. Frank

Laubach called for a "prayer army" of ten million people who "would start praying until our minds were in perfect harmony with the will of God . . . who would tip the balance and save the world." He called this a "war of amazing kindness." We have yet to see what could happen should such an army arise!

In the meantime, however, praying for others will bring you to love them. Loving them will lead you to serve them. Serving them will be the open door through which God can move in to save, heal, and make whole.

Make no mistake: the ministry of intercession is very demanding. To be serious about intercession is to be ready to give ourselves for the sake of others. This may be the very reason we don't take intercession to heart.

As Christians, when we look for our clearest picture of God, we look to Jesus. One of the most characteristic dimensions of Jesus' life and ministry was the attention he gave to people around him. He heard blind Bartimaeus call out from the roadside (Mark 10:46–52). Jesus felt the touch of the woman who had been hemorrhaging for twelve years when she reached out in the crowd and touched the hem of his garment (Matt. 9:20–22). He saw Zacchaeus up in the sycamore tree (Luke 19:1–10). He listened to the leper who came to him and said, "If you will, you can make me whole" (Matt. 8:2). If God is like Jesus, then we can know that no matter what we pray or who we're praying for, God hears us. Not only that, but he answers, as well. Just as surely as we speak to God, and as we seek to be related to God, God answers.

There is a marvelous word of the Lord, recorded by the prophet Isaiah, that speaks to this issue. "Before they call I will answer; while they are still speaking I will hear" (Isa. 65:24). What an extravagant word—God hears and God answers. And he waits for us to rise up, reach out, and love others as he has loved us.

THE HEART OF THE MATTER

❀ Do you consider prayer the least you can do for someone, or the most? Why do you think that is?

❀ Have you ever prayed for someone and seen that prayer answered? Remember the experience now. How did that encourage your faith—as well as the faith of the person you prayed for?

❀ Do you keep a list of people and situations to pray for? Some Christians find it helps keep them on track. If you don't have such a list, would you consider starting one now?

PRESENCE

*"Hallelujah! For our Lord God Almighty reigns. Let us rejoice
and be glad and give him glory! For the wedding of the Lamb
has come, and his bride has made herself ready."*
Rev. 19:6–7

Bishop James Baker lived to be ninety years old—
and even at ninety, he had a zest for life. He was
too blind to read during the last years of his life,
but volunteer readers kept him up on current events and
movements. His mind was agile and alert, and he possessed a
keen perception that got right to the heart of things and
probed their meaning with clear insight.

There were many glowing tributes at Bishop Baker's
memorial service. The one that came nearest to summarizing
the soul of this great man was a brief word by Bishop Marvin
Stuart of the Denver Area. Bishop Stuart told of how his son,
Rob, while a graduate student at the seminary in Claremont,
had been one of the persons who graciously read to Bishop
Baker. He also drove the bishop to church in Pasadena on
Sunday mornings and sat with him down front. Over the
weeks, the bishop had apparently noticed something he did
not quite like about the way Rob sang the hymns. So, one
Sunday, at the close of the final hymn, in a quiet voice that
could nonetheless be distinctly heard by many people sitting
around them, the bishop turned to Rob Stuart and remon-
strated, "Rob, don't fade out on the amen!"

Of course there is an admonition here about singing—
Methodists in particular are supposed to be a singing people.
Their theology and understanding of the gospel and the

Christian life is carried forward as much in Charles Wesley's hymns as in John Wesley's sermons. Bishop Baker reminded Rob of that: "Don't fade out on the amen!" Sing heartily. But this is more than direction for singing—it is direction for worship and all of life: don't fade out on the amen.

Amen means "So let it be! God's will be done." On the other hand, *hallelujah* means, "Praise Jehovah; praise the Lord Most High!" So we say both "amen" and "hallelujah," and we say them in a lot of different ways.

The primary meaning of worship—no matter the style—is to pay attention to God. In fact, I would go so far as to say that the primary task of the pastor is to pay attention to God and to inspire and guide the congregation to do the same. We need to be open to different styles of worship so that people will be able to say "amen" and "hallelujah" in their own tongue—we want to use any and all mediums that will enable them to express "amen" and "hallelujah" in the most authentic way.

What would happen in our worship if everything we did was an effort to lead people to pay attention to God? What would happen if we allowed persons in worship to express their "attention to God" in ways that were indigenous—that is, a part of their being, and their culture?

It's not easy—not easy at all—to say "amen" in worship. I don't mean the shout of a verbal amen, though unfortunately that would be out of place in most worship services. I mean affirming, "So let it be to the will of God."

We are self-centered people. Even at our best, when we are sincere about wanting our life to be filled with meaning and to count for something, it's not easy to say "amen" to the will of God. Worship with integrity is always calling people to pay attention to God, to deliberately put themselves in God's presence, and to say "amen" to God's will.

Simply being religious is not the answer. Having a particular ritual for worship is not the answer. Worshiping just to make ourselves feel good, to find comfort or escape from the world, is not what true worship is all about. The question is not whether our worship should be traditional or contemporary—to change or not to change—it's a matter of whether we are paying attention to God.

What Can Be

At the heart of worship is *hallelujah*—celebration and praise. We remember the mighty acts of God in history, but we also remember how God has acted in our lives and we give him thanks.

We shout *hallelujah* not only for the current state of our lives, but also for the promise of a future that rests in God's hands. Our circumstances may not be so good on any given Sunday morning. Some of us come to worship broken-hearted, grieving because a loved one has died, a spouse has left us, a child has fallen into the wrong crowd, and the future looks pretty grim. We may have lost a job or we may be struggling with an aged parent, where no decision we make can please everyone. Whether or not we come in joy, we come to worship ready to praise God for what is. But we can also come to praise God for *what can be.*

What does it mean to worship in confidence? The psalmist asked the question, "How can we sing the songs of the LORD while in a foreign land?" (Ps. 137:4). Because our day-to-day lives often seem bereft of God's presence, this same question lingers in our hearts today. In authentic worship, however, we bring the past into the present, and are empowered to believe that things really can be different in the future. We celebrate the past, knowing that just as God has delivered us before, so God will deliver us now. He has not brought us this far to forsake us.

Do people who worship in your church each Sunday experience that kind of confidence? Is the presence of a God who is acting now celebrated and made real? Is Christ, who walks the road of every day, walking the aisle of your place of worship?

There is nothing more essential for individual Christian growth and discipleship than worship. Certainly there is nothing more essential for the "body" (the congregation) than worship. So we vow to uphold the church with our presence. At a very foundational level, our worship defines who we are.

A COMMAND AND A CALL

Weekly worship wasn't meant to be seen as optional for God's people. Consider that one of the Ten Commandments instructs us to observe the Sabbath:

> Remember the Sabbath day by keeping it holy. Six days you shall labor and do all your work, but the seventh day is a Sabbath to the LORD your God. On it you shall not do any work, neither you, nor your son or daughter, nor your manservant or maidservant, nor your animals, nor the alien within your gates. (Exod. 20:8–10)

Some of us may not resonate with the idea of worship as a command, but consider this: our god is who or what we worship. God's chosen, covenant people were preserved in identity by their worship.

The early Christian community followed the command of God to worship; those first believers came together for worship more than once each week. I believe that's because they understood the true nature and dynamic of worship. When we join with them, when we remember who God is and when we rehearse his mighty acts, we too will say, "amen" and "hallelujah!"

My hope is that we have all taken the vow (or at some point will take it) to worship. And we faithfully keep that vow by gathering with our Christian family every Sunday. We remember God's mighty acts in history and we offer our lives afresh to God, that God may continue to act through us.

MADE READY

In worship, we not only remember God's history, we imagine God's future and we pray, "Thy kingdom come, thy will be done." Even though our vows of "prayers, presence, gifts, and service" can be an often-repeated promise, there are still those who miss the importance of simply showing up. Yes, we are called to be present for those around us in need. But as surely as Christ established the church, part of expressing our love for others means we take part in regular gatherings with members of our faith community. We cannot be responsible members of God's family without being willing to hang out with our siblings.

Again, worship is not an option; it is a command. Beyond that, it is a privilege and an honor. Worship allows us to connect with the one who made us, and that's exciting business, a far cry from the idea of just "paying back a debt to God" or being bored in a pew.

We must acknowledge, too, that the business of praise is not a professional business. It is not restricted to a chosen few, the ordained and the specially trained. It is the business of every believer, everywhere. Participation is essential— worship is not a spectator sport. It is everybody gathered and paying attention to God. Let everything that has breath praise the Lord!

Annie Dillard, in her book *Teaching a Stone to Talk,* asks this question: "Why do people in churches seem like cheerful, brainless tourists, on a packaged tour of the Absolute?" Then she shares this observation:

> On the whole, I do not find Christians, outside of the cata-
> combs, sufficiently sensible of conditions. Does anyone have
> the foggiest idea what sort of power we so blithely invoke? Or,
> as I suspect, does no one believe a word of it? The churches are
> children playing on the floor with their chemistry sets, mixing
> up a batch of TNT to kill a Sunday morning. It is madness to
> wear ladies' straw hats and velvet hats to church; we should all
> be wearing crash helmets. Ushers should issue life preservers
> and signal flares; they should lash us to our pews. For the
> sleeping god may wake someday and take offense, or the
> waking god may draw us out to where we can never return.

That's the awesome possibility that is present whenever we worship. As we pay attention to God, we may be drawn out of ourselves into a living relationship with God from which we can never return. And, if we are privileged to have it happen, we will shout with those gathered around the throne, *Amen! Hallelujah! For the Lord our God reigns. Let us rejoice and exalt and give him the glory, for the marriage of the Lamb has come and his bride—the church—has made herself ready.*

THE HEART OF THE MATTER

❀ Have you ever experienced a deeply moving worship service? How did you feel? How did that experience have an impact on your life?

❀ How are you doing with your commitment to attend worship? Are there areas where you could improve on your vow to be present in your family of faith? If you have any resistance to this idea, take it to God in prayer.

❀ Has your time in this study helped you focus more on paying attention to God? Have you experienced any changes as a result?

GIFTS

Do not wear yourself out to get rich;
have the wisdom to show restraint.
Cast but a glance at riches, and they are gone. . . .
Prov. 23:4–5

There's a wonderful story connected with the terrible earthquake that shook Alaska and almost destroyed the city of Fairbanks in November 2002. Following that earthquake, many people wrote the governor to describe the suffering they had endured and demanded that the state take responsibility. A few weeks later, the governor gave a news conference and reported that among all the correspondence he had received about the disaster, there was a letter from a small boy that included two nickels taped to an index card. The boy had written on the card: "Use this wherever it's needed. If you need more, let me know."

What a spirit! The amount of the gift is not nearly as important as the heart behind it. The real challenge for us is whether, in all things, we're giving our best to the Lord.

Many Christians don't like to talk about money, but it must be addressed. Jesus dealt with money and possessions in a radical way because he knew that our possessions too often possess us. It is a sign of our original sin that we are possessive. The unconverted self, the ego—by nature, it seems—is in bondage to things, slavishly persistent in acquiring and keeping. Apparently one of our natural instincts is acquisition. Children have to be taught to share. Owning and holding, not giving, are natural traits.

The discipline of generosity—the actual giving of money—is essential for spiritual growth. Because the acquiring and holding aspects of our being are so tenacious, generosity must begin with the giving of ourselves. That's what much of this study has been all about. Paul captured this concept succinctly in Second Corinthians 8:5. It is, I believe, the heartbeat of generosity in all things: "They gave themselves first to the Lord and then to us in keeping with God's will."

Committing time and energy to the family of faith comes easily to some of us, but when the offering plate is passed, our comfort turns to denial. We may believe the church doesn't really need our money, but that misses the point. As Christians, we *need* to give. Giving keeps things in perspective. Before we go any further, an explanation of tithing might help.

Tithing is the biblical pattern established for practicing generosity in the use of our money. The principle, which became a law in Judaism, began not with a focus on money, but rather on all we possess: land, animals, crops, even the bounty of war.

The story of the first offering in history is found in the fourth chapter of Genesis. This is the account of Cain and Abel making their offerings to God. In this story, Abel's offering was acceptable to God but Cain's was not. To understand why, we must look at the quality of the offering. Abel gave the firstlings of his flock, while Cain's offering seems to have been an indiscriminate collection of the fruit of the ground. The Genesis story may confuse us to some degree, but in the Epistle to the Hebrews there is this word: "By faith Abel offered God a better sacrifice than Cain did" (Heb. 11:4). That's because God requires the best we have to offer.

As for the first mention of tithing in the Bible, Genesis 14:18–20 contains the story of Abraham (then called Abram) paying tithes to Melchizedek, who was a king of

Salem as well as a priest of God. After Abraham had won a great battle, Melchizedek blessed him and said, "Blessed be Abram by God Most High, Creator of heaven and earth. And blessed be God Most High, who delivered your enemies into your hand." After receiving this blessing, Abraham gave the priest a tenth of everything.

The amount of the separated portion is designated here for the first time—it is the tenth. It was a common practice among ancient warriors to tithe the spoils of war. Abraham, no doubt, was familiar with this custom. Yet there was something different about this act of Abraham: it was an act of genuine devotion. He was worshiping the one true God and was giving to God a tenth of all he received. Therefore, it set the precedent of tithing.

The concept of tithing grows in the Old Testament, and Jacob is the first person on record to enter into a tithing covenant with God:

> Then Jacob made a vow, saying, "If God will be with me and will watch over me on this journey I am taking and will give me food to eat and clothes to wear so that I return safely to my father's house, then the LORD will be my God and this stone that I have set up as a pillar will be God's house, and of all that you give me I will give you a tenth." (Gen. 28:20–22)

To be sure, there is something far less than Christian about praying such a prayer. God is not one to be bargained with. We don't make deals with God—he is not one from whom we can buy favors. God is not a godfather in the mafia sense or a cosmic bellhop in some grand hotel. Even so, the story of Jacob and what Jacob is doing is something to reckon with.

When we read the story of Jacob's rising early in the morning, going out and setting up an altar and praying to God as a result of what had happened to him, then the story speaks to us. You remember that Jacob had dreamed that a ladder was set between earth and heaven. Angels of God were ascending and descending the ladder. Jacob beheld the Lord standing above that ladder and the Lord spoke to him, offering great promises, climaxing with the affirmation, "I am with you and will watch over you wherever you go, and I will bring you back to this land. I will not leave you until I have done what I have promised you." (Gen. 28:15). After awakening from that sleep, you will recall, Jacob uttered that famous witness, "Surely the LORD is in this place, and I was not aware of it" (Gen. 28:16).

Our relationship with God always involves giving to God a portion of that which God has already given us.

When, in reflection, Jacob prays again and enters into that tithing covenant with God, it is on the basis of having received the promise from God. It is as though he is testing that promise and seeking to offer a response to it. That is certainly only the beginning of the development of the tithe in the history of the Hebrew people and in the Christian church, but it symbolizes the fact that our relationship with God always involves giving to God a portion of that which God has already given us.

It is this principle—returning to God a portion of that with which God has blessed us—that must be at the heart of our understanding of the tithe. Moses formulated the principle into law that all faithful Jews were to keep. That law was expressed at the close of the book of Leviticus, after many new statutes, both moral and ceremonial, had been given. The ancient law of the tithe was added as a constant reminder and for preservation and emphasis. Listen to that principle stated as law:

> A tithe of everything from the land, whether grain from the soil or fruit from the trees, belongs to the LORD; it is holy to the LORD. . . . The entire tithe of the herd and flock—every tenth animal that passes under the shepherd's rod—will be holy to the LORD. (Lev. 27:30, 32)

After that final law, the Book of Leviticus closes with this word: "These are the commands the LORD gave Moses on Mount Sinai for the Israelites" (Lev. 27:34). The precedent was set firmly in the fabric of Jewish life.

The classic and most dramatic warning about tithes, however, came from Malachi. In language that is strong and unmistakable, this prophet pointed out that disobedience to the law of the tithe was the cause of Israel's apostasy in his day and that reformation in this regard was the sure and only way to the restoration of the divine favor and blessing. Consider it:

> "Will a mere mortal rob God? Yet you rob me. But you ask, 'How are we robbing you?' In tithes and offerings. You are under a curse—your whole nation—because you are robbing me. Bring the whole tithe into the storehouse, that there may be food in my house. Test me in this," says the LORD Almighty, "and see if I will not throw open the floodgates of heaven and pour out so much blessing that there will not be room enough to store it." (Mal. 3:8–10 TNIV)

For many Christians, the scriptural precedent set in words like these is reason enough to commit to tithing. It should be so for all Christians if we are going to be people of "the Book." But that's still not all there is to it.

WHAT MONEY CAN AND CAN'T DO

Earlier I mentioned perspective; giving my tithe to the Lord is an ongoing reminder of what money can and cannot do. As it is wrong to idealize poverty, it is equally wrong to characterize riches as though they were innately evil. Money can make an enormous positive difference in our lifestyles, but it is crucial to maintain perspective about the things money cannot buy. Money can't buy friendship. It can't buy love. It can't buy respect. It can't buy exemption from the problems that are common to everyone.

You see, we don't purchase character, meaning, and direction in life. We can't charge peace of mind, a sense of fulfillment, understanding, and wisdom to our credit cards. Death is the great equalizer—I've never seen a hearse pulling a U-Haul trailer. Eternal life is certainly not for sale, but how we spend our money may rob us of eternal life. Jesus said, "For where your treasure is, there your heart will be also" (Matt. 6:21).

On the other hand, what money *can* do is teach us to let go and let God, to fund ministries that help those in need, to pay the salaries of those who pastor and preach on our behalf, and to allow us to be part of something bigger than ourselves. That last one, I believe, is the reason we are to bring our tithes into the storehouse, that is, the church. The church can use that cumulative money to accomplish far greater things than we could ever accomplish on our own.

I recently discovered a marvelous verse of Scripture that was packed with meaning for me. Does that happen to you now and then? Maybe you've read the passage countless times, but suddenly something happens—a light goes on in your mind; your heart stands at attention as you read a word that never before had registered. For me, it was the ninth chapter of Second Corinthians. I was reading the New English Bible, and this is what verse 10 says: "Now he who provides seed for sowing and bread for food will provide the seed for you to sow; he will multiply it and swell the harvest of your benevolence, and you will always be rich enough to be generous."

Wow! Does it hit you as it did me? Rich enough to be generous! Oh, to be rich in that way! The good news is that any one of us can be; it has nothing to do with how much we earn, or how much we have—we all can be rich enough to be generous. And we will be, when we see life as an opportunity to live in the fullness of Christ, to understand God's great and gracious gifts to us, and to practice passing that generosity on to others however we possibly can. That truly is a life of riches—and definitely one worth living!

THE HEART OF THE MATTER

❋ Has tithing been a challenge for you? Why or why not?

❋ Has this study changed your perspective on generosity? If so, how?

❋ Why do you think it is important for Christians to model generosity to the world?

SERVICE

Day 40

*Sitting down, Jesus called the Twelve and said, "If anyone wants
to be first, he must be the very last, and the servant of all."*
Mark 9:35

Pastor Mark Trotter once told a story about a young
woman who lost her husband, a doctor in India
during the Second World War; he died from some
tropical disease. The shock of her husband's death sent her
into despair, and she lost all interest in life, not caring
whether she lived or died. She booked passage on a ship back
to America, and on that ship she met the survivor of another
tragedy, a seven-year-old boy, whose missionary parents had
been killed in the fighting in Burma.

The boy was drawn to the woman—a seven-year-old needs a
mother, especially under those circumstances. But she would
have nothing to do with him. In fact, she tried to avoid him. She
couldn't get outside of her sorrow long enough to comfort the
little boy. "I have my own problems to deal with," she said.

One night, the ship was torpedoed and slowly began to
sink. The woman came out on deck prepared to go down with
the ship. She had no will to live and decided not even to seek
an escape. But on the deck she saw the little boy, shivering with
cold and fright. He saw her, ran over, and clung to her.

Something came over the woman. She led the boy to one
of the lifeboats; they both got in, and for the next several days
until they were rescued, she held him. Her friends, looking
back on that incident, say they don't know whether the
woman saved the boy or the boy saved the woman.

What a true picture of kindness and servanthood; they were yoked together in a fashion that made the way easier for both of them. Why are we so blind that we fail to see how many among us share the same need?

I was with a man recently—a big, macho man, some would say—successful both in terms of professional recognition and material wealth. But that day, he was like a little child as he poured out his pain and talked about how desperately he needed to be loved, held, and yoked together in gentle kindness with his wife. We mistakenly think it is only the woman who needs that in a marriage, but that is not true. All people in all relationships need someone there with us, yoked as Jesus is to us, to help make the way easier. We all need to give—and receive—acts of kind service.

IN WORD AND DEED

Methodists, in particular, should not be surprised that when they become members of the church, they are asked to take a vow of service. Jesus launched his ministry in Nazareth with these words: "The Spirit of the Lord . . . has anointed me to preach good news to the poor . . . has sent me to proclaim freedom for the prisoners . . ." (Luke 4:18–19). When Jesus promised his followers the Holy Spirit, he said, "But you will receive power when the Holy Spirit comes on you; and you will be my witnesses . . ." (Acts 1:8). We see through these verses that word and deed go together. There are times when the word *is* the deed—the only deed we can perform. We must speak, even if we can't act. There are also times when acting is the word we speak. Of course, we are most effective when both word and deed are combined.

There is a marvelous statement about the necessity of word and deed in the First Epistle of Peter: "But even if you should suffer for what is right, you are blessed. 'Do not fear what they fear; do not be frightened.' But in your hearts set apart Christ as Lord. Always be prepared to give an answer to everyone who asks you to give the reason for the hope that you have . . ." (1 Pet. 3:14–15).

When teaching the Ephesians about gifts and service in the church, Paul also established the linkage between word and deed, and how both are essential:

> It was he who gave some to be apostles, some to be prophets, some to be evangelists, and some to be pastors and teachers, to prepare God's people for works of service, so that the body of Christ may be built up until we all reach unity in the faith and in the knowledge of the Son of God and become mature, attaining to the whole measure of the fullness of Christ. Then we will no longer be infants, tossed back and forth by the waves, and blown here and there by every wind of teaching and by the cunning and craftiness of men in their deceitful scheming. Instead, speaking the truth in love, we will in all things grow up into him who is the Head, that is, Christ. (Eph. 4:11–15)

Here is the conflict: even though we make the decision to serve, undisciplined as we are, we continue to choose when, where, whom, and how we will serve. Thus we continually run the risk of pride, and we are always vulnerable to a good-works mentality that sends us frantically to engage ourselves in whatever deeds of mercy we can devise. How do we deal with these snares?

First, Thomas Merton reminds us that:

> . . . he who attempts to act and do things for others or for the world without deepening his own self-understanding, freedom, integrity, and capacity to love, will not have anything to give others. He will communicate to them nothing but the contagion of his own obsessions, his aggressiveness, his ego-centered ambitions, his delusions about ends and means.

If we think we know others and their needs perfectly well, our serving will often hinder rather than help. To combat pride, we must be attentive to the other person (which is a form of submission) as well as having a patient intention to serve the genuine needs of the other, rather than serving our own need to serve. In this fashion, we will be open to the Spirit to guide us in discerning need and in making appropriate responses to need.

As for the good-works mentality—the mindset that tells us that, given a decision to serve, we must immediately spring into action—we must guard against two pitfalls. Our desire to serve may be poisoned by a desire to please. Also, there is the snare of turning our servant action into controlling power over another.

> *To be a Christian person, one fully alive in Christ, is to be one whose life reflects the life of Jesus.*

One antidote for a good-works mentality, then, is an ongoing sensitivity to our own unworthiness. The biblical witness is clear—awareness of a calling to service is accompanied by a sense of personal unworthiness. A good-works mentality is also dissolved by keeping alive the conviction that our salvation depends upon God's grace, not our performance. A third antidote to a good-works mentality is an ongoing awareness that our serving is not redemptive within itself; it simply provides the environment, sets the stage, and releases the energy for the person we are serving to be genuinely helped, even healed, by God.

The central issue, however, remains: we deliberately act as servants because we are servants of Christ. As such, our choosing to serve elicits no false pride. In a disciplined way, we choose and decide to serve here or there, this person or that person, now or tomorrow, until we take the form of a servant and our lives become spontaneous expressions of the cross. We begin to understand the difference between being a Christian—the noun form of the word—and being *Christian*—the adjective. To be a Christian is to be one who professes the Christian faith and has begun the journey. To be *Christian*—to be a Christian person, one fully alive in Christ—is to be one whose life reflects the life of Jesus.

THIS IS HOW WE KNOW WHAT LOVE IS

I know many people who are ready to give themselves to others and to causes. They are terribly unselfish, yet they don't stop to ask, "What worthwhile gift do I have to offer?" This question always precedes effective relationship. Our task is not just to help someone in a vague sort of way—we need to help them specifically, so they might become the unique person they were intended to be. We are never able to do that until we recognize and accept our own gifts. In fact, much of our "helping" may be just another escape from the demanding task of developing our own potential.

I want to close this study with a beautiful story, one that hits at the heart of selfless service. Beware its innate challenge.

Dr. E. V. Hill, a dynamic African American pastor, served a church in the Watts area of Los Angeles. In the 1960s, when horrible riots broke out in his neighborhood, he showed his courage. From his pulpit, he denounced his neighbors who were burning and destroying property and stealing from the merchants. His bold preaching provoked all kinds of threats.

Late one night, the telephone rang. There was something about the way Hill held the receiver that told his wife something was wrong. When he hung up, she wanted to know who had called and what they wanted. Hill didn't want to talk. She persisted, almost demanding that he tell her.

Finally he did. "I don't know who it was," he said, "but
they've threatened to blow up my car with me in it."
Throughout the night, Hill was restless and uneasy. He
couldn't sleep for the longest time, worrying about the threat
to his life. Finally his drowsiness caught up with him and he
fell asleep about 2 AM.

At seven o'clock in the morning he awakened, terrified. He
reached over to touch his wife and she was gone. He couldn't
find her anywhere in the house. He then looked out the window
to see if she had gone outside. To his great horror, she wasn't on
the patio or in the yard. He then realized the car was gone from
the carport. He was beside himself and was about to call the
police when he saw her turn in the driveway and park the car.

"Where have you been?" he almost shouted at her.

Do you know what she said?

"I just wanted to drive the car around the block to make
sure it was safe for you this morning."

"From that day on," the late Dr. Hill said, "I have never
asked my wife if she loved me!"

What a picture! Mrs. Hill was paying attention to Jesus;
she understood his call to serve in a way many of us can't
fathom. "This is how we know what love is: Jesus Christ laid
down his life for us. And we ought to lay down our lives for
our brothers" (1 John 3:16).

THE HEART OF THE MATTER

❋ How do you think serving others could help deepen your
relationship with God?

❋ Is there anything that hinders you from serving more
often? What would that be?

❋ How can serving others with the right motives help demonstrate Jesus' love to the world?

EPILOGUE

Day 41

Lately I've been hearing the same questions over and over. Where is all of this going to take me? What does it really mean to get serious about the Christian life? I can't answer those questions completely; I'm still trying to figure them out for myself. But I have learned one thing thus far: the life to which we are called as Christians is one of *holy recklessness.* Nothing short of utter abandonment to God will do.

I say this now because you have reached a threshold. You can no longer plead ignorance about what it means to be Christian, what it means to be extravagantly loved by God, what it means to be fully alive in Christ. You are responsible now for what you have learned. The invitation is to receive the extravagant love of God—an invitation that, when considered fully, is well nigh irresistible. If we respond to that invitation, we begin to live our lives in Christ, with the exhilarating possibility that we can one day say with Paul, "It is no longer I who live, but Christ lives in me" (Gal. 2:20 NKJV).

I don't want to scare you. Rather, my invitation to you is to take a leap of faith in your discipleship. This is your opportunity to walk in knowledge and faith, putting into practice everything that we have covered in the last six weeks. What an exciting journey awaits!

Understand that when we fully commit to Christ, our questions no longer matter. We are able to affirm with Paul:

> We are hard pressed on every side, but not crushed; perplexed, but not in despair; persecuted, but not abandoned; struck down, but not destroyed. . . . Therefore we do not lose heart. Though outwardly we are wasting away, yet inwardly we are being renewed day by day. For our light and momentary troubles are achieving for us an eternal glory that far outweighs them all. So we fix our eyes not on what is seen, but on what is unseen. For what is seen is temporary, but what is unseen is eternal. (2 Cor. 4:8–9, 16–18)

Understand, too, that every decision we make restricts the opportunity for every other decision and narrows the range of our choices. For this reason, the decision of our true relationship with Christ is basic—it is the momentous choice that we must all make and for which we are all responsible. When by some mysterious grace, God touches the intimate center of our lives, at that point we accept or refuse on the basis that henceforth we belong to God or we do not. It is this decision that precludes all other decisions and in which all other decisions are caught up and properly assessed.

Know that your decisions have eternal significance. I am continually challenged by Elie Wiesel. In his remarkable collection of Hasidic tales, he tells of a young couple discussing their marriage announcement with the rabbi. The announcement indicated that the wedding would take place in Berditchev, Poland, on a certain date. The rabbi, with that particular Hasidic wisdom, edited the announcement to read as follows: "The wedding will take place in Jerusalem, but if the Messiah has not come, it will take place in Berditchev."

So, the hour strikes for each of us. We stand before God. This is the day—a day of visitation and testing, a moment of judgment, but, praise God, a moment of grace. The past and the future meet and the source of life and freedom is ours. To miss it is to deny ourselves that for which we must forever seek, that which we eternally need. To miss it is to settle for the ordinary rather than the extraordinary; the natural rather than the supernatural; and to deny the extravagant, bountiful, beautiful gifts God wants to bestow not only on his children as a whole, but on each of us individually.

So, are you ready to turn the page? A new life awaits. May you walk into it boldly, immersed in grace, fully aware of the constant presence of Christ, who will be with us until he returns in glory.

ACCEPTING JESUS

If you don't remember ever confessing that Jesus is your Lord and Savior, you can take care of that right now. Just repeat the prayer listed below. Please let someone else know that you have done it—tell a member of your church or a friend whom you know is a Christian. They will help you take the next step.

> *God*, I know I have made a lot of mistakes in my life. I know that I have sinned. But I believe that you can help wipe the slate clean. I believe you sent your Son, Jesus, to die on the cross for me, and I accept him now as my Savior and Lord. God, I thank you for drawing me to you, I thank you for your forgiveness, and I thank you for the new life you have begun in me. I believe I am a new creation. *Amen.*

OTHER WORKS BY MAXIE DUNNAM

Alive in Christ: The Dynamic Process of Spiritual Formation
Barefoot Days of the Soul
Be Your Whole Self
Channels of Challenge: Fifty-six Meditations that Inspire and Challenge
Congregational Evangelism: A Pastor's View (The Denman Lectures, 1992)
Dancing at My Funeral
Direction and Destiny: Making Decisions that Shape Your Future
Jesus' Claims—Our Promises: A Study of the "I Am" Sayings of Jesus
Keeping Company With the Saints
Homesick for a Future
Let Me Say That Again: Maxims for Spiritual Living
Living Life on Purpose: The Joy of Discovering and Following God's Call
Living the Psalms: A Confidence for All Seasons
Pack Up Your Troubles: Sermons on How to Trust in God
Perceptions: Observations on Everyday Life
Praying the Story: Learning Prayer from the Psalms with John David Walt Jr.
Staying the Course
That's What the Man Said: The Sayings of Jesus
The Christian Way: A Wesleyan View of Our Spiritual Journey
The Devil at Noon Day: Battling Temptation in Daily Life
The Gospel of Mark: Bible Study for Christian Living
The Workbook of Intercessory Prayer
The Workbook of Living Prayer
The Workbook on Becoming Alive in Christ
The Workbook on Christians Under Construction and in Recovery
The Workbook on Coping as Christians
The Workbook on Keeping Company with the Saints
The Workbook on Lessons from the Saints
The Workbook on Living as a Christian
The Workbook on Loving the Jesus Way
The Workbook on Spiritual Disciplines
The Workbook on the Christian Walk
This Is Christianity
Twelve Parables of Jesus: Bible Study for Christian Living

With Kimberly Dunnam Reisman:

The Workbook on the Beatitudes: An Invitation to Kingdom Living
The Workbook on the Seven Deadly Sins
The Workbook on the Ten Commandments
The Workbook on Virtues and the Fruit of the Spirit

SOURCES

Albin, Thomas. "An Empirical Study of Early Methodist Spirituality," in *Wesleyan Theology Today*, ed. Theodore Runyan. Nashville, Tenn: Kingswood, 1985.

Atkinson, James, ed. *Daily Readings with Martin Luther.* Springfield, Ill.: Templegate Publishers, 1987.

Baillie, John. *Invitation to Pilgrimage.* Grand Rapids, Mich.: Baker Books, 1982.

Barclay, William. *The Acts of the Apostles.* Louisville, Ky.: Westminster John Knox Press, 1976.

Black, James M. "When the Roll Is Called Up Yonder." 1893.

Campbell, Will D. *Brother to a Dragonfly.* New York: Continuum Publishing Company, 2000.

Carruth, William Herbert. "Each in His Own Tongue" from *Each in His Own Tongue and Other Poems.* New York: P. F. Volland Company, 1920.

Cooley, Charles H. *Human Nature and the Social Order.* New York: Charles Scribner's Sons, 1922.

Covey, Stephen. *The Seven Habits of Highly Effective People.* New York: Simon and Schuster, 1989.

de Sales, St. Francis, quoted in *A Year with the Saints.* Translated by a member of the Order of Mercy (Mt. St. Joseph's Seminary, Hartford, Conn.) Rockford, Ill.: Tan Books and Publishers, 1988.

Dillard, Annie. *Teaching a Stone to Talk: Expeditions and Encounters.* New York: HarperCollins, 1983.

Eliot, T. S. "The Dry Salvages," from *Four Quartets.* New York: Harcourt, Inc.

English, Donald. Sermon excerpt from message at Christ United Methodist Church, August 1984.

Fox, H. Eddie and George Morris. *Faith-Sharing: Dynamic Christian Witnessing by Invitation.* Nashville, Tenn.: Discipleship Resources, 1986.

Fox, Matthew. *A Spirituality Named Compassion.* Rochester, Vt.: Inner Traditions, 1999.

Frost, Robert. "The Death of the Hired Man" from *North of Boston.* New York: Henry Holt and Company, 1915.

Gaither, Gloria and William J. Gaither. "Because He Lives." Hymn, ©1971 William J. Gaither, Inc.

Galli, Mark. "Saint Nasty." *Christianity Today,* June 17, 1996.

Gardner, John W. *Self-Renewal: The Individual and the Innovative Society.* New York: W. W. Norton & Co., Inc., 1981.

Hunter, George G. III. *Wesley's Approach to Evangelism and Church Growth: A Working Paper Presented to the Seventh Oxford Institute of Methodist Theological Studies.* Kebel College, Oxford, England, July 26–August 5, 1982.

Jordan, Clarence. *The Cotton Patch Version of Hebrews and the General Epistles: A Colloquial Translation with a Southern Accent.* New York: Association Press, 1973.

Julian of Norwich: *Showings.* Translated and with an introduction by Edmund Colledge and James Walsh. New York: Paulist Press, 1978.

Kagawa, Toyohiko. *Living Out Christ's Love: Selected Writings of Toyohiko Kagawa.* Nashville, Tenn.: Upper Room Books, 1998.

Keats, John. "Ode to a Nightingale," In *Selected Poems and Letters,* Boston, Mass.: Houghton Mifflin, 1959.

Langford, Thomas A. *Christian Wholeness.* Nashville, Tenn.: Upper Room Books, 1978.

Laubach, Frank. *Prayer, the Mightiest Force in the World: Thoughts for an Atomic Age.* New York: Fleming H. Revell Co., 1946.

Law, William. *The Life of Christian Devotion: Devotional Selections from the Works of William Law.* Nashville, Tenn.: Abingdon Press, 1961.

L'Engle, Madeleine, quoted by James A. Harnish. *Journeys with the People of Genesis.* Nashville, Tenn.: Upper Room Books, 1989.

Lewis, C. S. *Mere Christianity.* New York: MacMillan Paperbacks edition, 1960.

Logan, William M. *In the Beginning.* Richmond, Va.: John Knox Press, 1957.

Mead, Loren. *The Once and Future Church: Reinventing the Congregation for a New Mission Frontier.* Herndon, Va.: The Alban Institute, 1991.

Merton, Thomas. *Contemplation in a World of Action.* Notre Dame, Ind.: University of Notre Dame Press.

Michel, Otto. "The Conclusion of Matthew's Gospel," translated by Constance Femington, ed. Graham N. Stanton, *The Interpretation of Matthew.* Philadelphia: Fortress Press, 1983.

Milton, John. "On the Morning of Christ's Nativity."

Mugurag, Malcolm. *Something Beautiful for God*. New York: Harper and Row, 1971.

Murphy, Anne S. "Constantly Abiding." Hymn, 1908.

Olmstead, Bob. "Poets of the Manger," and "T. S. Eliot: The Hint Half Guessed." Sermons. Reno, Nev.: First Methodist Church, 1991.

Percy, Walker. *The Second Coming*. New York: Picador USA, 1999.

Redhead, John A. *Getting to Know God*. Nashville, Tenn.: Abingdon Press, 1954.

Ritter, William. "Clubs Are No Longer Trump." Sermon.

Rosser, Dois. I., Jr. and Ellen Vaughn. *The God Who Hung on the Cross*. Grand Rapids, Mich.: Zondervan, 2003.

Schell, Orville. *China: In the People's Republic*. London: Gollancz, 1978.

Seka, Joseph. "Will the Real God Please Stand Up?" quoted in *Pack Up Your Troubles: Sermons on How to Trust in God* by Maxie Dunnam. Nashville, Tenn.: Abingdon Press.

Stevens, R. Paul. *The Other Six Days: Vocation, Work, and Ministry in Biblical Perspective*. Grand Rapids, Mich: Wm. B. Eerdmans Publishing Co., 1999.

Wagner, James K. *Blessed to Be a Blessing: How to Have an Intentional Healing Ministry in Your Church*. Nashville, Tenn: The Upper Room, 1980.

Wesley, John. "The Character of a Methodist," in *The Works of John Wesley*, Thomas Jackson, ed. London: Wesleyan Methodist Book Room, 1872.

Wesley, John. *Letters, II*, p. 325, in Mack Stokes, *The Bible in the Wesleyan Heritage*, Nashville, Tenn.: Abingdon Press, 1981.

Whitley, Henry C. *Laughter in Heaven*. Grand Rapids, Mich.: Fleming H. Revell, 1963.

Widmeyer, Charles B. "Come and Dine." Hymn, 1906.

Wiesel, Elie from "The Authority of Hope" *Loving God with One's Mind: Essays, Articles and Speeches of F. Thomas Trotter* by F. Thomas Trotter. Nashville, Tenn.: Board of Higher Education and Ministry of the United Methodist Church, 1987.

Williams, Colin Wilbur. *John Wesley's Theology Today*. Nashville, Tenn.: Abingdon Press, 1972.

ABOUT THE AUTHOR

Maxie D. Dunnam is chancellor of Asbury Theological Seminary in Wilmore, Kentucky, where he also served as president from 1994 through 2004. Widely known as an evangelist, leader, and pioneer in small-group ministries, he organized and pastored three United Methodist churches before becoming the world editor of the Upper Room Fellowship. He created the Upper Room Cursillo that later became the Walk to Emmaus.

Dunnam served twelve fruitful years as senior minister of the six-thousand-member Christ United Methodist Church in Memphis, Tennessee. He has served as president of the World Methodist Council and is currently on its Executive Committee. He is a director of the Board of Global Ministries of The United Methodist Church and a member of the Executive Committee of the Association of Theological Schools.

In 1989, he was inducted into the Foundation for Evangelism's Hall of Fame. In 1992, he was awarded the Chair of Distinction by the World Methodist Council, and the following year he received the Philip Award for Distinguished Service in Evangelism.

Dr. Dunnam has authored more than forty books, most notably *The Workbook of Living Prayer*, which sold more than one million copies; *Alive in Christ; This Is Christianity*; and two volumes in *The Communicator's Commentary* series. He resides in Memphis, Tennessee, with his wife, Jerry.

IRRESISTIBLE *Invitation*

RESPONDING TO THE
EXTRAVAGANT HEART OF GOD

A STEWARDSHIP RESOURCE FOR
CHURCHES OF ALL SIZES

CAMPAIGN HANDBOOK

Abingdon Press
Nashville

IRRESISTIBLE INVITATION
CULTIVATING JOYFUL GIVING IN YOUR CHURCH
CAMPAIGN HANDBOOK
Copyright 2008 by Abingdon Press
All rights reserved.

This book is printed on acid-free, elemental-chlorine–free paper.

Original art, cover, and page design by Joey McNair

ISBN: 978-0-687-64849-8

17 16 15 14 13 12 11 10 09 08   1 2 3 4 5 6 7 8 9 10

MANUFACTURED IN THE UNITED STATES OF AMERICA

CONTENTS

INTRODUCTION

Dear friend, I'd like to tell you a story about a little boy in Alabama who had no shoes. Winter had arrived, and one day he was standing over a grate on a sidewalk to keep his feet warm. A woman came along, and when she saw the boy, her heart went out to him. She couldn't believe that he was standing there in the cold with no shoes and only a light jacket.

"Where are your shoes, young man?" she asked. He said he didn't have any. So the woman said to him, "Why don't you come with me and let's see what we can do about that?" Then she took him by the hand and led him into a nearby department store. There she bought him a new pair of shoes.

When they came out of the store, the little boy was so excited that he took off running down the street to show his family what he had been given. All of a sudden, he came to a halt, turned around and walked back to the woman. He thanked her, and then he asked, "Ma'am, could I ask you a question? Are you God's wife?" The woman smiled and said, "Oh, no, I'm not God's wife, just one of God's children." The little boy replied, "I knew it! I knew it! I just knew you were related!"

As Christians, we are all related to Christ; we are his disciples. The question is, however, how much do we look like our "relative" when it comes to our compassion and generosity?

Irresistible Invitation: Responding to the Extravagant Heart of God and its comprehensive, church-wide study, *Irresistible Invitation: Cultivating Joyful Giving in Your Church,* is one that can help your congregation take a good, hard look at such subjects, and come out the other side as a more tightly knit, singularly focused team that can truly partner with God in all he wants to do. *Irresistible Invitation* is set up as a forty-day study, and with an emphasis on becoming partners in the gospel, easily ties in to any church's stewardship campaign.

It is our hope that as you embark on this journey together, you'll find renewed commitment and faith—as well as increased financial giving—throughout your entire congregation. And in the process, may you all experience a greater measure of God's own generosity in return.

Sincerely,
Maxie Dunnam

Chapter 1

THE HEART OF
IRRESISTIBLE INVITATION

Do you sense the winds of change, the breeze of refreshment? They're about to head your way. You hold in your hands a tool that can lead your entire congregation to a greater understanding of God, his goodness, his mercy, his extravagant love, and his plans for their lives. This handbook—combined with prayer—will provide everything you need to know for the journey.

But before we take the first step, let's bring our efforts to God so they'll be firmly grounded. Let's take a moment to stop and pray right now. The pastor or stewardship committee chair should lead the committee in prayer:

> *Heavenly Father,* we thank you for the great opportunities for growth that lie before us. We praise you that you are leading us in a new adventure with you—one that can reap an incredible harvest for our families, our congregation, and our community. Help us to press into you, to see more of you, and to learn everything that you want to teach us in the coming days.
>
> We give you thanks in the mighty name of your Son, Jesus, our Savior. *Amen.*

SHOW ME THE MONEY

You'd better be sitting down for this one. We're going to tackle the issue of money right off, without any excuses. The reality is that churches need essential funds. Without them, benevolence programs flounder, community outreach falters, and church staff have difficulty making ends meet. It's long been said that money makes the world go 'round, but the truth is that it makes churches go 'round, as well.

You wouldn't know that, however, from many church coffers. There may be plenty of support for the church in word and deed, but when it comes to tithes and offerings, it can be a completely different case. Members of the congregation may privately resent feeling like they "have" to give, they may have different priorities, or they may have had inadequate teachings about God's view on tithes and offerings.

This is nothing new; it's a tale as old as time. How do we know this? Jesus spoke about money more than any other topic in the Bible. The people needed instruction then, as well as they do now. Yet today's church leadership is still somehow reluctant to give it.

Perhaps pastors are uncomfortable with the topic because they don't want to look like they have their hands out. Maybe church leaders are afraid that if they push the issue too hard, they'll actually push people out the door. But missing the importance of giving financially causes a much greater problem: it cuts people off from the understanding of how God wants to bless them, and how he longs to honor their sacrifice. In addition, it keeps those people from being able to walk in the fullness of God's grace.

In order to give financially—and by that, we mean joyfully and enthusiastically, rather than defensively and begrudgingly—people must learn how to give of themselves, as well. They must understand the extravagant goodness of God, and see how God longs for them to pour out blessings on others, also.

Find a person who willingly gives financial gifts to the church, and you'll see someone who understands the importance of prayer. Find someone with a rich prayer life, and you'll see someone who feels compelled to regularly attend worship services. Find someone who attends every Sunday, and you'll see that the person is also motivated to serve. It all fits together beautifully—just the way God intended.

Maybe you don't see many people in your congregation at that level of commitment. But they can be, and this resource will show you exactly how it can happen.

IT ALL COMES DOWN TO COMMITMENT SUNDAY

Irresistible Invitation: Cultivating Joyful Giving in Your Church is designed to be comprehensive. It's more than just a forty-day study that members of the congregation read on their own. Instead, it provides a consistent, often-reinforced message that will inspire church members in many different ways, on many different levels. In addition to the daily readings, there are tie-ins for weekly small-group sessions or class studies, as well as sermon points and other church-wide communications spread throughout the six weeks.

As we mentioned earlier, the study is designed to be incorporated into your church's annual stewardship campaign, with the last message given on Commitment Sunday. By that time, members of your church family will have moved from the "big picture" idea of God's extravagant love to how that holy love can flow out from their own lives toward others. Over the six weeks, participants will learn more about the life and love of Jesus, what it means to be fully alive in Christ, and how to be fit for kingdom living. They'll also learn about being part of the family of God and making the church a true home of grace. As such, Commitment Sunday offers a moment for the congregation to bring it all together and be a vital part of something larger than themselves.

Combining a stewardship campaign with a church-wide study may seem like a novel idea. You may not be familiar with some of the aspects of such a program—perhaps you have limited experience with a stewardship campaign, church-wide study, or small-group Bible study. Don't worry. This program will lead you—and your entire congregation—every step of the way.

As you move ahead, don't ignore the fact that there really is strength in numbers. Involving your entire congregation in moving toward a focused goal can be a powerful thing indeed. It will build bridges where there currently are none, and offer opportunities for discussion, prayer, and encouragement among people who might not previously have found anything in common. Members of your congregation will find open doors for talking about things like faith, money, and service. Most important, the unified church is one in which the enemy can't win. With everyone's eyes focused on the goal, there will be less emphasis on complaining, gossip, negativity, and other potentially damaging attitudes among members.

NURTURING GENEROUS HEARTS

At the very core of this study is a shift in overall thinking, a transition from the idea of "What's in it for me?"

to "How is God at work in me, and how can I share what I'm receiving with others?" The reality is that this goes against our very nature—not to mention our self-focused culture. But once Christians grasp the truth about God's extravagant love—and experience the ways that God rewards a generous heart—they are never the same again. New areas of faith begin to surface, especially faith that God will supply each and every need, no matter how much we give away. Consider Matthew 6:32–33: "For the pagans run after all these things, and your heavenly Father knows that you need them. But seek first his kingdom and his righteousness, and all these things will be given to you as well."

There's also Psalm 23, which begins: "The Lord is my shepherd, I shall not be in want," and First Timothy 6:17, which urges:

> Command those who are rich in this present world not to be arrogant nor to put their hope in wealth, which is so uncertain, but to put their hope in God, who richly provides us with everything for our enjoyment.

Of course, this is not just about money. Generosity also includes being willing to be present for others in need, offering an ear to listen or a shoulder to cry on, as well as serving in other areas of ministry. It includes the blessing of intercessory prayer, and being prepared to go before the Father with the needs of those around us, as well.

This new understanding of generosity offers a tremendous place of growth for any congregation; imagine what it would be like if every member was willing to give, to serve, and to pray, fully understanding that they were walking in the fullness of the Christian life?

It sounds impossible, but it's not. The way to get there, however, is to start with the idea that God himself is a generous force, and that God is for us rather than against us. It begins with a true understanding of the concept of grace; God is not just a dour-faced judge up in heaven, waiting to punish us at every turn. It continues with a study on the life of Jesus, delving into his teaching and focusing on his Resurrection. We are invited to accept God's offer of new life in Jesus, and given the keys to embracing this holy lifestyle. The study culminates in a fresh look at what it means to be the body of Christ in a hurting world, and how we as individuals can become partners in the gospel by renewing our vows of prayers, presence, gifts, and service.

Perhaps the best part, however, is that this study offers something for everyone. Whether new believers or seasoned followers, we can all continue to grow in the ways we demonstrate God's generosity and grace in our daily lives. It truly is a lifelong journey.

The study will take forty days for your congregation to complete. Of course, it will take a little more time than that to pull it off from an organizational standpoint. That's what this book is all about. You'll find suggested time lines, tips, and more in the following pages, but don't be afraid to make this campaign your own. Nobody knows your church like your church's leadership, so there may be places that need to be tweaked for a better fit. Go for it. With God on your side, you will certainly win.

Chapter 2

WHY FORTY DAYS?

The Israelites wandered in the desert for forty years (Deut. 8:2–5); Jesus was tempted by Satan for forty days (Mark 1:13); Noah built his ark in preparation for a rain that lasted forty days and forty nights (Gen. 7:4); and Moses was on Mount Sinai for forty days and forty nights speaking with God about commandments and laws (Exod. 24:18).

Throughout the Bible, the number forty is used to denote a season or preparation of trial. Forty days is roughly six weeks. It's not that the number of days is magical—on a practical level, six weeks is the length of time experts say it takes to develop a new habit. A forty-day study, then, divided into six weeks, can be long enough to make a significant difference in the habits of your congregation.

The span of six weeks isn't so long that people will lose interest. It's brief enough to see the proverbial light at the end of the tunnel, or the goal everyone's working toward. It's also a familiar marker of growth. Remember six-week progress reports from school? Think of this study, then, as a crash course in growing closer to God. At its close, the progress will be apparent to all.

Imagine what your church could be like if every member was committed to daily study and each one was on the same page with everyone else—literally. What would it be like if members came to Sunday worship with expectancy and excitement, knowing what topic would be discussed?

Imagine, too, the possibilities of continuing that sense of anticipation long after the forty-day campaign is complete. Since the campaign concludes with filling out commitment cards and service commitment forms, it's more like a new beginning, rather than an end.

The best part is that everyone likes being part of a team and working toward common goals. As such, *Irresistible Invitation* can help your church family grow in unity, creating long-lasting relationships along the way.

The idea of forty days, then, isn't arbitrary—even if this is the first time you've seen it linked to a stewardship campaign. It is simply a period of time to which people can commit, having a defined goal in sight. And once the good habits of increased prayer, godly introspection, willingness to serve, and understanding of tithes and offerings are set, they can continue for a lifetime and propel your church family truly into a world-changing congregation.

Chapter 3

CULTIVATING JOYFUL GIVING

A woman named Doris Hier tells a great story in *Christian Reader* magazine. Her daughter worked in Chicago before she was married, and one day she got off the commuter train to go to her job, and a scruffy-looking panhandler stopped her, asking for a quarter. The young woman was never one to cast judgment or ignore need, but she was absolutely penniless and couldn't help the fellow. Looking him straight in the eye, she said, "I'm sorry I don't have a quarter. I don't have any money to take the bus to work today." She couldn't believe what happened next. Without saying a word, the fellow reached into his pocket and gave her a quarter.

It's a wonderful tale about generosity, and not just one about money. Instead, it's about generosity of spirit. The sad thing is, in our "always-looking-out-for-number-one" society, this story is so unusual that it's almost unbelievable. But it doesn't have to be.

WEEK ONE: COMING HOME TO GOD

When it comes to the topic of generosity, there simply is no greater example than God. He is the ultimate act to follow. God does not consider generosity simply in a financial sense, but in one that is played out through an abundance of love, grace, commitment, and presence. Once we, as Christians, truly begin to plumb the depths of that generosity, we can't help but want to give back. We can't help but want to return our love, our devotion—and yes, even our finances—to those God puts in our path.

This forty-day study can help us understand that profound truth on a deeper level. It's based on the prolific teachings of Maxie Dunnam, breaking down the idea of God's extravagant love into bite-sized, yet still life-changing, pieces.

The first week starts with the broad concept of God's goodness, played out through the great and amazing love God has for each of us. It was through the generosity of his love, after all, that he sent his Son to die for our sins. It is also through his great generosity that we are given the chance to "come home" and find forgiveness; to accept freedom from our sins; and to gain new life.

Each day of the first week challenges misconceptions we may have of our Heavenly Father, clearing the path for deep truths to be revealed and accepted in the weeks ahead. The seventh day serves as a review; key concepts are repeated, and probing questions are asked so that the reader can make the study a truly relevant, individual experience.

WEEK TWO: A LOVE LIKE NO OTHER

The second week of the study focuses on the life and love of Jesus. It's not just that his very coming to Earth is a prime example of God's extravagant love for us; it's also that while here, Jesus lived a life poured out for others. Key concepts for this week, then, include the importance of understanding—and still preaching—the cross, as well as the chance to see Jesus as one who still comes to us in peace, compassion, and judgment. The week incorporates numerous Scriptures about Jesus' days on Earth, making his experiences newly applicable to our lives today. Again, the week ends with a review of main points, so these can be firmly planted before moving on.

WEEK THREE: ALIVE IN CHRIST

Different people have different ideas about what it means to be Christian. We believe it can be much more than simply accepting Jesus as a personal Lord and Savior. Instead, through this study, we focus on the idea of being alive in Christ—walking in all of the fullness of God's grace, love, direction, kindness, and power. Getting there, however, is not an instantaneous thing. Rather, it takes a depth of commitment and willingness to walk side by side with God on a daily basis. That's what this week is all about.

We look at the person who is alive in Christ as one who is prepared for the flow of the Holy Spirit both in and out of season; one who walks in power; one who constantly abides with the Father; one who is humble and willing to serve; one who remains accountable and repentant of sin; and one who is confident of who he or she is in Christ. This week does not offer a list of have-tos that must be accomplished or rules that must be followed to get on God's good side. No, this is not legalistic at all. Rather, it considers the practices that can cultivate a life of fullness in the believer. Stories, Scriptures, and thoughtful questions help guide the reader to a deeper hunger for all that God has to offer.

WEEK FOUR: FIT FOR KINGDOM LIVING

There is so much more to walking with God than many of us realize. Again, this week's lessons are not about shoulds, but being fit for our lives in the kingdom. Christians are called to a higher standard of living, incorporating service, prayer, discipleship, and the idea of being crucified with Christ. As with other weeks, these lessons use both Scripture and testimonies from saints and others to help us understand what it means to be sheep guided by the mighty Shepherd.

WEEK FIVE: THE HOME OF GRACE

In many congregations, it can be a challenge to get members of the family to show up for regular meal times. Beyond that, there may be a number of people who will make it there on Sunday mornings, but that's where the level of commitment stops. Obviously, this isn't God's best. If he has called people to be part of a congregation, he has called them to be a vital part, and this week's lessons will drive the point home. The church is to be a true home of grace, a place where all are welcomed, and all have a significant part to play. This section's lessons are a great lead-in to the final week, which tackles the idea of personal responsibility in prayer, presence, gifts, and service. All of these things are tied into grace, and as a result, this week offers a deeper level of understanding of just how generous is this God that we serve. By this point, members of the congregation should be well versed in the concept of generosity in the life of the Christian, as evidenced by God, his Son, his followers, and his Word.

WEEK SIX: PARTNERS IN THE GOSPEL

The final week, which culminates with Commitment Sunday, brings it all together by giving members of the congregation an outlet for walking out everything they've just learned. The week leans heavily on the tenets of prayer, presence, gifts, and service, with an added idea thrown in: the importance of extending grace to others, and allowing them to be all that God has called them to be, as well. Under the umbrella of living a life of generosity toward others—using God's example—the financial offerings for Commitment Sunday are a natural fit. This is not, however, just a warm-up for congregants to make a big, one-time pledge. Instead, it is a call to a continued life of giving, one that includes regular tithes and offerings for both now and the days to come. Commitment Sunday, then, becomes a beginning, rather than an end.

THE MOST GENEROUS ACT OF ALL

One final note, before your church begins its campaign. We don't want to take anything for granted—and that includes where individual members stand in their commitment to Jesus. In a time when many churches report few or no professions of faith or baptisms, the focus of this study may cause some participants to examine their commitment or make a new or renewed profession of faith. It can be a tricky subject for some pastors, especially those who are afraid they'll offend congregants if they ask. We'd like to help you out.

Because a commitment to Christ is an essential part of this study—not to mention the basis for all that God wants to do in a person's life—we've included the option right there in the book. An appendix includes an explanation and prayer for accepting Jesus as Lord and Savior. If the person reading it is doing so for the first time, they're instructed to let someone else know. There's also an opportunity built into week two of the *Irresistible Invitation Leader's Guide.*

Don't be surprised if *Irresistible Invitation: Responding to the Extravagant Heart of God* results in changes and salvations among your church body; it's designed to meet people wherever they are, and some people may not be exactly where you think.

WEEKLY STUDY SEQUENCE

There is an important concept to make clear to the church leaders, staff, and participants throughout the planning and progress of this study: the weekly sequence of sermons, bulletin inserts, newsletter articles, and timing of small-group or Sunday school class discussions. Without careful explanation groups can get off track and it can become confusing.

The planned weekly sequence is as follows:

SERMONS

Each week's sermon is planned to be preached the Sunday prior to the upcoming readings. This sets the tone and lets the congregation anticipate what is ahead.

DAILY READINGS

These will follow during the next seven days. Participants should read Day One of the first week on a Monday, thus establishing the correct progression of weekly reading for the entire six weeks of the study.

SMALL-GROUP/SUNDAY SCHOOL DISCUSSIONS

These discussions will occur after the group has completed each week's reading. Many small groups will be meeting at time intervals that do not exactly coincide with the completion of the week's readings, so some small groups may have only read a few of that week's readings prior to the group discussion. While less than ideal, it is unavoidable and acceptable. Maxie Dunnam's DVD message will provide a good introduction to the material for each gathering. Sunday school classes, or better yet, small groups scheduled on Sundays, will have the benefit of having read the full week's readings, ending with the seventh entry that day. Remember, however, the pastor's sermon preached that same morning will be focused on the upcoming week's theme.

BULLETIN INSERTS

The inserts will review the past week's readings, providing a look back to establish closure for the theme and setting the stage for the pastor to introduce the new theme for the week ahead.

NEWSLETTER/WEB SITE ARTICLES

Churches have many different patterns of midweek communications—ranging from weekly traditional mailings or e-mails to Web site-only postings. Others issue printed communications only on a biweekly or monthly basis. Each newsletter article is written so that it can be used at any time during the appropriate week. The steering committee should evaluate the best usage of the newsletter articles, noting that they contain excellent reflections and are an important part of the program's message.

Chapter 4

WHO'S ON YOUR TEAM?

Behind every winning team, there is strong leadership. In the case of *Irresistible Invitation: Cultivating Joyful Giving in Your Church*, the head coach won't necessarily be the pastor. Instead, the majority of the effort will come from the members of your stewardship committee. Even if your church is small, it's important to consider developing such a committee; it can take the pressure off of the pastor, as well as help develop a level of peer acceptance when it comes to things like committing to presence, service, giving, and prayer. In most cases, members of the congregation will be much more likely to respond favorably to needs presented by their peers than to any special influence from the pastor.

Now, this is not to say that the pastor's role is diminished when it comes to stewardship. The pastor should be in regular contact with the stewardship committee leader, offer theological and biblical counsel as needed, and talk about how God meets us as we give of ourselves, our time, our prayers, and our finances. The pastor can set a good example for the congregation by regularly giving of his or her own finances and openly talking about money, tithes, offerings, and stewardship.

Developing a stewardship committee also gives the pastor the option of not knowing how much money individual members of the congregation give. Pastors who choose to distance themselves from specific knowledge of individual giving levels have greater freedom in their pastoral ministry. Allowing trusted lay leadership or other church staff to work with the specific financial commitments gives the pastor the option of not knowing the information.

The stewardship committee doesn't have to be a large group, especially if the congregation isn't large. But it is important that it's made up of a cross-section of members to ensure that different economic groups are fairly represented. Don't make the mistake of putting only the wealthiest folks on the committee, and expect that they'll be able to understand the needs of the congregation as a whole. A single mother struggling to make ends meet, for example, brings a completely different voice to the table than a successful entrepreneur.

Wanted: Generous Hearts

The choice of who should be involved begins with a search for those with generous hearts. Chances are, you already know who they are. They're not necessarily the ones with the most cash, but they are the ones with an infectious attitude of selflessness, always willing to put other people's needs before their own.

In addition, look for members who are enthusiastic about church and spiritual growth. They'll be the ones who get excited about learning new truths, digging into the depths of God's Word, and sharing with others what God has done in their lives.

You might also consider people who have financial work experience. This is not to say they're chosen solely for that reason, but an understanding of investments and the way money works can be a great asset to any team.

In addition, look for members who aren't afraid to dream big. Any successful stewardship committee needs both people who can see the big picture and the ones who can figure out the details to make it happen. Too much of one side or the other won't get you anywhere. Visionaries can offer excitement and possibility, while the detail folks can balance it out with practicality and planning.

Finally, resist the temptation to only fill the committee with seasoned church members and traditional leaders. Too often, church leadership can become stale or tired when the same people attempt to implement the church's programs. The committee can also provide an entry into leadership for newer church members. It can be a chance for them to grow into future front-runners, rubbing shoulders with those who are already in positions of authority and learning along the way. They can also bring fresh ideas to the table and maintain a voice with their peers. Remember, your more seasoned members may welcome an opportunity to serve in some other capacity.

FOLLOWING THE LEADER

The first person that should be chosen for any committee is its leader, and that's a decision to be considered with much prayer. The leader should offer insight, accountability, and vision for the entire church body—not just the committee—so it's important that you carefully consider all the talents and skills that your potential candidates offer. It might help to come up with a job description for the leader so it's easier to see who fits. A list of desirable traits, for example, could include:

- Evidence of a consistent Christian walk, displayed through commitment to attendance, tithing, service, and prayer;
- A heart turned toward God and to living a clean, holy, and just life;
- Leadership/managerial skills;
- Humility and a teachable spirit;
- Honesty and trustworthiness;
- Enthusiasm for growing the church and congregation;
- Confidence about the connection between a Christian's money and his devotion to God and a willingness to promote it;
- A positive relationship with the pastor;
- A positive reputation within the congregation; and
- Previous experience in working with church fundraising, stewardship, or development campaigns (not necessary, but helpful).

Obviously, the leader should also be willing to lead. Most stewardship committees meet about once a month throughout the year, probably more in the months leading up to the church's annual stewardship campaign. As the chair of the stewardship committee, then, the leader would be responsible for planning and facilitating the meetings; helping appoint committee members; delegating and following up on assigned tasks; regularly reporting progress to the pastor; coordinating with other church committees; helping develop and implement the church budget; promoting stewardship throughout the congregation; and offering a personal example of commitment.

How much time all this will take depends on a number of factors, including the leader's ability to delegate, the committee's willingness to participate, the size and intricacy of the church budget, and the amount of confidence the pastor places in the committee chair. At any rate, it is not a position to be taken lightly.

THE ROLE OF THE COMMITTEE

The stewardship committee does a lot more than just spearhead the *Irresistible Invitation* campaign. Anyone knows that programs and facilities require money, so the committee actually serves as a dream team for helping guide the path of the overall church. The committee must be clear on the vision of the pastor and be enthusiastic about helping carry it out.

In regard to this particular study, the committee also has an opportunity to help people grow in their perceptions of commitment through time, service, and prayer. It's an opportunity to affect not only the outcome of the church's annual budget but also scriptural foundations for generations to come. To prevent members of the committee from being overloaded, delegation is essential. Various roles might include:

BOOK DISTRIBUTION COORDINATOR

Develop a sales/distribution plan, help determine whether the books and workbooks are underwritten by the church or have the cost passed onto recipients, and develop a master checklist of all church families. If your church chooses to give thank-you gifts to members who turn in commitment cards and service commitment forms, the book distribution coordinator could have responsibility for distributing the gifts as well.

SMALL-GROUP COORDINATOR

Work with other leaders involved in the church's education ministry for Sunday school/small-group studies, recruit small-group leaders for short-term studies, heavily promote the study for full congregational participation, determine the quantity of resources to order, train small-group leaders, coordinate the program with youth leadership, and ensure the availability of DVD players for Sunday school/small-group meetings.

VOLUNTEER COMMITMENT COORDINATOR

Work with individual church committees to develop the service commitment materials, develop a method for recording volunteer's responses, and communicate volunteer responses to appropriate church leaders for follow-up and eventual integration into the specified ministry areas.

COMMUNICATIONS COORDINATOR

Work with church staff to coordinate mailings, newsletter text, and bulletin inserts; hang posters and distribute materials for the program; and communicate with church webmaster (if applicable) regarding possible online elements.

PRINT RESOURCES COORDINATOR

Develop a schedule for all printed components, review the CD-ROM Toolkit for program-furnished graphics, customize or develop new graphics as appropriate, draft/edit/design/adapt all printed components, and establish print quantities and secure printing.

PRAYER COORDINATOR

Recruit participants for continual prayer throughout the forty-day period and coordinate a prayer vigil to commence twenty-four hours prior to Commitment Sunday.

TESTIMONY COORDINATOR

Recruit church members to give brief personal testimony related to the study during each week of the campaign.

FOLLOW-UP COORDINATOR

Obtain lists of individuals who have not returned commitment cards or service commitment forms and ensure that follow-up letters are sent to those individuals.

COMPARATIVE STUDY COORDINATOR

Gather statistics for comparison before and after the campaign.

HOSPITALITY COORDINATOR

Make arrangements for a leadership prayer dinner (if your church opts to do one), coordinate refreshments/decorations for Commitment Sunday, and organize the Commitment Sunday concluding meal or event, including menu planning, purchasing supplies and/or decorations, and recruiting volunteers to help with the event.

Chapter 5

HOW THE CAMPAIGN WORKS

At the heart of the *Irresistible Invitation: Cultivating Joyful Giving in Your Church* campaign is the individual reading of *Irresistible Invitation: Responding to the Extravagant Heart of God.* It's only through reading the book that members of the congregation can personally apply the principles to their lives. As such, every effort should be made to put books in the hands of members, and to encourage participation across all levels.

Different churches might go about this in different ways. Regardless, the best bet is to create an atmosphere in which people will truly feel left out if they're not participating. Church leadership should be encouraged to talk up the campaign in the days leading to its start, during the six weeks it takes place, and especially on Commitment Sunday. Rather than presenting the campaign as a requirement, however, introduce it as an exciting, potentially life-changing event not to be missed.

The campaign theme offers an excellent opportunity to reach out to inactive or marginally active members. By playing up the invitation theme, these members and visitors can be encouraged to become involved in new ways, strengthening your congregation and reaching out to draw them into the full life God desires for them. You'll find a number of resources on the CD-ROM Toolkit that will help you do that, including fun bulletin inserts and letters the pastor or the stewardship committee chair can sign and send directly to members of the congregation. But don't be afraid to be creative. Incorporate your church sign, consider hanging posters or banners, and if your church has something like a drama ministry, ask it to prepare a skit or two to be presented to the congregation.

Remember: the higher the expectancy of the congregation, the more likely they are to see God move in and among them.

KEEPING THE GOAL IN SIGHT

Throughout the campaign, don't forget to emphasize that it will end with a commitment. As the campaign progresses, continue the countdown to Commitment Sunday, but be careful that it's not seen as simply a day for financial commitments. Rather, it's a time for commitment in all areas, representing a generosity of spirit rather than just generosity with cash. Money is only part of the picture. Continue to emphasize the fact that God—and the church—wants every aspect of each member's life, not just his or her dollars.

As such, be as open about the importance of tithes and offerings as you are about service and presence. If you, as a leader, have any reservations about asking people to fully participate, work through those reservations now.

GROUP DISCUSSIONS

In addition to the individual study of *Irresistible Invitation: Responding to the Extravagant Heart of God*, group discussion during Sunday school or small-group meetings is a key aspect of the overall *Irresistible Invitation* campaign. This element builds bridges between members, and it helps establish common ground.

First, the *Participant's Workbook* offers a review of key concepts so they're not forgotten over the course of the week. Repetition can greatly aid in learning, so this step helps ensure that those key concepts are established before the next topic is introduced.

Group discussion also allows church members to hear other viewpoints. Those who are lacking faith in certain areas, for example, might find encouragement through others who are a little further along. The group meetings, which are clearly outlined in both the *Participant's Workbook* and the *Leader's Guide*, also incorporate opportunities for the participants to break into even smaller groups and share on a more personal level. This builds intimacy as well as humility as members learn to be more open with their thoughts.

Again, the *Participant's Workbook* and the *Leader's Guide* clearly outline the format for each meeting, and also give tips for first-time leaders on facilitating discussion. The meetings will run most smoothly, however, when the leaders are familiar with the key concepts and book chapters and are willing to rely on God for guidance. Pre-meeting prayer can definitely change the course of the gathering, and leaders should be chosen based on their ability to follow the lead of the Holy Spirit as much as their ability to help people learn.

The meetings are designed to last from forty-five minutes to an hour, so they can easily be covered in a traditional Sunday school format. Should your church have small-group meetings at other times during the week, however, that's another option for group study. Suggestions for incorporating that into the campaign time line are included.

If there's any question about the efficacy of small groups, keep in mind that Jesus did most of his work in small groups. Small groups and Sunday school classes offer intimacy, a chance for everyone to share and grow, and a safe place for people to participate. If your church doesn't currently offer small groups or Sunday school classes, the *Irresistible Invitation* study is an excellent opportunity to start or expand participation in such programs. A strong emphasis on starting new small groups could begin a movement in your church that will last for many years to come. Many individuals may choose to continue their group meetings with new topics and studies.

THE PASTOR'S ROLE

Each Sunday during the campaign, the pastor will present a message that incorporates the key concepts of the upcoming week's readings. The CD-ROM Toolkit includes sermons written by Maxie Dunnam, which can be used as is, or as a jumping-off point for the pastor in preparing his or her own messages.

The best-case scenario, however, is for the church pastor to read through each week's lessons and craft a personal message based on the insight learned. This is recommended for a number of reasons. Not only will it give the messages a personal touch, it will also allow members of the congregation to see that the entire church family really is in the campaign together, including the pastor. It will also demonstrate that no matter how mature we become in our walk with the Lord, we always have more to learn. This gives the pastor an opportunity to model unity and new ways of looking at tried-and-true ideas.

Beyond that, however, a pastor who crafts original messages has the opportunity to gear them toward the specific needs and challenges of the congregation. One church might find attendance issues its biggest concern; another might be challenged by a lack of consistent financial support; and yet another might have trouble encouraging people to step into acts of service. Regardless, the campaign covers them all and allows the pastor to offer messages that can speak to the heart.

But the pastor's role doesn't end there.

The CD-ROM Toolkit also includes sample letters that can be sent from the pastor and/or stewardship committee chair to the congregation. One encourages participation before the study begins, and another is designed to be mailed to church members along with commitment cards and service commitment forms a few weeks before Commitment Sunday. In addition, it's crucial for members of the congregation to see the pastor actually involved in the process and excited about it on a personal level. Otherwise, the campaign comes across as something that the stewardship committee has concocted simply to raise funds.

The pastor is the one who has the opportunity to lead the flock by personal example, which is always easier for people to follow. Keep the focus on "us" and "we" rather than on "you."

MAXIE DUNNAM'S LEAD

Throughout the study, there's a name and face that will become familiar to members of your church family:

Maxie Dunnam. In addition to writing the text, Dunnam has prepared DVD messages for this kit. They allow everyone involved to experience Dunnam speaking straight from his heart. Brief introductory DVD messages feature Dunnam at the start of each Sunday school/small-group meeting, and these help set the tone for discussions, provide consistency, and allow participants to hear Dunnam's personal insights on the key concept for each week in the study. There's also an introductory message for the church leadership, to give them special guidance for the campaign ahead.

TESTIMONY TIME

To be truly successful, *Irresistible Invitation* has to get more than just the church leadership talking. And that's where personal testimonies from members of the congregation come in. Incorporating these testimonies can help drive important messages home from a peer perspective, and in many cases, they can easily be incorporated into Sunday services. Testimonies are particularly effective when they relate to the overall themes of each week of the *Irresistible Invitation* study. The week about the church being the home of grace, for example, might include a brief word from someone whose walk has been positively affected by the kindness of another member of the congregation.

But feel free to keep things simple. Place a member of the stewardship committee in charge of finding and scheduling those who are willing to speak. Work in consultation with the pastor, who may choose to stand with the person and interview him or her to help keep the message relevant and on point. Sharing testimonies helps generate excitement for the campaign and encourages people who are not yet fully committed to take part.

COMMITMENT CARDS AND SERVICE COMMITMENT FORMS

As the *Irresistible Invitation* campaign comes to a close, members of the congregation should find themselves ready and willing to enter new levels of commitment in a variety of areas. That's where the commitment cards and service commitment forms come in. Sample copies are included on the CD-ROM Toolkit, but it will be necessary to tailor the service commitment forms to include areas of service specific to your church family.

The commitment cards and service commitment forms will be mailed to church members individually a few weeks before the campaign ends. This allows members enough time to give proper thought and prayer to their response.

It's important that no member of the congregation be surprised by the introduction of these documents. Throughout the campaign, the church family will be preparing for new levels of commitment, so the receipt of these items comes simply as the next step in the process. The entire study is based on a heart change, rather than strong-arm tactics. By Commitment Sunday, members should commit out of a desire to serve God, to grow closer to him, and to participate in the work he's doing, rather than feeling like it's something that they have to do.

That said, each member should be strongly encouraged to sign a commitment card and service commitment form for each area of prayer, presence, gifts, and service, no matter what that commitment is. Encourage members to take part immediately, so they don't miss the opportunity for God's blessings and so they can experience the fullness of heart that comes with venturing into deeper levels of faithfulness.

As for what's actually on the cards, that will vary depending on the congregation. It's important, though, that the cards incorporate all elements of the study: prayer, presence, gifts, and service. There may be a listing of various opportunities for serving, blank lines that allow people to commit to a certain amount of money per week or month, and a section that commits support through prayer and attendance. Don't forget to include a place for each member to actually sign his or her name, giving added credence to the commitment. Some examples of commitment cards and service commitment forms are provided on the CD-ROM Toolkit and are shown in the appendix.

For those who attend but don't turn in a card, a letter can be sent to their home. A sample of such a letter is provided on the CD-ROM Toolkit and is shown in the appendix.

The actual giving back of a completed commitment card and service commitment form on Commitment Sunday should be done in a spirit of reverent celebration. It can be a moving, beautiful experience to see every person or family in a worship service come up to the front of the church to reverently and publicly give their commitment to the church by placing their cards and forms in a basket.

To make the moment even more special, you might consider giving a commemorative gift to each family or individual that turns in a commitment card and service commitment form. Such gifts don't need to be expensive, but communicate that their offering is valued. Since

Commitment Sunday frequently comes right before Thanksgiving, your church might want to give a special Christmas tree ornament imprinted with the campaign logo and/or your church name. Other gift examples might be mugs, umbrellas, pens, keychains, or other personalized gifts. If you choose to thank your members with a gift, these could be handed to people when they deliver their commitment cards and service commitment forms during worship.

PRAYER

If there's only one thing you remember from this entire campaign handbook, let this be it: God must remain an essential part of everything you do. He is ready and willing to offer insight and help wherever it is needed. To help things run as smoothly as possible—and to give members of the church family an opportunity to stretch in their own prayer lives—*Irresistible Invitation* has a prayer element built right in. Your church might establish a schedule of volunteers to pray continuously throughout the forty-day period. The beauty of it is that once it's set in place, you might find a core group willing to continue it long after the campaign has finished.

You might also consider organizing a vigil for the last twenty-four hours prior to Commitment Sunday. This can be a great time of worship and praising God for all that he's done and all he's yet to do. Additionally, you may want to consider holding a leadership prayer dinner about a week before the campaign kicks off. That can help build excitement, as well as express gratitude for those who have led the way thus far.

Commitment Sunday Celebration

A beautiful opportunity for corporate celebration, the *Irresistible Invitation* campaign should end with a public event commemorating the completion of the church-wide study. Each member of your church should receive a special invitation using the campaign logo that asks them to be present for the recognition of their personal commitment. Just as the completion of the pledge cards and service commitment forms is a vital time in the life of the church, the opportunity for renewing spiritual commitments is also an important occasion worthy of being celebrated.

Decisions to Be Made

Irresistible Invitation: Cultivating Joyful Giving in Your Church can be adapted for literally any church, whether big or small. Depending on the church structure, budget, and goals, however, some decisions will need to be made about how the study is actually implemented. The following questions should be addressed by the pastor, stewardship committee, and possibly other church leadership before the study begins.

How Should a Date Be Determined for Commitment Sunday?

If you have a day that's traditionally set aside for Commitment Sunday, this will be an easy substitution. Many churches already have an annual stewardship campaign each fall to help support the budget for the following year.

If you don't already have a date in mind, autumn is a good time for many reasons. The main one is that we have all been programmed to expect autumn as a time of new beginnings. As we were growing up, there were always new school years, new semesters, new school clothes, and new friends to look forward to each fall. As such, we innately understand that this season is one for something new, and it's the season for learning.

There's one caveat, however: if you're setting an autumn date for your Commitment Sunday, don't wait so late that you get close to the Christmas season. You don't want people to miss weekly events due to holiday obligations, plus you want people to establish their new habits of increased giving, service, and prayer before extra holiday outings and responsibilities distract them. The Sunday prior to Thanksgiving, then, could be an ideal time.

WHO PAYS FOR THE BOOKS?

Personal reading of *Irresistible Invitation: Responding to the Extravagant Heart of God* is an essential part of the study for the congregation. Without the books, the campaign becomes nothing more than a series of messages from the pastor. You must decide, however, who will cover the cost.

- ❋ Will the church purchase the books in advance, and then ask members of the church family to reimburse the church when they pick them up? (This will be the most common approach.)
- ❋ Will the church cover the cost of the books to distribute to the congregation for free?
- ❋ Or will the solution fall somewhere in between, with the church picking up part of the cost and offering the books to the congregation at a discounted rate?

The answer depends entirely on your congregation.

Low-income families, for example, may see the cost of the book as prohibitive. You want to be careful that people aren't left out if they can't afford to purchase one. If the books are sold to members of the congregation at full or reduced costs, consider a special appeal, asking members of the church family if they'd be willing to sponsor someone in need by adding in a little extra cash.

HOW WILL THE BOOKS/WORKBOOKS BE DISTRIBUTED?

Copies of *Irresistible Invitation: Responding to the Extravagant Heart of God* should be available on Sunday mornings before and after worship services. To keep a close eye on the number distributed, they could be picked up at a table in the church narthex. Have church members initial or sign to be sure people have received copies and to keep track of inventory.

The books are intended for individual study, but one copy per family should work just fine (sharing can be good). The associated *Participant's Workbook*, however, should be available per person, since it contains journaling space and areas to fill in the blanks and take notes. Remember to include sufficient copies for teens and older children when figuring out how many workbooks to order.

Throughout the campaign, it will be a good idea to keep extra copies at the church office so those who missed the original distribution won't be penalized. If your church office does not keep regular hours during the week, appoint someone as a contact for materials, making sure that person's phone number is listed in conjunction with church bulletin inserts, newsletter articles, and the like for anyone who decides to join in.

WILL YOUR CHURCH USE THE PROVIDED PROGRAM THEME AND GRAPHICS, OR WILL YOU DESIGN YOUR OWN?

The answer to this depends entirely on the creativity, skill, and time available for planning. You've been provided with everything you need, but if there's enough time and interest within the stewardship committee, feel free to make it your own.

Whatever you decide, remember to be consistent. A graphic like the cover invitation—if repeated on newsletter articles, bulletin inserts, posters, and banners—can help instill the idea that the study reaches all members of the church and touches all church programs.

Creating wearable stickers with the campaign logo to every person at worship each week of the study can also reinforce the theme and unity. Stickers aren't expensive and are disposable, but entering church on Sunday and seeing everyone wearing the same lapel sticker helps create an atmosphere that says we're all together and this is a special season.

WHAT ARE THE ADDITIONAL PROGRAM EXPENSES?

Don't forget to factor in incidental costs such as printing, postage, the creation of signs and banners, or refreshments for Commitment Sunday. Discuss beforehand where the money will come from in the church's budget. Consider whether you want to reinforce the unified theme by passing out campaign stickers at all services and if you want to give thank-you gifts.

INCORPORATING THE CHURCH WEB SITE

One of the most important aspects of *Irresistible Invitation* is that it's a program the entire church can experience together. The reality, however, is that someone is bound to miss an occasional group meeting. Maybe someone serving with the children doesn't get a chance to attend Sunday school. Maybe someone who's sick or homebound misses out on one of the pastor's sermons. Maybe someone else with a third-shift work schedule is finding it hard to link up with others for community discussions.

The answer to this situation could come through technology. An increasing number of churches have Web sites. Some are even incorporating regularly updated components that appeal to those who might otherwise be out of touch. Digital availability is also high on the priority list for many teens and young adults, who increasingly receive information and insight through the Internet.

If your church already has a Web site, consider incorporating *Irresistible Invitation* as a component. You might post a key question or two from the individual lessons of the *Participant's Workbook* during the week after each meeting takes place. For an interactive experience, consider including some of the workbook's fill-in-the-blank questions.

If you'd like to take it a step further, your church's Web site could incorporate a blog or commentary section through which people could post their own thoughts or respond to those of others. One of the most exciting things about that approach is that people outside the church walls would also have access to view the comments. People who might be hesitant to set foot inside the actual church building would still be able to take part in intriguing dialogue about important spiritual topics. If you decide to go this route, however, it's important to appoint a Web moderator who can make sure comments stay on track.

Another option is to post the pastor's sermons (either portions or the entire messages) on the Web site as text, audio files, or even video files. Reinforcing the campaign in a Web format could be a good kicking-off point for incorporating more multimedia into your church programs. The CD-ROM Toolkit has jpeg files of the graphics, as well as the contents of the newsletter articles and bulletin inserts.

Other ideas for Web site content include:

- A sample commitment card and service commitment form showing the variety of places where people can plug into the church;
- A reminder of the Scripture verse for each week;
- A countdown ticker to Commitment Sunday to build excitement; and
- Previews of the coming week's message.

ADAPTING FOR YOUTH AND FAMILIES

You might think that the *Irresistible Invitation* campaign is only for the church's adults. But that's not necessarily so; *Irresistible Invitation* and its workbook are both at a level that could be understood by teens. Consider involving your church's youth leadership as soon as possible so they can incorporate the program into their own activities. Youth participation in servant activities, prayer, attendance, and financial gifts could be increased by incorporating teen-specific elements into the study.

In addition, you may want to develop separate commitment cards and service commitment forms for youth. Sample cards are included on the CD-ROM Toolkit. These could include servant opportunities that have to do with youth events or with general church activities, showing teens how to find places to give of themselves. You may want to consider incorporating the taking of tithes and offerings into youth activities. Provide opportunities for teens to share input into where money could be spent to improve youth programs, and help them see that their own financial gifts could help those things happen.

On a more individual level, as teens go through the program with their own peers, they'll also have a shared experience and point of conversation with their parents. Families should be encouraged to talk about the various topics of *Irresistible Invitation* with each other, opening up discussions on prayer, giving, service, and the like.

Engaging in family discussions doesn't just apply to teens. It's never too early to begin teaching children such biblical concepts as giving back to God and putting others before yourself. Children learn great things by seeing their parents actively model prayer, tithing, service, and regular church attendance.

THE BEFORE AND AFTER

Each of us has our own idea of success, and that's true even when it comes to a campaign like *Irresistible Invitation*. Before you begin, then, it's important to give some thought and prayer to what kind of results you'd like to see before it's all over.

As you consider the results you'd like to see, think about how the campaign might impact your church long-term. Think about what can be done to facilitate future growth and development. Discuss how people can be regularly reminded of the things they've learned and the new goals they've set. Consider if there's a way to incorporate Sunday school/small-group accountability. And be sure to determine how the service commitments will be followed up on by leadership to ensure that all members who volunteer are used in their appropriate areas of ministry.

This isn't just an individual thing. It might not be a bad idea to bring it up during the first meeting of the stewardship committee. Have everyone take out a piece of paper and write down three goals for discussion. The goals don't necessarily have to be shared with the entire congregation. They could simply be discussed among the members of the committee, helping define the purpose of the campaign.

Now, when it comes to those goals, it's important to be as specific as possible. It's easy to say, "I'd like to see greater unity among the congregation," but that's not really measurable. Instead, consider something like, "increase attendance in weekly Sunday school classes by 25 percent," "have at least 75 percent of members involved in specific ministries or service," or "secure $200,000 in commitments for the church's building project."

Your goals might seem lofty, but again, if the goals are set through prayer and communion with God, who says they can't be met? It's so important that we give God room to work.

To help keep things in perspective, it's a good idea to take inventory before the program begins so you can compare the status of the church after the campaign ends. For example, take note of the following:

- ❈ Average attendance for Sunday morning worship;
- ❈ Average attendance for Sunday school/small-group meetings;

- Attendance figures as a percentage of overall membership;
- Number of church members;
- Average amount given in tithes and offerings per person each week;
- Percentage of church membership actively involved in one or more areas of service;
- Current church budget;
- Current financial commitments for growth, development, or building campaigns; and
- Number of ministries with unmet financial or staffing needs.

As you can see, there are many ways a study like *Irresistible Invitation* could offer measurable results. That's important for a variety of reasons. First, it ensures you a return on your investment, so you'll know whether your time and efforts were worthwhile when you consider another such endeavor. Second, it can build great faith to see God move in ways that only he can, and bring results in ways that only he will. And finally, should you choose to share some of these results with the entire congregation, they'll also get a lift in their faith.

Those involved will have an opportunity to see how their individual efforts are part of the greater good and how effective a team can be when it works together. In addition, marked levels of success establish a new culture in the church, one in which every member is committed, involved, and enthusiastic about continuing the new norms. It's a built-in accountability so that the church doesn't fall back on its old habits once the campaign is through.

Chapter 6

COMPONENTS OF THE CAMPAIGN

This program kit contains the key components you need to carry out an *Irresistible Invitation* campaign in your church. Each element of the campaign was briefly mentioned in the first chapter of this handbook, but here's a closer look:

CAMPAIGN HANDBOOK

This handbook serves as your roadmap, checklist, strategy plan, and communication material source for the entire campaign. It explains the campaign, defines the how-tos, lays out a chronology for tasks, and includes samples of materials you can create or use as they are.

IRRESISTIBLE INVITATION: RESPONDING TO THE EXTRAVAGANT HEART OF GOD

This book by Maxie Dunnam takes us from the big picture idea of God's extravagant love to the individual responsibility of passing that love on to others. It helps participants recognize any misconceptions they may have about God, as well as discover greater understanding of Jesus and how his example can enrich our lives. The book is broken into forty separate lessons, with a review at the end of each week. Each day's lesson offers an opportunity for readers to prayerfully answer a handful of introspective questions, thereby deepening the experience.

PARTICIPANT'S WORKBOOK

The workbook is meant to be used alongside the book, and includes space for individual journaling. It's also intended for use in small groups and/or Sunday school classes. The workbook includes six weekly lessons, complete with fill-in-the-blank components and questions for group discussion.

LEADER'S GUIDE WITH DVD

The *Leader's Guide with DVD* has all the same information as the *Participant's Workbook,* but also includes scripts of six video messages from Maxie Dunnam as well as strategic tips and guidance for facilitating the small-group meetings.

Each small-group meeting and/or Sunday school gathering during the forty-day period will integrate the *Irresistible Invitation* study. To help set the tone for those meetings, the facilitator will begin by playing a brief introductory DVD segment. The six messages add a personal touch to each topic, as well as provide consistency to each lesson.

CAMPAIGN MEDIA KIT

CD-ROM TOOLKIT
SAMPLE SERMONS

During the forty-day study, pastors are strongly encouraged to present sermons related to the upcoming week's readings, bringing home the message in a corporate worship setting. Maxie Dunnam has prepared one or more sermons for each week based on that idea, and you can use them as they are, or look to those messages for ideas and inspiration. The text for each sermon is on the CD-ROM Toolkit in a Microsoft® Word document.

BULLETIN INSERTS

The more a message is repeated, the more likely it is to stick. As such, in addition to daily readings, weekly small-group meetings, and Sunday sermons, church members can find a brief summary—and also a look ahead—in the church bulletin. You'll find the eight inserts in the appendix of this book. The inserts are also included as PDF files and as text in Microsoft® Word documents on the CD-ROM Toolkit.

NEWSLETTER ARTICLES

Since so many churches offer midweek newsletters, this is a way to maintain enthusiasm on the days away from the church building. These articles are found in the appendix, and the text is also on the CD-ROM Toolkit in a Microsoft® Word document. Each column will serve as a reminder to keep up with the week's daily readings, so church members won't miss out on all of the great things going on.

SAMPLE SERVICE COMMITMENT FORMS

Service commitment is crucial to the lifeblood of the church and the spiritual growth of members. Having a method people use to volunteer for and commit to areas of service is just as critical. Included are two modifiable versions (in Microsoft® Word) of service commitment forms that your church can use to assist in this indispensable area.

ADDITIONAL MATERIALS

The CD-ROM Toolkit also contains a poster, campaign theme sticker, commitment cards, congregational letters, graphics, etc. Feel free to use the ones provided or to develop your own.

DVD

"IRRESISTIBLE INVITATION FOR LEADERS"

Nobody says it like Maxie Dunnam, and this part of the *Irresistible Invitation* campaign offers an opportunity to hear straight from his heart. He introduces the idea of true giving, which goes beyond simple concepts of money, and personally encourages leaders to catch hold of the themes presented and blaze a trail for the rest of the congregation. The video also touches on the how-tos of pulling together a stewardship committee that can take the church to the next level.

Chapter 7

MINISTRY BY THE PEOPLE

bove all else, it's important to remember that
Irresistible Invitation isn't just about money. That's
certainly a big part of it, but the goal here is not
just to have people release more from their checkbooks; it is
to help them release more of themselves. In addition to
financial gifts, service is an aspect of the Christian walk that is
too powerful to be ignored. This campaign can help
members of the congregation understand that by giving of
their time and talents, they can walk more closely with God
and can better understand his purposes for their lives.

So how do you get people involved? It starts with a
focus on service based on the concept of volunteerism.
Rather than arm-twisting or manipulation, volunteering
can be presented as meaningful, fun, and exciting—and
when it is, that attitude is contagious. When lay members
share about specific ministries they're involved in and
what that involvement has meant to their lives, others start
thinking about areas in which they can volunteer, as well.

Irresistible Invitation talks about the importance of each
person being a vital part of the church family, but it's important to understand that the impetus for service must come
straight from leadership. Rather than something that's
simply hoped for, commitment to volunteerism and service

shows that being involved is an expected part of church life, just like showing up on Sunday mornings. It's not something that's mentioned once and then forgotten; it needs to be reiterated again and again, echoed from the pulpit, the Sunday school classrooms, and person to person.

SERVING IS BELONGING

When people join an organization, church or otherwise, their level of commitment has a lot to do with the level of expectation they find. As such, when people join your church, they should be given an opportunity right away to say where they feel called to serve. That will help them feel like they belong—quite a different scenario from one in which people have to wait to be asked to do anything. Those who are new or not well known may fall through the cracks, while the people who already do a lot may continuously be asked to keep doing more. Aside from all that, trying to figure out who would be good at what task can add up to a tremendous waste of time for the church leadership.

Volunteering is always better than being recruited. Keep in mind that most people are uncomfortable saying no to the pastor. If the pastor (or someone else in leadership) asks someone to be involved in a certain area of ministry, that person may say yes even if they really have no interest in serving there. That can lead to problems in the long run, as well as a general lack of enthusiasm—and therefore, effectiveness—along the way.

The involvement of all church members in service can be the most powerful method of transforming congregations and developing deep commitment. Get people involved and they change in many areas, including financial giving. So even though soliciting volunteers during the course of your stewardship campaign may seem like extra work, it's important. Your church will have far better results if it embraces and implements the service commitment part of the *Irresistible Invitation* program.

SERVICE MADE EASY

If your church already has a structure in place for identifying service needs and soliciting volunteer workers, consider the following ideas simply as new ways to keep your volunteer recruitment fresh. If your church doesn't have a systematic method of linking service needs with volunteers, the *Irresistible Invitation* program makes it simple.

Begin with identifying service needs by meeting with lay leaders and staff to solicit a list of service opportunities. Make the list as complete as possible; consider things as large as finding someone who will overhaul your Web site to needs as small as vacuuming the carpet in the church. Look for ongoing needs, such as ushering on a weekly basis, as well as one-time-only services, like mulching church flower beds in the fall.

Once you have a comprehensive list, you'll be ready to develop your own service commitment forms. The CD-ROM Toolkit has a sample template in Microsoft® Word of the form shown in the appendix. This document can be easily modified to accommodate the specific ministries in your congregation. (This particular commitment form was based on one developed and used successfully by a small-membership congregation, and it's patterned after a model used by Frazer Memorial United Methodist Church in Montgomery, Alabama, a congregation known for its every-member-in-ministry focus.)

Send the commitment card and service commitment form to each church member by mail, noting it is to be returned on Commitment Sunday. After members have turned in their service commitment forms, have someone go through them all and compile the responses and areas of service. Some churches use computer software programs to track volunteers and the areas of service in which they volunteered.

It's really important that the person in charge of the service area diligently follows up on the volunteer responses. There is perhaps nothing more demoralizing to someone who has volunteered than to not be contacted to serve. Make it a goal to contact each new volunteer within two weeks of receiving the service commitment form. Equally important is to have each new volunteer begin service as soon as feasible, reinforcing the fact that volunteers are both needed and valued.

RELEASING AUTHORITY
TO VOLUNTEER LAITY

When you open the door for people to volunteer, you might have people offering themselves in areas you wouldn't have expected. And they may not be the people you would have picked for the job. Occasionally, church staff and leadership can feel a little intimidated by the laity. There can be a fear of losing control as responsibilities are handed off to people who aren't on staff. But when members of the laity are released to grow in their giftings, wonderful things can happen. The congregation as a whole becomes more vibrant, committed, and involved. Energy and excitement become tangible, and with more hands on deck, the church is able to greatly expand its offerings to both its members and the outside community.

With a volunteer emphasis, the pastor may not know everything that the laity is doing, but that's not necessarily a bad thing. It's been said that if a pastor knows everything going on in the church, there's not enough going on. Instead of a frustration, this can actually be a freedom for the pastor who helps his congregation realize that everyone is in it together. It also allows the pastor to focus on the things that only the pastor can do, and to release the rest to others.

Since ministry is initiated by God, allowing people to volunteer for areas of service—and encouraging them to grow in those areas of service—helps them learn to make effective decisions with God's guidance, and to grow in their ability to walk with him and hear him. Of course, training can and should be offered in various areas of ministry, but at the same time, allow room for creativity.

EACH MEMBER IN MINISTRY IS IMPORTANT

If we truly believe that we're the body of Christ—and that every part of that body is important for it to function as a whole—then every member of the church must have some vital role to play. Now, not every person will be gifted in the area of leading worship, teaching Sunday school, or singing in the choir. But each person brings something to the table, and by helping people find what their gifting is, you can help them grow in confidence and maturity.

Keep in mind that a task one person has no interest in doing could be an absolute delight for someone else. It doesn't really matter if the task is large or small, as long as it's done in love. One person might like to write letters to new members or people in times of need, for example. Another might make sure the pew racks are stocked with appropriate materials and sharpened pencils. Another might want to develop the church Web site. And yet another may be willing to stand in the parking lot and help people into the church building as needed. Each task can have a significant impact on both the congregation and the person who volunteers to do it.

No doubt, as your church moves to an understanding that everyone is expected to be involved, there will be members who feel they have nothing to offer. If members struggle with the issue, try a few exercises. Ask them what they're passionate about, and what they're doing when they feel the most joy or peace. Ask them where they have particular skills or interests, and look for creative ways that those can be plugged into the church. Finally, ask them to pray for direction. God may lead them to a particular area of service that they may not have imagined for themselves.

Each church will have its own set of needs and opportunities for service, and it will be up to your leadership to determine what might be listed on your church's service commitment form. There are some generic categories that most congregations are involved in. As such, we've included a service commitment form that can help you get started, as well as a couple of actual examples from churches.

Pray it through, though, and prepare to see God raise up unlikely leaders in your midst.

Chapter 8

CAMPAIGN CHRONOLOGY

E ven though *Irresistible Invitation* is billed as a forty-day, or six-week, program, the planning must begin before that. Ideally, the clock starts ticking several months before the campaign begins, allowing ample time to effectively delegate tasks. This will also create an opportunity for excitement and momentum to build within the church, rather than forcing a last-minute, rushed effort that doesn't come across as important or well planned.

Ideally, the campaign schedule should flow backwards from your planned date for Commitment Sunday. Starting with that date, the campaign should kick off eight weeks prior. That allows time for the congregation to move through all six weeks of the program.

If you've just received this study and there are fewer than three months until your church's annual stewardship campaign, don't panic. Just do the best you can, consolidating steps as necessary. God will work with you no matter where you are.

THREE MONTHS OR MORE BEFORE KICKOFF

____ Pastor watches DVD segment *Irresistible Invitation for Leaders*

_____ Pastor appoints chair of stewardship committee, if no such committee is in place

_____ Pastor and committee chair read *Irresistible Invitation* devotional book

_____ Stewardship committee job descriptions are reviewed and accepted by lay leadership

TWO MONTHS BEFORE KICKOFF

_____ Chair of stewardship committee, with the help of the pastor, appoints committee members

_____ Stewardship committee holds its first meeting and watches DVD segment *Irresistible Invitation for Leaders*; pastor meets with the committee to encourage full participation

_____ Copies of *Irresistible Invitation: Responding to the Extravagant Heart of God* are ordered for committee members

_____ Program graphics and printing strategies are determined and initiated

_____ Work on the service commitment form begins, with church leadership determining areas of service needs

_____ Optional program features such as providing thank-you gifts or sticker giveaways are discussed and committee decides if they'll be implemented

SIX WEEKS BEFORE KICKOFF

_____ Stewardship committee holds second meeting after books arrive; books are distributed to committee members

_____ Roles are delegated during the meeting
  * book distribution coordinator

- small-group coordinator
- volunteer commitment coordinator
- communications coordinator
- print resources coordinator
- prayer coordinator
- testimony coordinator
- follow-up coordinator
- comparative study coordinator
- hospitality/Commitment Sunday event coordinator

ONE MONTH BEFORE KICKOFF

____ Stewardship committee meets to discuss progress in each delegated task

____ *Irresistible Invitation* books, *Participant's Workbooks*, and *Leader's Guides with DVD* are ordered for the congregation (see Cokesbury ordering information enclosed with *Irresistible Invitation* program kit)

____ Statistics are gathered for pre- and post-campaign comparison, such as average Sunday attendance, average amount of giving, etc. This continues weekly through end of campaign

____ Sunday school/small-group leader recruitment begins (if not already in place in your church)

____ Church webmaster is contacted about including online elements of study during the campaign

____ Youth leaders are contacted to discuss incorporation of youth activities in regard to the campaign

____ Posters/banners/etc. are displayed in church announcing an upcoming event

____ Congregational Letter #1 from pastor or stewardship committee chair mailed to congregation to introduce the campaign

_____ Arrangements made for a leadership prayer dinner to be held one week before kickoff

_____ Committee brainstorms appropriate Commitment Sunday event, concluding meal, or other final event

TWO WEEKS BEFORE KICKOFF

_____ Copies of *Irresistible Invitation: Responding to the Extravagant Heart of God* and the *Participant's Workbook* are made available to congregation

_____ Recruitment of Sunday school/small-group leaders continues

_____ *Leader's Guide with DVD* distributed to Sunday school/small-group leaders

ONE WEEK BEFORE KICKOFF

_____ Copies of *Irresistible Invitation: Responding to the Extravagant Heart of God* and the *Participant's Workbook* are made available to congregation members who have not yet received one

_____ Recruitment of Sunday school/small-group leaders ends; *Leader's Guide with DVD* distributed to any leaders who haven't yet received copies

_____ Ensure Sunday school/small-group leaders have all necessary materials to begin the campaign the following week

_____ Complete design of commitment card and service commitment form, including areas of service, prayer, attendance, and financial commitments, and take to printer or make arrangements for duplication

_____ Invitation to the Commitment Sunday or concluding meal or event is designed and approved

_____ Pastor gives brief introduction to the study and encourages church members to participate

_____ Newsletter article #1, "You're Invited to an Exciting Journey," and bulletin insert #1, "A Special Invitation Just for You" appear in church newsletter and bulletin

_____ First witness is secured to give testimony about the study during the following week's worship service, with a focus on the goodness of God

_____ Hold leadership prayer dinner

KICKOFF WEEK

_____ Copies of *Irresistible Invitation: Responding to the Extravagant Heart of God* and the *Participant's Workbook* are made available to congregation members who have not yet received one

_____ Newsletter article #2, "The Choice Is Yours" and bulletin insert #2, "Kickoff Sunday" appear in church newsletter and bulletin

_____ Pastor gives sermon related to Week One of *Irresistible Invitation,* "Coming Home to God"

_____ During worship service, first witness gives testimony related to Week One of *Irresistible Invitation* with an emphasis on the goodness of God

_____ Congregation begins daily readings of *Irresistible Invitation,* Week One, "Coming Home to God," after the Kickoff Sunday launch

_____ Second witness is secured to give testimony about Resurrection and new life in Christ during the following week's assembly

_____ If some small groups will hold midweek meetings, those meetings take place this week, with groups discussing Week One, "Coming Home to God"

[Handwritten margin notes: "if Sept. 14th" with a bracket; "?" mark; "of the sermons listed 1-7 which one is the 1st for the week"]

SECOND WEEK OF THE CAMPAIGN

Sept. 21

✳ ____ Sunday school/small groups watch first DVD segment and discuss Week One of *Irresistible Invitation*, "Coming Home to God"

____ Newsletter article #3, "Are You Ready for the Perfect Gift?" and bulletin insert #3, "Responding to Week One" appear in church newsletter and bulletin

____ Campaign theme stickers are passed out as members enter church on Sunday

____ Pastor gives sermon related to Week Two of *Irresistible Invitation*, "A Love Like No Other"

Testimonies ____ During worship service, second witness gives testimony related to Week Two, with a focus on Resurrection and new life in Christ

____ Third witness is secured to give testimony with a focus on the guidance of the Holy Spirit and living a life of grace

____ On Monday, congregation continues daily readings of *Irresistible Invitation* with Week Two, "A Love Like No Other"

____ Invitations to Commitment Sunday or concluding meal or event are mailed

THIRD WEEK OF THE CAMPAIGN

____ Sunday school/small groups watch second DVD segment and discuss Week Two of *Irresistible Invitation*, "A Love Like No Other"

____ Newsletter article #4, "What a Feast" and bulletin insert #4, "Responding to Week Two" appear in church newsletter and bulletin

____ Campaign stickers are passed out as members enter church on Sunday

_____ Pastor gives sermon related to Week Three of
      Irresistible Invitation, "Alive in Christ"

_____ During worship service, third witness gives testi-
      mony related to Week Three, with a focus on the
      guidance of the Holy Spirit and living a life of grace

_____ Fourth witness is secured to give testimony about the
      study during the following week's assembly, with a focus
      on reading the Bible and communicating with God

_____ Commitment cards and service commitment forms
      are prepared for mailing the following week

_____ On Monday, congregation continues daily readings of
      Irresistible Invitation with Week Three, "Alive in Christ"

FOURTH WEEK OF THE CAMPAIGN

_____ Sunday school/small groups watch third DVD
      segment and discuss Week Three of *Irresistible
      Invitation*, "Alive in Christ"

_____ Campaign theme stickers are passed out as
      members enter church on Sunday

_____ Newsletter article #5, "Math for Christians" and
      bulletin insert #5, "Responding to Week Three"
      appear in church newsletter and bulletin

_____ Pastor gives sermon related to Week Four of
      Irresistible Invitation, "Fit for Kingdom Living"

_____ During worship service, fourth witness gives testi-
      mony with a focus on reading the Bible and
      communicating with God

_____ Fifth witness is secured to give testimony related to
      Week Five about being a part of the church family

_____ Congregational Letter #2 from the pastor or steward-
      ship committee chair (or jointly from both) is sent to
      the congregation on Monday, encouraging continued

participation in the study; commitment cards and service commitment forms to be turned in on Commitment Sunday are included in the mailing

_____ Stewardship committee meets to discuss progress of campaign and discuss ideas in more detail for continuing the momentum once the campaign ends

_____ On Monday, congregation continues daily readings of *Irresistible Invitation* with Week Four, "Fit for Kingdom Living"

FIFTH WEEK OF THE CAMPAIGN

_____ Sunday school/small groups watch fourth DVD segment and discuss Week Four of *Irresistible Invitation*, "Fit for Kingdom Living"

_____ Newsletter article #6, "Welcome Home" and bulletin insert #6, "Responding to Week Four" appear in church newsletter and bulletin

_____ Campaign theme stickers are passed out as members enter church on Sunday

✳ _____ Pastor gives sermon related to Week Five of *Irresistible Invitation*, "The Home of Grace"

_____ During worship service, fifth witness gives testimony related to Week Five, focusing on being a part of the church family

_____ Sixth witness is secured to give testimony related to Week Six, with a focus on sacrificial giving and service

_____ On Monday, congregation continues daily readings of *Irresistible Invitation* with Week Five, "The Home of Grace"

SIXTH WEEK OF THE CAMPAIGN

____ Sunday school/small groups watch fifth DVD segment and discuss Week Five of *Irresistible Invitation,* "The Home of Grace"

✳ ____ Newsletter article #7, "Van Gogh on Tithing?" and bulletin insert #7, "Responding to Week Five" appear in church newsletter and bulletin

____ Campaign theme stickers are passed out as members enter church on Sunday

____ Pastor gives sermon related to Week Six of *Irresistible Invitation,* "Partners in the Gospel"

____ During worship service, sixth witness gives testimony related to Week Six, with a focus on continuing to grow in our relationship with God

____ Leadership meal is held for stewardship committee and other church leaders who have been key to implementing the campaign

____ On Monday, congregation continues daily readings of *Irresistible Invitation* with Week Six, "Partners in the Gospel"

COMMITMENT SUNDAY

____ Congregation has completed daily readings of *Irresistible Invitation: Responding to the Extravagant Heart of God*

____ Sunday school/small groups watch sixth DVD segment and discuss Week Six of *Irresistible Invitation,* "Partners in the Gospel"

✳ ____ Newsletter article #8, "A Brand-New Day" and bulletin insert #8, "Becoming Partners in the Gospel" appear in church newsletter and bulletin

____ Campaign theme stickers are passed out as members enter church on Sunday

____ Pastor gives sermon concluding the study and thanking the congregation for participating

✳ ____ Commitment cards and service commitment forms are turned in during worship service

____ Communion held during worship service

____ Thank-you gifts given to members turning in forms (optional)

____ Commitment Sunday or concluding meal or event is held

WEEK FOLLOWING COMMITMENT SUNDAY

____ Congregational Letter #3 is sent to thank those who turned in commitment cards and service commitment forms

____ Congregational Letter #4, commitment cards, and service commitment forms are sent to follow up with those who have not yet responded

____ Commitment cards and service commitment forms are distributed to appropriate leadership for follow-up

____ Final statistics are gathered for post-campaign comparison

TWO WEEKS AFTER COMMITMENT SUNDAY

____ Stewardship committee meets to go over pre- and post-campaign comparison

____ Formal report is prepared for pastor, including what worked best during the study, what didn't, and what can be done in the future to make similar campaigns even more effective

Appendix

This appendix contains a number of resources that may be used to help spread the word about your church's *Irresistible Invitation: Cultivating Joyful Giving in Your Church* campaign. Each element of the campaign was briefly mentioned in the first chapter of this handbook, but here's a closer look. Many of them are designed to be used as they are by copying directly from the CD-ROM Toolkit, and others might only need a church letterhead or name attached to the copy. All resources are formatted as Microsoft® Word files or Adobe© Acrobat© (.pdf) files.

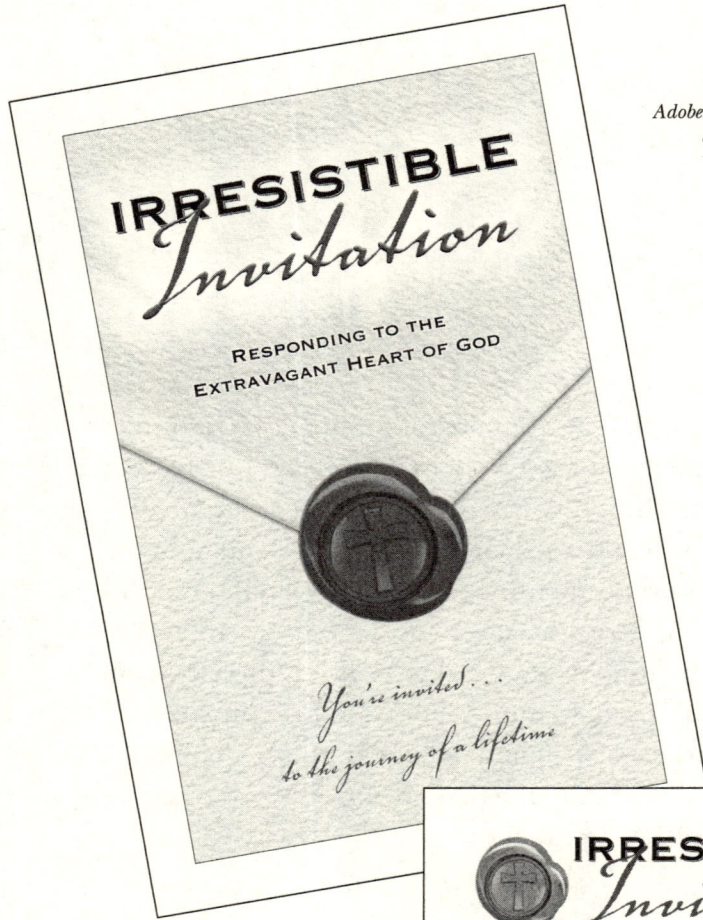

11 x 17 color poster.
Adobe PDF graphic file available
on CD-ROM Toolkit.

1-color, standard letterhead and envelope.
Modifiable text in MS Word
available on CD-ROM Toolkit.

Campaign theme/lapel sticker

Commitment Sunday invitation
Modifiable text available on CD-ROM Toolkit.

Dear family member,

Exciting days are ahead! We're preparing to embark on a life-changing journey for our church family, and it's a chance for us to fully embrace all that God has for us, both individually and as a congregation. Our goal as a church is to have as close to 100 percent involvement in this study as possible. That means each of us will be asked to accept the invitation to take part.

In coming weeks, you'll be able to pick up a copy of *Irresistible Invitation: Responding to the Extravagant Heart of God* immediately before or after the worship service. This book includes forty daily readings that will challenge you in your perceptions about God, Jesus, and the Holy Spirit, and you'll have the chance to ask yourself some probing questions about what you believe and why. Please take advantage of all that this book has to offer. Set aside a few brief moments for introspection each day, and I guarantee that the Lord will meet you exactly where you are. He'll begin to fulfill desires of your heart that you might not even realize you have.

To deepen your experience, we'll be discussing each week's topics in both our small-group/Sunday school meetings and in worship. That way, we'll all have the opportunity to grow as one, reaching for a common goal—a rich, rewarding, blessed life of adventure, joy, peace, and purpose.

At the end of the study, we'll all take part in Commitment Sunday, when we'll have a chance to put our faith into action. That will be here soon enough. For now, let's focus on the task at hand.

Do your best to attend worship services in the coming weeks, and keep your eye out for the start of the campaign. I'd hate for you to miss a moment as we all embark on this journey together. And please, join me in prayer that God would indeed "throw open the floodgates of heaven," as he promises in Malachi 3:10 (NIV), and pour out so much blessing individually and corporately that we don't have room to contain it.

There's so much more to God than we can even imagine. During the course of this forty-day study, however, we'll have an opportunity to see God and his presence in our lives in an entirely new way.

Sincerely,

Dear family member,

What an incredible time we have had during this study!

Hard to believe, but our *Irresistible Invitation: Responding to the Extravagant Heart of God* study is quickly passing by. Commitment Sunday is just a few weeks away.

At this point, I'd like you to revisit some of the key concepts from the study and recall what your expectations were. Did God meet you there? Have you found a new understanding of God, and experienced renewed communication with him? How is God continuing to deepen your trust, faith, and wisdom as you continue your daily readings?

Personally, I believe this study is bringing us closer as a congregation, and truly establishing the idea that the church is family. I'm excited to see how this new unity will make us even more effective in showing Christ to our community. I'm excited, too, about new commitments through service, prayer, and financial gifts.

But we can't keep taking it all in without giving anything back. So now's the time to put your faith into action. There's a commitment card and service commitment form for each family member enclosed with this letter, and I'd like you to begin thinking about how you'll fill them out, so they will be ready to turn in on Commitment Sunday. As you'll notice, you have the opportunity to be specific about which areas of service you'd like to take part in, and how much you plan to give financially. Do you remember that the more you're willing to share in terms of time, money, and effort, the more opportunity you give the Lord to bless you in return? The life poured out, after all, is the one that God can more easily fill.

I'd like to remind you to consider your commitments with much prayer. God wants to partner with you in his work, and involving God in the decision-making process ensures that his will is done, rather than our own.

I do hope this experience has been a rich, rewarding one for you, and I'd like to encourage you to continue any good habits in regard to prayer, Bible study, community, or group discussion you're picking up along the way. This is by no means an end. Rather, it's a beginning to a new life that God has called us to, one that we can enjoy both as individuals and as part of the church family.

See you on Sunday!

Sincerely,

Congregational letter #2.
Modifiable text available on CD-ROM Toolkit.

Dear family member,

Thank you!

I've just received word that you turned in a commitment card and service commitment form during Commitment Sunday, and I'd like to personally thank you for taking the time and making the effort. May the Lord richly bless you in return!

This campaign has been such an incredible time for our church, but the truth its, there's no point in doing it without the enthusiasm and dedication of people like you. It is my hope and prayer that your experience with *Irresistible Invitation: Responding to the Extravagant Heart of God* has been a rich one, and that the lessons learned would be ones that stay with you for the rest of your life.

As you move forward in your new commitment to prayer, presence, service, and financial gifts, keep in mind that the Lord will be by your side every step of the way. He will provide in ways you've yet to imagine, and watching him work is half the fun.

Thanks again for being a vital, irreplaceable part of our church family. You are loved.

Sincerely,

Congregational letter #3.
Modifiable text available on CD-ROM Toolkit.

Dear family member,

We recently wrapped up our *Irresistible Invitation: Responding to the Extravagant Heart of God* campaign, culminating with Commitment Sunday. It was an awesome opportunity for every member of the church to make a fresh commitment in regard to service, prayer, attendance, and financial gifts, as well as a chance for the church to move ahead as a unified team.

But as we've been going through the cards and forms that were turned in, we've noticed that there aren't any from you.

First of all, if you did indeed turn in a card and form and you have received this letter in error, please let the church office know. We're excited to help you begin serving as soon as possible.

If, for some reason, you never received a commitment card and service commitment form, it's not too late to turn them in. I've included copies with this letter so you can still take part. Simply drop these in the offering plate on Sunday.

You know, you can also use these if you've simply been undecided until now. If that's the case, I'd encourage you to take a small step of faith and remember that God will meet you wherever you are.

This study has been such a blessing for our entire church family, and I want to make sure that you don't miss out. Our body simply isn't complete with the gifts, talents, and presence you bring to the table. Won't you join us?

Sincerely,

Congregational letter #4.
Modifiable text available on CD-ROM Toolkit.

You're Invited to an Exciting Journey

It's so easy to make snap judgments about others, isn't it? Though we may try our best to see others through eyes of grace, fully understanding that they're still works in progress, just as we are, it can happen so quickly that we barely recognize it. In the blink of an eye, we size someone up according to their gender, their clothing, their race, and maybe what we consider their level of attractiveness. And based on all that, we form expectations about who they are.

Sometimes, if we take the time to get to know those people, we discover that they are indeed like we thought. But other times, they offer us a surprise; we find ourselves completely amazed at their depth, or character, or even life experience. Can you relate?

The tragic thing is that we don't just do this with other folks here on earth. All too often, we do it with God, as well. We think we know God based on a picture someone else has shown us. We are quick to guess God must be aloof, disinterested in our lives, or worse yet, angry and vengeful. But if we take the time to know him, we may well be surprised here, too. We may just find that he truly is good, loves us more than we can imagine, and he longs for us to walk with him daily and partner with him in his works.

Starting this Sunday, our church family will have the chance to encounter God in a variety of fresh ways. We're about to embark on a forty-day study called *Irresistible Invitation: Responding to the Extravagant Heart of God*, and through individual devotions, Sunday school/small-group discussions, and related sermons, we'll all grow in faith together.

Our goal is to have 100 percent participation in this life-changing event. Each of us will be asked to accept the invitation to take part. All of it culminates with Commitment Sunday, when you'll have a chance to put your faith into action. Sounds exciting, doesn't it?

Please don't miss this church-wide opportunity to grow in your faith and to experience new levels of relationship with God. He is more than able to surprise you with his blessings and surround you with his love. Make plans now to join us for this Sunday's worship service, so you can pick up your copy of *Irresistible Invitation: Responding to the Extravagant Heart of God* and get started. There's no telling what we can find when we're willing to take a closer look.

Newsletter article #1.
Modifiable text available on CD-ROM Toolkit.

THE CHOICE IS YOURS

Had any good surprises lately?

This past Sunday, we began distributing copies of Maxie Dunnam's *Irresistible Invitation: Responding to the Extravagant Heart of God*. The book is a forty-day study that shows us how extravagant God's love has been toward us, and how we can turn that into lives poured out for others. It is hoped by now you've accepted the invitation and started digging in.

You could go about this study one of several ways. First, you could ignore it. You could allow that book to gather dust on your bedside table, and figure that you'll get the main points by hearing the pastor's sermons and listening to the discussions in Sunday school.

Second, you could read the entire week's lessons in one sitting, maybe even on Saturday night or early Sunday morning. That way, you figure, you can catch up and still know what everybody is talking about.

Or you could set aside a little bit of time each day, going over the daily readings and prayerfully considering the answers to the probing questions. You could allow God to speak to both your heart and mind. You could openly discuss what you're learning in your small group, and you could gain from the insights of others as you find yourself sharing in humility, as well.

Really, the choice is yours. This isn't school, after all, with someone looking over your shoulder and grading you on your level of participation. No, this is between you and God.

You could look at this as simply one more thing to do in your already-busy schedule, or you could see it as the chance of a lifetime to press in and know God as you've never known him before.

E. Stanley Jones once said that, "Life in our hands is life on our hands—a problem. Life in the hands of Jesus is no longer a problem; it is a possibility."

So what's the greatest of possibilities today? Are you ready to take a deep breath, grab the hand of God, and respond, "I'm willing"?

Newsletter article #2.
Modifiable text available on CD-ROM Toolkit.

ARE YOU READY FOR THE PERFECT GIFT?

Which do you prefer: to give the perfect gift—something you know for sure that the recipient will absolutely treasure—or to receive the perfect gift yourself?

There's no right or wrong answer here; most of us would admit to finding value in both. There's a certain satisfaction in showing someone that you care in a way that's meaningful to them, but there's also great joy in discovering that someone cares enough about you to know what you'd like.

On the other hand, consider the disappointment of receiving a gift that doesn't interest you at all, or in giving a gift that you can tell the other person doesn't really like.

This week, *Irresistible Invitation: Responding to the Extravagant Heart of God* looks at the life of Jesus. He is, of course, God's precious gift to us, a sacrifice with no equal. And through this sacrifice, we also receive new life.

You'll see this represented in the Scripture memory verse you'll go over with your Sunday school/small group: "For it is by grace you have been saved, through faith—and this not from yourselves, it is the gift of God" (Eph. 2:8 NIV).

At this point, however, we have to ask ourselves a serious question: how well have we received that gift in our own lives? Have we recognized it, as precious as it is? Have we realized that it really is exactly what we need—as well as what our heart truly desires?

We can spend a lot of time searching for other things that will satisfy us, other gifts that might somehow, some way, make us feel complete. But that search won't be fruitful. Jesus is the only one who offers us the great gift of eternal life, and the chance to choose new life every single day.

So, what's your choice on this day? Are you in the mode of giving or receiving? God stands ready to meet you in either place, welcoming you into his presence, and providing your deepest heart's desire.

Newsletter article #3.
Modifiable text available on CD-ROM Toolkit.

WHAT A FEAST!

Imagine the scene: you're headed to a party, but you don't know that much about the host. There may be some food there; there may not. And even if there is, you may not like it. So, what do you do? You scrounge around at home, looking through leftovers and prepackaged goods to make a quick meal to tide you over. Even if you're not fully satisfied, at least you won't be hungry, right?

Well, get this: you arrive at that party, and the host has laid out the most incredible buffet you've ever seen. It includes an abundance of all of your favorites—even the things that you've never told anyone you desired—and the host invites you to have your fill. The problem is, you already have. You had enough of that less-than-satisfying food to quell your appetite, and frankly, there's no room left.

It's a sad state of affairs when we settle for less than we knew was coming, isn't it? How much more so when that settling is not just about our meal choices, but rather about our relationship with God.

See, God doesn't just want more from us; he wants more *for* us, as well. He wants us to be alive in Christ, fully walking in his grace, his love, his joy, his peace, his power, and his strength. That's what this week's lesson of *Irresistible Invitation: Responding to the Extravagant Heart of God* is all about. Through prayer, Bible study, fellowship, an understanding of Jesus' sacrifice, and a dependence on the Holy Spirit, we too can approach that buffet of all that God has for us, and we can confidently dig right in.

So where are you in all of this? At the table? Seeing it for the first time? Or standing at the door, wishing you hadn't already filled up on empty calories? Please take advantage of this precious time, when you and your church family can approach the buffet together. It's guaranteed to be the most satisfying, richly rewarding meal of your life.

Newsletter article #4.
Modifiable text available on CD-ROM Toolkit.

MATH FOR CHRISTIANS

Sooner or later, you'll discover it.

It's not some new math, some twisted form of algebra, or even a modified version of addition and subtraction. Instead, it's often described as God math, and it defies all sorts of human logic.

It works like this: you give money to the church or to someone in need, even though you don't really have it to give. You make a sacrifice. God then does a miraculous thing: since you've done his business, he takes care of yours. You find that your own need is satisfied, sometimes in a surprising way.

Anne Frank summed it up this way: "No one has ever become poor by giving."

Did you ever wonder why?

It could be that being generous with our finances allows us to be rich in faith. The more we see God math in our own lives, the more confident we become that God really will meet all of our needs.

Besides all that, though, giving a regular tithe demonstrates to God that we consider him more important than we consider money. It keeps us from allowing money to become an idol in our lives. Have you ever thought about it that way?

The truth is, God doesn't just want our cash—even if it does help fund church programs and ministries. What he really wants is our hearts. He wants us to turn to him and say, "Whatever I have, it's yours."

This week, our *Irresistible Invitation* study focuses on being fit for kingdom living, and the Scripture memory verse you'll go over in your Sunday school/small-group meeting is this: "I tell you the truth, anyone who has faith in me will do what I have been doing. He will do even greater things than these, because I am going to the Father" (John 14:12 NIV).

That said, consider this: what more has God done than give? This reminds us that we can never pay back God for his great gifts to us. One thing we can do, however, is cheerfully start with the tithe, the very least he asks of us. Set aside that 10 percent every week as soon as you get a paycheck, and you'll never miss it. It will show God that you're serious about putting him first—and it will continue to give him opportunities to supply your every need, just as he promised he would.

Newsletter article #5.
Modifiable text available on CD-ROM Toolkit.

WELCOME HOME

What does home represent to you? Hopefully, the word conjures up an image of the place where you belong. It's the spot you can be who you really are, where you're accepted, loved, encouraged, and nurtured so you can face the rest of the world with confidence.

Granted, not everyone is blessed with that kind of scenario. Some deal with abusive situations, hurtful relationships, and negative influences that can make things more uncomfortable than they should be. And that's all the more reason why the church needs to step up to the plate.

In this week's readings of *Irresistible Invitation: Responding to the Extravagant Heart of God*, we see the church called the "home of grace." It's a beautiful image, isn't it? That concept of grace means that everyone—no matter who they are, no matter what they've done—can find acceptance, love, and rest. But that's not always an easy pill to swallow. Sometimes it's hard to accept people who are different than us. In God's eyes, though, it doesn't matter. When we truly understand the acceptance that God offers us through Jesus, we find ourselves extending that grace to others. We also find that we want to do more for others, and cultivate the practice of putting them before ourselves.

This week, as you consider what you individually can do to help make this church more of a welcoming presence, keep this Scripture in mind: "Dear friends, let us love one another, for love comes from God" (1 John 4:7 NIV).

As Christians, we have been tasked with passing on what we have received from God, and acceptance of others is just the start. The church has a mighty calling to fulfill, but without everyone's help—even those we wouldn't have chosen ourselves—it won't happen.

Never forget that you love because God first loved you. Who, in your own life, could you help welcome home?

Newsletter article #6.
Modifiable text available on CD-ROM Toolkit.

VAN GOGH ON TITHING?

Remember being a kid and waiting expectantly during the days leading up to Christmas? You were probably on your best behavior, making sure that if Santa really did check that list twice, you'd be on the right side of it. Hours felt like days, and days felt like weeks, until the moment finally arrived: Christmas morning.

If you were like most children, you probably hopped out of bed before dawn, before your parents were even awake, and headed expectantly for the gifts wrapped and waiting under the tree. Who knew what wonders awaited?

This week, as we read through the last part of *Irresistible Invitation: Responding to the Extravagant Heart of God*, we're headed toward another wonderfully special event: Commitment Sunday. That's the day you'll be able to commit your prayers, presence, service, and financial gifts to the church for the coming season. And just like Christmas morning, you have no idea what wonders await.

See, God always meets us where we are, and anytime we take a step closer to him, he responds likewise by stepping closer to us. When we're ready to say yes to all that he asks of us, we can know for certain that he will richly reward us for it, and continue to draw us closer into relationship with him.

This Sunday, even if you feel the tiniest bit apprehensive about taking the next step, rely on your faith to get you there. Consider what Vincent van Gogh once said about doubt: "If you hear a voice within you say 'You are not a painter,' then by all means paint, and that voice will be silenced."

The master painter, the one who created you with beautiful strokes of his brush, still stands with that brush in hand. So as your special day arrives, greet it with expectancy and know that God will honor your new levels of commitment and help you stand firm. Keep this in mind:

> And now, just as you accepted Christ Jesus as your Lord, you must continue to live in obedience to him. Let your roots grow down into him and draw up nourishment from him, so you will grow in faith, strong and vigorous in the truth you were taught. Let your lives overflow with thanksgiving for all he has done. (Col. 2:6–7 NLT)

Newsletter article #7.
Modifiable text available on CD-ROM Toolkit.

A BRAND-NEW DAY

There's nothing quite like the afterglow of a really good party.

Once the last guests have left, the dishes are done, and you can finally sit down and relish the memories of the evening, it hits you: it may have taken some preparation and some sacrifice, but the result was worth it. Your home became a haven of peace, welcome, and joy.

This past Sunday, you had the opportunity to commit to new levels in your relationship with God. You boldly filled out your card, and in a wave of momentum, turned in it.

Hopefully, you're not having second thoughts. Hopefully, you're not still looking at that pile of plates and cups, wondering how you'll ever make it through. But let's be honest: have you had any doubts that you'll actually be able to meet that financial commitment, or fit that area of service into your busy schedule? If so, it's not such a bad thing. It means that you've given God room to work, and without new dependence on him, it's not going to happen.

God delights in our dependence on him, you know. He waits for us to ask for help. But when we have all the answers already or we do things in our own strength, we leave no opportunity for him to be glorified. It becomes about what we can do, rather than what he can do through us.

In coming weeks, as the lessons of *Irresistible Invitation* settle into your consciousness, it will be possible for you to lose steam and to forget what it was all about. On the other hand, you could take what you've learned and build on it.

Remember that very first chapter, the one that talked about incandescent amazement? Over the past forty days, you've had the opportunity to grasp that sense of wonder and amazement, and learn how to funnel God's great love, power, and peace through your own life into the lives of others. You've learned the importance of generosity of spirit as well as the significance of living a life fully alive in Christ.

But please, don't stop there. Consider this a beginning rather than an end, an invitation not just to a single event, but rather to a brand-new life. Today is a day for looking forward with confidence and security. And while you're at it, keep your eyes peeled; you never know just when that next invitation will arrive.

Newsletter article #8.
Modifiable text available on CD-ROM Toolkit.

IRRESISTIBLE *Invitation*

A SPECIAL INVITATION JUST FOR YOU...

IRRESISTIBLE *Invitation*

RESPONDING TO THE
EXTRAVAGANT HEART OF GOD

MAXIE D. DUNNAM

The honor of your presence is requested at the event of a lifetime—it's called *Irresistible Invitation: Responding to the Extravagant Heart of God.* Our entire congregation will have the privilege of taking part in this transformative forty-day study. Together we'll explore the heart of our faith, and open the door to a fresh experience of God's presence. *Irresistible Invitation* is loaded with insight that can take us from where we are to places we never imagined we could be.

You can start by picking up your own copy of *Irresistible Invitation,* the book from noted Methodist leader Maxie Dunnam. We'll all begin reading the book after next Sunday, when we'll officially kick off the campaign. As a companion to our daily reading, we'll discuss what we've learned in our Sunday school classes and/or small-group meetings. Along the way, the pastor's messages will bring us to a common understanding of the weekly themes.

So get ready to RSVP—God is waiting to reveal himself in new ways as we devote ourselves to private times of prayer and reflect on the daily readings. The next couple of months could be a chance for you to see God in a whole new way. Pray expectantly—knowing that God will be faithful to meet you wherever you are—and keep your eye on this spot in the bulletin for the latest notes of encouragement!

Bulletin insert #1.
Adobe PDF graphic files available on CD-ROM Toolkit.

IRRESISTIBLE
Invitation

KICKOFF SUNDAY

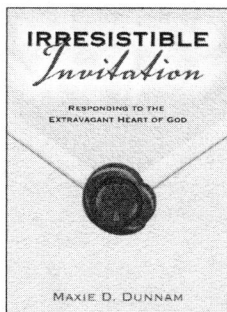

IRRESISTIBLE
Invitation

RESPONDING TO THE
EXTRAVAGANT HEART OF GOD

MAXIE D. DUNNAM

Before you leave today, if you haven't already, be sure to pick up your copy of *Irresistible Invitation: Responding to the Extravagant Heart of God*. It's a forty-day study that our entire church will be going through together, and you simply don't want to miss it. This is going to be a great opportunity to grow in faith and stretch your spirit. It's the event of the season, and your name is on the list.

So what should you expect? For starters, plan now to set aside a few extra minutes each day to go over the readings and prayerfully consider the topics presented. They're certain to speak straight to your heart. Count on something else, too: being a part of the big picture as our entire congregation moves through the study together. We'll talk about the concepts in our Sunday school/small group meetings, and the pastor's messages will offer further insight each week. There's no telling how God can move among us when we're all on the same page—literally.

The study will finish with Commitment Sunday, a chance for you to renew your vows of commitment and see what God will do in return. Now's the time to start fresh, to look ahead, and to be expectant that God will accomplish great things right here in our church body. What are you waiting for?

Coming up next week: Coming Home to God

Bulletin insert #2.
Adobe PDF graphic files available on CD-ROM Toolkit.

IRRESISTIBLE
Invitation

RESPONDING TO
WEEK ONE: COMING HOME TO GOD

Once an invitation arrives, there are really only three ways to deal with it. You can excitedly sign up right away; you can discard the envelope, deciding it doesn't really fit in with your goals, schedule, or interests; or your can toss it into the pile marked "get to it later."

So, how have you responded to the call to join *Irresistible Invitation: Responding to the Extravagant Heart of God*? Have you fully hopped on board, opening your arms wide to all that God has to offer? Have you dismissed the thought, believing it isn't for you? Or are you still undecided? By now, participants have read through the first week of the book, but it's not too late to join in. Any idea what could be standing in your way?

If you haven't already noticed, pastor Maxie Dunnam is simply amazed by God. For more than forty years, he's been helping others share that sense of amazement, as well. This week, the first chapter of *Irresistible Invitation: Responding to the Extravagant Heart of God* talked about how very good our Heavenly Father is—and how much good God wants for us, as well. Remember, as you read through each chapter, to take a few minutes and prayerfully consider your answers to the Heart of the Matter questions. You might even make a few notes in the accompanying workbook. Remember: the more you put into this study, the more you'll get out of it in return. Prepare your heart now to receive a message on a topic related to the study, and prepare your spirit to be renewed by God's extravagant love.

Coming up next week: A Love Like No Other

IRRESISTIBLE
Invitation

RESPONDING TO
WEEK TWO: A LOVE LIKE NO OTHER

At this point, you've probably finished reading the second week of *Irresistible Invitation: Responding to the Extravagant Heart of God*. As you read the daily chapters, how did you feel about Jesus loving you as though you are the only person in the world to love? Do you know who you are, viewed through the eyes of Christ? What does the cross represent to you?

Remember that all too often, we feel that God disapproves of us and thinks we are nothing, but that couldn't be further from the truth. Our value in God's sight has been affirmed once and for all by the gift of Jesus in death on our behalf. Yes, our behalf—and that includes you. How would your life be different with a full understanding of the cross?

Are you ready to discuss your thoughts about these powerful ideas in your Sunday school/small-group meeting? During our worship service, the pastor's message will provide a glimpse into the new life we have in Christ, and you'll have the chance to look ahead to the coming week. But we must remember that we can only experience that new life by choosing to enter through the door of Christ's sacrifice on the cross.

Coming up next week: Alive in Christ

Bulletin insert #4.
Adobe PDF graphic files available on CD-ROM Toolkit.

IRRESISTIBLE
Invitation

RESPONDING TO
WEEK THREE: ALIVE IN CHRIST

Here we are at the end of the third week, halfway through *Irresistible Invitation: Responding to the Extravagant Heart of God*. This week, it's important to keep in mind that we're responsible for what we know. If you've been reading that there's more to this Christian walk than you've been experiencing, you can no longer plead ignorance. It's up to you to accept God's irresistible invitation to a new kind of life.

Since we worship an extraordinary God, our lives should be anything but ordinary. But it's not all God's doing; we have to partner with him in the work. This week's readings focused on becoming alive in Christ by allowing the Holy Spirit to take up residence in our hearts. Remember that there's a difference between following Jesus and being *in Christ*.

Being in Christ means fulfilling a calling that only you can carry out. It means supernatural guidance, peace, love, forgiveness, joy, and all the other things that we'll miserably fail at if we go it alone. The good news, however, is that God really is right there, ready to offer it all.

Once we become aware of the ways that God is always at work around us, we may wonder why it took us so long to notice. So are you finding God's love to be extravagant indeed? Have you given the ho-hum life the boot?

Coming up next week: Fit for Kingdom Living

IRRESISTIBLE *Invitation*

RESPONDING TO
WEEK FOUR: FIT FOR KINGDOM LIVING

How good is your word? Do you always make good on your promises? Most of us do the best we can, but we're still human. The thing is, God is not. Yes, we're made in his image, but God is perfect in a way that we aren't. When God makes a promise, he keeps it. Period.

This week, as we've read about being "fit for Kingdom living" in *Irresistible Invitation: Responding to the Extravagant Heart of God*, we were reminded that God has promised that we will do even greater things than Jesus. He has also promised that he will never forsake us, that he will give us life, that he will offer us rest, and that we will receive power through the Holy Spirit. Hopefully, as you've devoted yourself to daily readings, prayer, and introspection, you've begun to experience these truths for yourself.

For faith to be authentic, it has to have legs. In other words, it can't be just a private affair. God calls us to be in community with others, to encourage, to intercede, and to serve. Has this study prompted you to think twice about the way you walk out your relationship with God and with others? In what areas are you giving of yourself? Here's hope that this churchwide study will continue bringing you into a deeper understanding of all that God is—as well as a richer relationship that truly does offer you rest, power, and new life.

Coming up next week: The Home of Grace

Bulletin insert #6.
Adobe PDF graphic files available on CD-ROM Toolkit.

IRRESISTIBLE *Invitation*

RESPONDING TO
WEEK FIVE: THE HOME OF GRACE

Now that our church is knee-deep in *Irresistible Invitation: Responding the Extravagant Heart of God*, you may be wondering where all of this is going. Yes, there's been talk about Commitment Sunday happening next week in our very own "home of grace." But are you still unsure about what that means?

Making a commitment to your church family is so much more than a pledge of money. Being committed—truly being part of the family—means doing your part in all areas: prayers, presence, gifts, and service. It means being willing to offer whatever you have for a cause you believe in—and whatever you can give to a God who's already given so much to you.

As we approach the grand finale that will be Commitment Sunday, then, search your heart for any areas where you may be holding back from God—or from others around you. How can God help you overcome those fears, doubts, and discomforts so that you can run unencumbered into the very arms that made you?

This morning, as you prepare to hear a message related to this study, take a moment to look around. No doubt, you'll see faces you recognize, but also some others that you don't. If we really are the family of God, these folks are your relatives. So why not introduce yourself? It doesn't have to be anything formal, and it doesn't have to be awkward. Just take a moment to look someone in the eye that you don't know, and say hello. If they're reading this too, they'll know exactly what you're after: building a new sense of community, a true home of grace where there's room—and a warm welcome—for all.

Coming up next week: Partners in the Gospel

IRRESISTIBLE
Invitation

BECOMING
PARTNERS IN THE GOSPEL

Here we are—the grand event has finally arrived. It's Commitment Sunday, and this is when it all comes together. Today you have the chance to stand up and be counted. Will you rise to the occasion?

First, let's admit the truth: no one likes to talk about money. We don't like anyone telling us what to do with it, either. This week, our daily readings in *Irresistible Invitation: Responding to the Extravagant Heart of God* talked about returning to God a portion of that which he has given. Obviously, money is part of that picture. But so are our time and resources. Today, then, our challenge is to avoid compartmentalizing our faith. The task at hand is to open your heart, your soul, your mind, your strength, and all that you have in response to the many ways God has so extravagantly poured out his love toward you.

Over the last six weeks, we've all had the opportunity to see ourselves, the world around us, and our God in new ways. As a member of this church family, you've had a chance to read the book, to discuss the concepts, and to hear the pastor's related messages. So what will your response be? Have you prayerfully considered how to fill out your commitment card and service commitment form? Are you ready to turn them in? If you never received them or you forgot to bring them today, don't worry; we have extras available for you to pick up.

As you prepare to turn in these commitments, think back over the previous weeks. Remember the insights you've gained and the challenges you've encountered. Above all, remember that God's love for you is big enough to handle whatever will come in the days ahead. So, are you ready to join the celebration? Your extravagant Host awaits.

Bulletin insert #8.
Adobe PDF graphic files available on CD-ROM Toolkit.

IRRESISTIBLE
Invitation

Irresistible Invitation
Service Commitment
[Year]

Church Name
Church Address
Church Phone

Yes, I am/we are ready to become a partner in the gospel—connecting more with others, acting as God's hands and feet on earth, and serving enthusiastically. Therefore, I/we commit to serve in the following areas in the coming year.

	M	F
Administrative (Office help, finances, library, mailings, answer phone, etc.)	( )	( )
Adult Ministry (Sunday school, small groups, classes, men's or women's ministry activities, etc.)	( )	( )
Church Building and Grounds Care (Gardening, maintenance, housekeeping, painting, etc.)	( )	( )
Communications (Web site, newsletter, photo or videography, publicity, sign messages, etc.)	( )	( )
Congregational Care (Visit homebound, hospitals; prepare meals; assist seniors, etc.)	( )	( )
Evangelism (Follow up with visitors, new member assimilation, organize attendance records, etc.)	( )	( )
Fellowship Activities (Book club, work with senior adults, churchwide retreat, etc.)	( )	( )
Hospitality (Usher, greeter, follow up with visitors, parking, etc.)	( )	( )
Music/Arts (Choir, drama, handbell choir, assist children's music, etc.)	( )	( )
Nursery (Childcare, Mother's Day Out, etc.)	( )	( )
Outreach (Food pantry, clothing ministry, *Volunteers in Mission*, children's center, etc.)	( )	( )
Prayer Ministry (Prayer tree, prayer vigils, coordinate prayer requests, etc.)	( )	( )
Student Ministry (Teach or assist grades K–5, middle school, Vacation Bible School, etc.)	( )	( )
Wednesday Night Activities (Kitchen, clean up, serve food, lead class, etc.)	( )	( )
Worship (Prepare communion, lay reader, altar preparation, flowers, etc.)	( )	( )
Youth (Assist with meetings, chaperone trips, events, etc.)	( )	( )
Wherever the church needs me	( )	( )
Other_____	( )	( )

Irresistible Invitation Service Commitment

Name: _____   Name: _____

E-mail Address: _____   E-mail Address: _____

Cell Number: _____   Cell Number: _____

Home Address: _____

Home Phone Number: _____

Signed _____   Signed _____

Service commitment form—short version.
Modifiable text in MS Word available on CD-ROM Toolkit.

IRRESISTIBLE *Invitation*

Church Name
Church Address
Church Phone

Irresistible Invitation
Service Commitment
[Year]

Yes, I am/we are ready to become a partner in the gospel. I/we want to connect more with others, act as God's hands and feet on earth, and serve enthusiastically. Therefore, I/we commit to serve in the following areas in the coming year.

Welcoming (Evangelism)

M F
1 ( ) ( ) Parking lot greeter
(_____ service time)
2 ( ) ( ) Greeter (_____ service time)
3 ( ) ( ) Usher (_____ service time)
4 ( ) ( ) Follow up with visitors
5 ( ) ( ) Adopt a new member
6 ( ) ( ) Assemble new member packets
7 ( ) ( ) Other_____

Learning

8 ( ) ( ) Attend _____ class
9 ( ) ( ) Participate in *Walk to Emmaus*
10 ( ) ( ) Attend Sunday school
11 ( ) ( ) Attend Wednesday Bible study
12 ( ) ( ) Attend *DISCIPLE Bible Study*
13 ( ) ( ) Attend new members' class
14 ( ) ( ) Other_____

Discipleship

15 ( ) ( ) Invite a friend to church
16 ( ) ( ) Learn to share my faith
17 ( ) ( ) Lead a small-group study
18 ( ) ( ) Lead where needed, if qualified
19 ( ) ( ) Other_____

Administrative

20 ( ) ( ) Help in office
21 ( ) ( ) Maintain bulletin boards
22 ( ) ( ) Assist in library
23 ( ) ( ) Work on history committee
24 ( ) ( ) Other_____

Nursery Ministry

25 ( ) ( ) Early service nursery helper
(Sunday school)
26 ( ) ( ) Late service nursery helper
(Worship)
27 ( ) ( ) Wednesday service volunteer
28 ( ) ( ) Mother's Day Out
29 ( ) ( ) Other_____

Student Ministry

30 ( ) ( ) Teach K–1st grade
31 ( ) ( ) Teach 2nd – 3rd grade
32 ( ) ( ) Teach 4th –5th grade
33 ( ) ( ) Assist in elementary grades
34 ( ) ( ) Teach middle school

M F
35 ( ) ( ) Teach high school
36 ( ) ( ) Assist in middle/high
school classes
37 ( ) ( ) Teach/help with Vacation
Bible school
38 ( ) ( ) Assist with activities for K–5
39 ( ) ( ) I have a special skill or interest I'd
like to share with children:
_____
40 ( ) ( ) Other_____

Youth

41 ( ) ( ) Volunteer for Sunday youth
meeting
42 ( ) ( ) Volunteer for youth program
43 ( ) ( ) Chaperone mission trip
44 ( ) ( ) Chaperone youth trip
45 ( ) ( ) Work with youth on ongoing basis
46 ( ) ( ) Other_____

Adult Ministry

47 ( ) ( ) Teach an adult class
48 ( ) ( ) Establish/lead new adult class
49 ( ) ( ) Participate in small group
50 ( ) ( ) Lead small group
51 ( ) ( ) Participate in women's ministries
52 ( ) ( ) Participate in men's ministries
53 ( ) ( ) Other_____

Wednesday Night Activities

54 ( ) ( ) Kitchen committee
55 ( ) ( ) Assist with children's
programming
56 ( ) ( ) Youth helper
57 ( ) ( ) Lead adult class
58 ( ) ( ) Help serve food
59 ( ) ( ) Help clean up
60 ( ) ( ) Collect money
61 ( ) ( ) Close and lock building
62 ( ) ( ) Other_____

Worship

63 ( ) ( ) Lay reader
64 ( ) ( ) Altar arrangement coordination
65 ( ) ( ) Prepare sanctuary for Sundays
66 ( ) ( ) Restock pew supplies
67 ( ) ( ) Communion preparation
68 ( ) ( ) Communion servers
69 ( ) ( ) Special and seasonal decorations
70 ( ) ( ) Assist with acolytes
71 ( ) ( ) Operate sound system
72 ( ) ( ) Other_____

Service commitment form—long version, page 1.
Modifiable text in MS Word available on CD-ROM Toolkit.

Music/Arts Ministries
73 ( ) ( ) Sing in chancel choir
74 ( ) ( ) Handbell choir
75 ( ) ( ) Direct beginning handbell choir
76 ( ) ( ) Set up and take down bell tables
77 ( ) ( ) Lead youth music ensemble
78 ( ) ( ) Assist in children's music
79 ( ) ( ) Play special musical instruments:
　　　　　_____
80 ( ) ( ) Serve as accompanist
81 ( ) ( ) Help maintain music library
82 ( ) ( ) Participate in drama group
83 ( ) ( ) Maintain choir robes
84 ( ) ( ) Other_____

Congregational Care
85 ( ) ( ) Visit homebound members
86 ( ) ( ) Visit hospital patients
87 ( ) ( ) Write/send cards
88 ( ) ( ) Organize meals for families
　　　　　experiencing childbirth,
　　　　　illness, etc.
89 ( ) ( ) Organize meals at church after
　　　　　funerals on request
90 ( ) ( ) Drive for those needing
　　　　　transportation
91 ( ) ( ) Do light home maintenance
　　　　　for seniors
92 ( ) ( ) Other_____

Prayer Ministry
93 ( ) ( ) Participate in prayer tree
94 ( ) ( ) Maintain prayer tree
95 ( ) ( ) Participate in prayer vigils
96 ( ) ( ) Coordinate prayer requests

Fellowship Activities
97 ( ) ( ) Book club
98 ( ) ( ) Work with senior adults
99 ( ) ( ) Churchwide retreat
100 ( ) ( ) Work with young adults
101 ( ) ( ) Other_____

Outreach
102 ( ) ( ) Clothing ministry
103 ( ) ( ) Food pantry
104 ( ) ( ) Volunteers in Missions participant
105 ( ) ( ) Indigent ministry
106 ( ) ( ) Local missions
107 ( ) ( ) Volunteer in shelter program
108 ( ) ( ) Children's center
109 ( ) ( ) Community outreach
110 ( ) ( ) Housing trust
111 ( ) ( ) Disaster relief
112 ( ) ( ) Multicultural awareness team
113 ( ) ( ) Other_____

Communications
114 ( ) ( ) Assist with Web site
115 ( ) ( ) Write newsletter or Web articles
116 ( ) ( ) Photography/video
117 ( ) ( ) Newspaper communications
118 ( ) ( ) Change sign messages
119 ( ) ( ) Other_____

Church Building and Grounds Care
120 ( ) ( ) Unlock and lock building Sunday
　　　　　mornings
121 ( ) ( ) Adopt a flower bed
122 ( ) ( ) Rake leaves
123 ( ) ( ) Prune shrubs
124 ( ) ( ) Pick up lawn litter
125 ( ) ( ) Water/maintain indoor plants
126 ( ) ( ) Dust and clean building interior
127 ( ) ( ) Participate in clean-up day
128 ( ) ( ) Redecorate/paint building interior
129 ( ) ( ) Other_____

Miscellaneous
130 ( ) ( ) Wherever the church needs me
131 ( ) ( ) Other_____

IRRESISTIBLE
Invitation

Irresistible Invitation Service Commitment

Name: _____   **Name:** _____
E-mail Address: _____   **E-mail Address:** _____
Cell Number: _____   **Cell Number:** _____
Home Address: _____
Home Phone Number: _____

Signed _____   **Signed** _____

Service commitment form—long version, page 2.
Modifiable text in MS Word available on CD-ROM Toolkit.

IRRESISTIBLE
Invitation

Youth Service Commitment

Church Name
Church Address
Church Phone

Yes, I am ready to become a partner in the gospel—connecting more with others, acting as God's hands and feet on earth, and serving enthusiastically. Therefore, I commit to serve in the following areas in the coming year.

Youth Choir (Attend rehearsals, sing as scheduled, choir tours as scheduled) ( )
Contemporary Worship Committee (Help plan contemporary worship events) ( )
Song Leader (Lead hymns in contemporary worship) ( )
Youth Communications (Web site, newsletter, photo or videography, publicity, sign messages, etc.) ( )
Sound System Volunteer (Operate sound systems at Sunday morning worship or at youth worship events) ( )
Instrumental Musician (Play a musical instrument in worship or at special events) ( )
Acolyte (Light candles or help lead Sunday worship or other worship events) ( )
Youth Evangelism (Follow up with visitors, make newcomers feel welcome) ( )
Liturgical Dancers (Perform at worship services or special services; practice as necessary) ( )
Youth Hospitality (Help with refreshments on Sunday morning or at youth events) ( )
Music/Arts (Choir, drama, handbell choir, assist children's music, etc.) ( )
Church Nursery (Help in church nursery on Sundays or other times; *requires special training*) ( )
Outreach Activities (Half-day or full-day local mission projects for youth) ( )
Prayer Ministry (Prayer tree, prayer vigils, coordinate prayer requests, etc.) ( )
Tutoring Ministry (Assist another student in a subject area in which you are strong) ( )
Youth Mentor (Mentor younger youth by being a friend, inviting them to events, etc.) ( )
Church Usher (Usher at the church's main Sunday morning services) ( )
Lay Reader (Read Scripture at church's main Sunday morning services or youth worship services) ( )
Church Maintenance (Assist in church maintenance projects, yard work, landscaping, etc.) ( )
Wherever the church needs me ( )
Other_____ ( )

Youth Service Commitment

Name: _____
E-mail Address: _____
Cell Phone Number: _____
Home Address: _____
Home Phone Number: _____

Signed: _____

Youth service commitment form.
Modifiable text in MS Word available on CD-ROM Toolkit.

IRRESISTIBLE *Invitation*

COMMITMENT CARD

please print:

name(s) _____

address _____

city, state, zip _____

signature(s) _____

I'm ready to become a partner in the gospel!

❑ My/our commitment to prayer is to pray for our church and other needs _____ times each week

❑ My/our commitment to presence this year is to attend worship service _____ times each month

❑ My/our commitment to gifts is to give to this church $ _____ per *circle one* (week / month / year)

❑ My/our commitment to service is to volunteer this year in the area(s) checked on the separate service commitment form

---

IRRESISTIBLE *Invitation*

Children's Commitment Card

please print:

name _____

address _____

city, state, zip _____

signature _____

I'm ready to become a partner in the gospel!

❑ I will pray for my family, friends, church, and world.

❑ I will attend worship and Sunday school.

❑ I will give to this church.

$ _____ per circle one (week / month / year)

❑ I will serve this year!

   ❑ I will sing in my age group choir.

   ❑ I will bring my Bible to church.

   ❑ I will attend children's activities.

IRRESISTIBLE *Invitation*

YOUTH COMMITMENT CARD

please print:

name _____

address _____

city, state, zip _____

signature _____

I'm ready to become a partner in the gospel!

❑ My commitment to prayer is to pray for our church _____ times each week

❑ My commitment to presence this year is to attend worship service _____ times each month and youth activities _____ times each month

❑ My commitment to gifts is to give to this church $ _____ per *circle one* (week / month / year)

❑ My commitment to service is to volunteer this year in the area(s) checked on the service commitment form.

Commitment cards.
Adobe PDF graphic files available on CD-ROM Toolkit.

IRRESISTIBLE
Invitation

RESPONDING TO THE
EXTRAVAGANT HEART OF GOD

LEADER'S GUIDE WITH DVD

IRRESISTIBLE INVITATION
RESPONDING TO THE EXTRAVAGANT HEART OF GOD
LEADER'S GUIDE WITH DVD

Copyright 2008 by Abingdon Press

All rights reserved.

This book is printed on acid-free, elemental-chlorine–free paper.

Original art, cover, and page design by Joey McNair

Leader's Guide with DVD
ISBN: 978-0-687-64859-7

Scripture quotations marked NIV are taken from HOLY BIBLE, NEW INTERNATIONAL VERSION®. Copyright © 1973, 1978, 1984 by International Bible Society. Used by permission of Zondervan Publishing House.

Scripture quotations from *The Message* Copyright © by Eugene H. Peterson 1993, 1994, 1995, 1996, 2000, 2001, 2002. Used by permission of NavPress Publishing Group.

08 09 10 11 12 13 14 15 16 17   10 9 8 7 6 5 4 3 2 1

MANUFACTURED IN THE UNITED STATES OF AMERICA

CONTENTS

GUIDELINES FOR LEADERS

Dear leader: This one has your name all over it. Yes, *Irresistible Invitation: Responding to the Extravagant Heart of God* is all about drawing people into a richer, deeper relationship with God. But if you're reading this, you've likely received yet another special offer as well: the chance to guide a Sunday school class or small group through the study. What great news!

Somebody obviously sees something in you—a leadership quality, a certain spiritual maturity, or maybe even just a contagiously joyful attitude. Then again, maybe it was God who put you up to leading the group, and you found yourself volunteering for the position before you realized what was happening.

Regardless, know this truth: no matter what doubts or concerns you may have about leading this study, God will fill in the gaps. The most important thing to remember is that no matter what happens, you're not alone. God has plans for each and every person in your small group—including you—and his purposes will be accomplished.

So, how can you make sure that happens? First and foremost, you have to pray. Only by staying connected to the Source can you find out what God truly wants you to do. And only through prayer can you receive the encouragement and support your heart will need.

This study is about transforming lives, and it's unfortunate that we have a very real enemy who will try to keep that from happening. Prayer will help keep you on your guard and will help thwart the enemy's schemes to make this a difficult study.

Pray for your ability to lead well, and remember to also pray regularly for the people in your small group. Pray that their hearts and minds would be open to whatever God has for them.

PREPARATION

In addition to prayer, something else is very important: taking the time to prepare for each week's study in advance. That will help you feel comfortable with the subject matter and enable you to keep things on track during the meeting. Read through the week's chapters a couple of times, go over the leader notes at the start of each section, and review the answers to the fill-in-the-blank questions. In the *Leader's Guide*, the answers are listed both in the text and the appendix, but in the *Participant's Workbook*, they are only in the appendix. Give some thought to the associated discussion questions so you can offer suggestions if your group members are not participating as much as you had expected.

Arrive a bit early to your small-group meeting so you won't be rushed. Check your audio/visual equipment, and make sure everything is working properly for playing the week's DVD message. When you're done, take a few moments to read through the leader notes at the end of each section, reviewing how things went, as well as beginning to prepare your heart for the week ahead.

AD HOC SMALL GROUPS

If, however, the small group you're leading has been organized specifically for this study and isn't a regularly meeting group, you'll probably want to begin the first couple of meetings with general introductions, since it's possible that not everyone in the group will already be acquainted. Introduce yourself, and perhaps tell the group how long you've been a member of the church. Then ask the others to introduce themselves, one at a time, to the rest of the group. You might begin with someone you know or you might select the person nearest you. If you have several members who don't know each other, consider providing name tags for the first couple of meetings.

LEADING THE MEETING

It's always good to start the meeting with prayer. You can pray, or you can ask someone else to pray, if you so desire. An appropriate prayer might be something like this:

Dear Heavenly Father, thank you for this opportunity to come together as a group and to share our thoughts, insights, and prayers regarding this forty-day study. We thank you for your presence with us now and as we go through these six weeks. We ask for your involvement and guidance for our entire congregation as we participate in this life-transforming program. We ask you to guide our discussion today, and we ask that your will be done. We ask this in Jesus' name. *Amen.*

Your main responsibility in leading this study is to facilitate a flow of conversation. It's not necessary for you to have all the answers. In fact, it's probably a good thing if you don't have all the answers. Asking for input from others can help them better relate to you.

Sometimes, one or two individuals will tend to dominate the discussion. If this happens, thank them for their input, scan the room, then ask if anyone else has something they'd like to add. It's okay to encourage people by making eye contact and calling on them if they seem to have something to contribute.

While going over the discussion questions, it might help to have a poster board and a marker (or even a chalkboard) at the front of the room to write down responses. The more senses that are involved in learning something, the better your group will remember it. Enabling people to both hear and see the responses, as well as encouraging them to take notes, will help the answers stay with them.

If you don't get through all of the discussion questions before it's time to move on, that's all right—as long as the discussion is still fruitful. Remember that the Holy Spirit might take things in a slightly different direction than you had planned; do your best to remain flexible. If some questions remain, simply tell the group that it's time for discussing personal application, and encourage them to answer the questions on their own later.

When it is time to divide into smaller groups for personal application, limit each group to no more than five people, so they'll each have an opportunity to share. You can determine who will be in which group in a number of ways: group people together according to where they're sitting, separate according to gender, allow people to choose groups for themselves, or have them pick numbers from a hat as they arrive for the meeting.

Some people will feel more comfortable sharing if they're in a group with people they don't know as well as the ones they came with; others will want to share with their friends. How you divide into smaller groups is really your choice.

Be clear at the outset about how long they're supposed to be in the smaller groups, and give a one-minute warning to wrap up when the time draws to a close.

Speaking of time, here's a general outline of how long to spend on each activity:

Prayer	1–5 minutes
Weekly Introduction	10–15 minutes
DVD Message	8–10 minutes
Post-DVD Discussion	20 minutes
Personal Application	10–15 minutes
Looking Ahead	5–10 minutes

You probably noticed that there's a little flexibility in the number of minutes for each activity. This study was designed to work for groups that meet for approximately forty-five minutes to one hour. Feel free to adjust the time to meet your group's specific needs.

STRATEGIC SCHEDULING

In most cases, this study will be done on Sunday mornings, on the same day the pastor delivers a message on the week's topic. In some instances, however, groups may be scheduled to meet during the week, such as on Wednesday nights. If that's the case, try to schedule the study so your group finishes the week's reading before the pastor speaks on the topic, rather than after. This gives the members of the small group a chance to cover all of the materials and have a few days to pray and further consider their responses before the topic is covered in the large assembly. It will mean a little more work during the first week to fit seven days' worth of lessons into a shorter time span, but it will be worth the effort.

SETTING AN EXAMPLE

Finally, keep in mind that it's important for you to provide a positive example. Your level of enthusiasm, excitement, and commitment to the study will be contagious. As the saying goes, "The speed of the leader is the speed of the gang." As such, do your best to keep up with daily readings, prepare responses, share what you're learning, and encourage participation among your church family. You have the opportunity to help the individuals in your small group change before your very eyes—and the whole experience could be even more gratifying than you could imagine.

INTRODUCTION TO THE WORKBOOK

J ust picture it: a big, beautiful house on a hill. It's different than the rest in the neighborhood somehow, with beautiful gardens, spacious rooms, and all that you could possibly want—but more than you probably think you could ever afford.

Maybe you've heard about the gatherings that go on there, joyful occasions that draw people from far and wide. Maybe you've heard how guests were treated like kings and queens, and even though you'd been invited yourself, you never thought you'd fit in, so you didn't go.

Well, friend, another invitation has just arrived. How will you respond?

What that "house" represents is the fullness of relationship with God. It's not just about accepting him as your Lord and Savior. That's just the start. It's about the richness of a life lived with abundant grace, love, and communication with the very One who made you.

From the outside looking in, that house may appear too good to be true. But once you step inside, you'll discover an amazing truth: it feels just like home. This is, after all, the place you were made for, a daily existence that goes beyond just "getting by." It is a place of acceptance, of purpose, and of fulfillment—and the door is standing wide open.

Over the next six weeks, we'll be approaching that door together. Through questions, discussion, Scripture, and personal application, you'll have the opportunity to discover new truths about God and his extended hand toward you. It doesn't matter whether you're brand new at all this or you've been walking with the Lord a while; there's always more to know. Keep in mind, though, that you'll get out of it what you put into it. If you're willing to wholeheartedly commit to prayer, study, and conversations with others about what you're learning, there's no telling the depths of transformation God can bring to your life.

STUDY FORMAT

This workbook is designed to be used in tandem with *Irresistible Invitation: Responding to the Extravagant Heart of God* by Maxie Dunnam. That text is grouped into six parts, with forty days' worth of personal readings and introspective questions. It is hoped that as you read through the book and work on the study, you'll take these questions seriously, reaching into the very corners of your heart with thoughtful consideration and prayer, asking God for his revelation and guidance.

The *Participant's Workbook* also contains space for insight and application at the beginning of each week's lesson. These Insight/Application pages will help your group reflect on what they've read and on what God is revealing to them through this study. They are for each person's private observations; what they write down won't be shared with your small group. Encourage your group members to record their personal reflections—any thoughts, observations, or revelations that they discover in reading *Irresistible Invitation: Responding to the Extravagant Heart of God*. Also, invite them to consider how they might make positive changes in their lives or ways of thinking in response to what they have read.

If you'd like to take notes on what you discover along the way, you're encouraged to keep a separate journal. In order to provide more leadership guidance, the Insight/Application pages are not included in this *Leader's Guide*. It is strongly recommended, however, that you join your group members in recording your thoughts each day in a journal. This daily writing is a key discipline that promises to bear much fruit in your spiritual life.

This *Leader's Guide* is designed to be the compass for making sure you get everything out of each week's study that you possibly can. Keep it handy while you read the daily book chapters, bring it with you when you lead your weekly small-group session, and expect God to move as he ties it all together.

Here's how the six weeks will unfold. Your *Leader's Guide* includes a brief summary of each week's topic to focus your understanding and shape your group's discussion. You will begin each small-group gathering with a short DVD message from Maxie Dunnam. The script for each video is included in this *Leader's Guide*; you may choose to read and reflect on the video content before you lead the group discussion. After watching the video, you'll review the main points of that week's chapter using a fill-in-the-blank format, and initiate some preliminary discussion.

You will then divide into smaller groups or pairs to give you the opportunity to share on a more personal level. At the close of each meeting, you'll look at Scripture that will help your group remember what you've learned.

During our six-week study, you'll notice that other activities in the church body will tie into the weekly subjects as well. That's because we're all in this together. No matter where we are in our walk with God, there's always more to learn, share, and receive.

Remind the group that this discipline will assist them in remembering and possibly sharing with the group or class some of the reflections that come to them during this forty-day journey.

COMING HOME TO GOD

As we go about the details of living our lives, it's easy for us to lose sight of the big picture. But if we allow God to teach us new things and reveal himself in new ways, there's no telling what could happen next. We may begin with lots of doubts and questions, but if we will focus our thinking on the beautiful miracle of creation, we can begin a new conversation with our Creator.

We all carry images of God that may be distorted from the truth of who God really is, but if we will look again at the witness of the saints and the words of the Bible, we'll discover a God of extravagant love and sheer joy who longs for communion with us. No matter who we are, no matter where we are, we can always come home to the idea that there is a loving Father ready to receive us.

One way we become reacquainted with God is by reading the Bible. Meditating on the Scriptures on a daily basis offers us hope, wisdom, knowledge, promise, joy, direction, and more. Are there any places you haven't yet "come home," or admitted your need for God's love, grace, and acceptance? Have you been able to develop a regular diet of the Word that can help you grow? What's standing in your way, and what can be done to remove those obstacles?

SMALL-GROUP MEETING

Ready to get started? By now, you've had time to read through this week's lesson—as well as the first seven chapters of the book—and have given some thought to how the questions might be answered, so you can help facilitate the discussions. At this point, then, it's time to let go just a bit and let the Holy Spirit work. Allow God to take control of the meeting, and he'll accomplish more than you thought possible. Take a deep breath, put on a smile, and dive in.

INTRODUCTION

Welcome—we're glad you're here. A place has been prepared just for you. Today marks a special occasion as we begin our group study of *Irresistible Invitation: Responding to the Extravagant Heart of God*. Let's begin with a word of prayer that God will bless this time together and open our eyes to more of him. (*prayer*)

Next, we'll turn to this workbook's introduction and study format. I will look to one of you to volunteer to do the reading.

So, ready to dig a little deeper? Let's watch a brief DVD message by Maxie Dunnam, author of the book.

VIDEO SCRIPT

Hi, I'm Maxie Dunnam. I'm excited to be with you as we begin this adventure of exploring God's irresistible invitation to us.

In my life, I've worked as a minister, teacher, and seminary president. I've written books and traveled around the world. In all these settings, I've observed the Spirit of God at work in the lives of countless people. You can count on it—that's what God wants to do—to be present in your life and mine, loving us and providing us with the power to be all we are created to be.

It is my privilege to welcome you to the start of a powerful new study exploring God's extravagant love, and to share with you some lessons I've learned over the last fifty years.

Before we move into the first week's theme, let's take a moment to look at our itinerary.

Over the next forty days, we'll journey deep into the heart of our faith—further, I hope, than each of us has ever gone. Our goal is to experience authentic spiritual growth that will prepare us to become more effective agents of Christ in this world. We've only got six weeks, and if you're going to accept this invitation, you need to be committed. Here are some ground rules.

1. Be Faithful—It is important that each one of you agree to be faithful in reading the daily chapters, reflecting on the Scripture passages, and perhaps most important, answering the Heart of the Matter questions. These materials will challenge you to think about relationships in a new light—certainly your relationship with God, but also your relationships with loved ones, friends, coworkers, and even strangers.

2. Be Real—There will be times of sharing throughout this study in which very personal issues are entrusted to the group. It is essential that we agree to be true and authentic with ourselves and with the group. Spiritual growth only happens in a place where our deepest truths can be shared with trust and security. What happens in the group, stays in the group. If we give each other respect and room to grow, the Holy Spirit will be free to work within each of us in God's own timing.

3. Be Prayerful—We'll be talking a lot about the power of prayer over the next several weeks. Nothing is more important. As we cultivate our ongoing conversation with God, look forward to becoming more and more comfortable praying with others. Lift up in prayer those on your heart—your brothers and sisters within this group, your families and communities, and extend your prayerful reach around the world. God will surprise and bless you when you allow him to work in and through you as you meet to study, pray, and learn together.

*4. **Be as One***—As you accept God's invitation to this forty-day study, I pray that your group will be knit together in the overwhelming awareness of God's infinite goodness and his personal love for you. Congratulations for choosing to take part in this life-changing event. Remember what Jesus promised: "Where two or three are gathered in my name, I will be present there." Be as one in Christ.

Now let's begin by addressing an important question: who is God, anyway? As the deer longs for flowing streams, we all carry deep within us a longing to know God. Passionately seeking God, as it turns out, is the best direction any of us can take, because God reveals himself to those who earnestly seek him.

As a pastor, I learned early on that many of us hold on to a mental image of God that is, to be honest, a little scary. God is seen as an angry judge who condemns, or a referee keeping a score of sins. If anything like this is your idea of who God is, you're probably uncomfortable with the idea of seeking after God. What if the God you discovered was just as frightening as you imagined?

There are so many misconceptions of who God is. The sad truth is that these wrong ideas keep us from experiencing the full measure of God's blessing in our everyday lives. If we can stop for a moment, take a deep breath, and step away from our own ideas, is there room for another, truer picture of God?

I want to let you in on a secret—this may be the biggest headline the newspapers never printed: *God is good!* And God loves each one of us as though we are the only person in the world to love. If we will look again at the Scriptures and the witness of believers through the ages, we discover that God really does love us. He cares for each one of us as a father or a mother—offering us grace, forgiveness, love, acceptance, and even new life. God does this with a generosity that can sometimes—let's be honest, *most of the time*—be hard to comprehend.

That's why I've written this study—to help you embrace this powerful understanding of God. "God loves me. I am a unique, unrepeatable miracle of God." The daily chapters, Bible verses, and Heart of the Matter questions will lead you, guiding your steps as you make your way into the full life promised in the Scriptures.

The road you'll travel has been illumined by the lives of saints and tread by ordinary people, and it always leads to the same destination: the kingdom of God. Each of the luminary Christians I've studied through the years experienced this soul-searching as the starting point of their relationship with God. I'll be sharing some of their stories with you during this study. I encourage you to reflect on them to discover how your life might be enriched by their timeless wisdom.

All seekers need directions, and the truths we'll study in the next few weeks will serve as the roadmap to our shared desti-nation. As much as we want instant solutions, we must remember that it's in the process of our time together that we'll find our way.

Here's a glimpse of the things we'll explore over the next few weeks:

* Opening ourselves to God in an ongoing conversation called prayer;

* Studying and reflecting on Scripture, which is God's breathed Word;

* Focusing on Jesus' life, teaching, death, and Resurrection as our hope and purpose in life;

* Allowing the Holy Spirit to take up residence in our hearts;

* Following God's guidance in our daily decisions;

* Experiencing relationship with God and his people in communities of grace; and

❈ Becoming a partner in God's work in the world by giving ourselves to others in the name of Jesus.

We must commit ourselves to this new way of being, this new style of living that will inform every choice we make and eventually conform us to the image of Christ.

So this is your invitation and your passport. Now, as you begin today's discussion, I pray and believe that God will speak to you in fresh and exciting ways.

POST-DVD DISCUSSION

We'll open our discussion time today with a few questions and statements from the DVD. First, we'll fill in the blank for each statement, then we'll look a little closer at each concept. Is there a volunteer who will read the first one out loud?

1. For this small group to be effective, it must become a place where deepest truths can be shared with security and _____. **(trust)**

    ❈ Why is it important that what is shared within this group stay within this group?

2. As we go through this study together, it's important that we regularly _____ for one another. **(pray)**

    ❈ How can lifting other group members up to God make this study more meaningful for all?

3. Deeply rooted misconceptions of God (such as thinking of God as an angry judge or scorekeeper) can prevent us from experiencing the full measure of _____ _____ in our everyday lives.
    (God's blessing)

    ❈ Where do misconceptions of God come from?

4. _____ _____ _____ is the best direction any of us can take. **(Passionately seeking God)**

❋ Why is it important for us to seek God, rather than just waiting for him to find us?

5. Above all, we must remember that God is _____; he is for us, not against us. **(good)**

    ❋ How could a deep understanding of this truth affect a person's walk with God?

6. We must embrace this powerful understanding: God _____ _____. I am a unique, unrepeatable _____ of God. **(loves me/miracle)**

    ❋ Where will this understanding take you?

PERSONAL APPLICATION

One of the most important parts of this small-group study is the opportunity for personal application. To make sure everyone has time to participate and respond, we'll break into small groups. Begin with the key discussion questions about this week's readings, and if there's still time after each person has had time to share, move on to the supplemental questions.

KEY QUESTIONS:

❋ What foundational ideas do you have about God? What life experiences or teachings have led to that belief?

❋ What things could stand in the way of a deeper relationship with God?

SUPPLEMENTAL QUESTIONS:

❋ Have you ever been amazed by God? How so?

❋ How could regular study of the Bible affect a person's relationship with God?

❋ What do you hope to get out of this study?

LOOKING AHEAD

During the next week, we'll take a closer look at the life of Jesus and what impact it has on our own lives. In the meantime, however, commit to memory the following verse so what we've learned this week won't be forgotten.

I have come that they may have life, and have it to the full.

—John 10:10

Write the verse below:

_____

_____

_____

_____

_____

LEADER NOTES

Take a few moments to review this week's meeting. What went well? What unexpected challenges surfaced? Was there any time you felt you could have been more prepared? How could you remedy that for next week? Thank God for his guidance, and ask him to lead you through the coming week's readings so you'll have insight and understanding of the concepts presented. Write down any thoughts about the meeting here. You might also want to use this space to write down any prayer requests that arose during your group meeting.

_____

_____

_____

_____

Week Two

A LOVE LIKE NO OTHER

As humans, we sometimes feel that we're merely guessing at the meaning of the mysteries of our faith, especially Jesus' life, death, and Resurrection. The fact that Jesus went to the cross for our sins and yet still lives is a deep mystery, but it is also the shaping dynamic of the Christian life.

As Christians, with Jesus as our central character, we can walk in confidence knowing that God loves us unconditionally, and there is nothing we can do to earn or justify that love; it just is. When we are able to accept that, we can become the secure, whole people God intended us to be all along. When we receive the gift of God's extravagant love, it both transforms us and re-creates us. Christ becomes alive in us, alive to provide forgiveness of our sins, healing in our brokenness, direction in our disorientation, joy in our sadness, and one day, Resurrection from the dead for eternal life with him. Is anything standing between you and this great, generous gift?

SMALL-GROUP MEETING

Now that you have at least one meeting under your belt, face your facilitating duties with confidence. God is on your side, and will help you draw out answers and discussions that may reach deeper into people's hearts than you realize. As always, keep an eye out for participants who may try to dominate conversations, and do your best to make sure everyone has a chance to share. Don't be afraid of pauses in discussions; wait long enough for others to speak up. Be on the lookout for pairs/groups that tend to get off track. One more thing: the personal application time of this section gives people an opportunity to receive Jesus as Lord and Savior if they have not yet done so. In case this happens, be prepared to either lead that person in a private prayer after the meeting, or take them to someone who can.

INTRODUCTION

Hello and welcome! Shall we open in prayer? (*prayer*) Can anyone recite last week's Scripture verse? Let's take a moment to write it on the lines provided below:

_____

_____

_____

_____

Now, as we begin our second small-group meeting for *Irresistible Invitation: Responding to the Extravagant Heart of God,* here's something to ponder: how is Jesus portrayed in movies and on TV, and how is that different than what the Bible teaches? Does Jesus represent weakness or strength? Futility or hope? Compassion or judgmentalism? How we understand Christ will have a definite impact on our level of relationship with God.

With that in mind, let's continue with a brief DVD message by Maxie Dunnam, followed by a few questions.

VIDEO SCRIPT

Hello again. I'm Maxie Dunnam. As we gather to reflect on the past week and begin another week of our forty-day study, I hope each of you will take a moment to share your thoughts with the group. Developing dialogue and remaining in conversation about the ideas and feelings stirred by your reading and reflection is an essential component of this study. In conversation, we grow individually and we forge bonds that will reinforce the foundation of our church family.

During your time reading the daily chapters, reflecting on the Bible verses, and answering the Heart of the Matter questions, I hope you've experienced a fresh encounter with God. I'm sure there is at least a stirring in your soul that is leading you deeper into prayer. Whatever you have experienced, I invite you to talk about it together.

This week we ponder the biggest mystery of all time: Jesus' death on the cross and his Resurrection from the tomb.

Now if you're like me, you've spent your life surrounded by crosses. We see them in church, on jewelry, in books, and on buildings. Although we find crosses all around, have you ever considered that perhaps we don't really see them at all? We've grown so accustomed to crosses that we can almost ignore their true meaning. The pretty gold cross dangling from a necklace becomes an empty symbol without the deeper significance of the death and passion of Christ.

As humans, we're all guilty of taking for granted the extravagant love of God through the sacrifice of his only son. We may wince when we pause, for a moment, to think about the suffering of Jesus, whipped and beaten, scorned and mocked, barbarically nailed to the cross to hang on Golgotha's hill. Yet it is almost too painful to remember that Christ chose this fate in his unfathomable love for us. He did this for me, for you. But the cross is so horrendous that it's easy to understand our desire to move quickly beyond the passion of Good Friday to the promise of Easter morning.

But the path to kingdom living must pass, not by, but through the cross.

Dying to our old selves, surrendering our selfish agendas, and receiving Jesus' miraculous gift of new life is the only way to the Father. When we choose to enter into Jesus' death and Resurrection, we begin a new adventure with God and are empowered to become agents of his love in the world.

Our handbook on this journey is the Bible, and in it we find rich history, living wisdom, and practical instruction that jumps off the pages into our daily lives. Jesus was a master of painting word-pictures, and the Gospels contain many poetic images Jesus used to teach.

One way that Jesus described himself was as a gate, or a door. If we are to experience eternal life, we have to enter through the gate of Jesus Christ, and walk through the door with him.

I love this picture of Jesus—not only because of the beautiful landscape we can envision on the other side of the garden gate, but also because once I choose to enter new life through Christ, God closes a door on my past. All my sins are forgiven. Everything I am has a new definition. I'm reminded of the television commercial for allergy medication—there is that moment when the blurry film is removed to reveal a crisp and colorful image that we always knew was there.

Another of my favorite ways Jesus describes himself is as a shepherd. I'm guessing that most of us don't spend a lot time around livestock. In fact, I probably wouldn't recognize a shepherd if I ran into him at Starbucks. But, in Jesus' day, this image really spoke to his listeners. Let's listen to Jesus' description of shepherds and the business of leading sheep in John's Gospel:

> I tell you the truth, the man who does not enter the sheep pen by the gate, but climbs in by some other way, is a thief and a robber. The man who enters by the gate is the shepherd of his sheep. The watchman opens the gate for him, and the sheep listen to his voice.

He calls his own sheep by name and leads them out. When he has
brought out all his own, he goes on ahead of them, and his sheep
follow him because they know his voice. But they will never follow
a stranger; in fact, they will run away from him because they do not
recognize a stranger's voice. . . . I tell you the truth, I am the gate
for the sheep. All who ever came before me were thieves and
robbers, but the sheep did not listen to them. I am the gate;
whoever enters through me will be saved. He will come in and go
out, and find pasture. (John 10:1–9)

I don't know much about sheep, but I do know that they don't
all live in smooth, grassy fields. In Jesus' setting, they had to navigate
rocky terrain, and danger lurked at every turn. Also, sheep are not
the smartest animals, and they spook easily, so they're constantly
wandering away from the path and getting lost in the scrub.

Sound familiar? As much as we hate to admit it, how many of
us are like sheep? We're confused and wandering, not sure of
where we should go in life, needing someone to point us to the
path with the surest footing. If we're honest with ourselves, we
know we get frightened by many things and we spend a lot of
time worrying. But deep inside, we're also aware of our needs, so
we begin to listen for direction from beyond, from our Shepherd.

Jesus' story about the sheep is a graceful picture and a gentle
instruction of how we are to follow him. The sheep know their
shepherd's voice because of an established relationship in which
he nurtures and cares for his flock. He has earned their trust, and
they honor him by listening to his voice and following his guidance. If another voice comes along and tries to direct them
elsewhere, they run back to their shepherd, so deep is their faith
in his protection. Sounds like those sheep may be smarter than
people some of the time. . . .

And what does Jesus promise for those who journey with him
through the gate of the cross, through the rocky terrain of their
days? "Pasture." Green pasture has such a rich meaning. It is a
dwelling place where the sheep feel safe and secure, knowing

they are protected. It is a place of provision, where they can graze on good food to nurture their bodies. It is a place of rest and renewal. It is home.

And that is where we are headed: home. What a beautiful image of God's extravagant goodness! As you spend time in your group today, I invite you to share your thoughts, feelings, and spiritual insights. My prayer is that each of you, as you ponder the meaning of Christ's death and Resurrection, will respond anew to his irresistible invitation. May you be blessed with a cross-bearing life that opens the gate to God's pasture, God's joy and peace, each day of your life.

POST-DVD DISCUSSION

Begin by filling in the blanks for each statement, then we'll look further at each concept. Who would like to read the first one for the group?

1. If we are to truly know God and experience the joy of the kingdom, we must enter through the _____. **(cross)**

   ❋ What does it mean to share in the death and Resurrection of Christ?

2. When God gives us new life, all of our _____ are forgiven. **(sins)**

   ❋ Why is it important for our wrongs to be confessed and forgiven?

3. God is able to close the door to my _____. **(past)**

   ❋ What does it mean to let go of the past?

4. Jesus is often presented as the _____, caring tenderly for his sheep. **(shepherd)**

   ❋ What might be some characteristics of a good shepherd, and how might those apply to God?

5. The sheep follow the shepherd because they have a
_____ with him; they recognize his
_____. **(relationship/voice)**

> ❈ What's the difference between knowing God and knowing *about* him?

6. Just like the shepherd offers the sheep _____,
Jesus offers his followers a place of provision, security, and rest. **(pasture)**

> ❈ In what ways could God provide security or rest?

PERSONAL APPLICATION

Personal application is next, so let's go ahead and break into small groups. Remember that each person should have a chance to participate and respond to the key questions first, and if time allows, the group can move on to the supplemental ones.

KEY QUESTIONS:

❈ Why was the death of Jesus necessary?

❈ What happens if we leave Jesus on the cross without considering his Resurrection?

SUPPLEMENTAL QUESTIONS:

❈ What does it mean to find yourself "not guilty," and how could an understanding of that truth affect your choices in life?

❈ What is the difference between optimism and hope?

❈ Is there anyone here who has not yet accepted Jesus as Lord and Savior, but would like to? (If so, please make the small group or Bible study leader aware.)

LOOKING AHEAD

Next week, we're going to dive into the concept of being alive in Christ. Before we do that, however, let's learn another Scripture verse to remind us of this week's riches.

> For it is by grace you have been saved, through faith—and this not from yourselves, it is the gift of God.
>
> —Eph. 2:8

Write the verse below:

_____

_____

_____

_____

_____

LEADER NOTES

So, how did the meeting go? How was it different than the previous week's session, and were those changes positive? Ask God to grow you in the areas you feel the least confident in your leadership.

_____

_____

_____

_____

_____

_____

_____

Week Three

ALIVE IN CHRIST

With Jesus, the Word truly did become flesh. Jesus is central to the gospel because he is God's invitation to salvation and eternal life. Not only does Christ justify us by providing full pardon for our sins, but he also dwells within us to give us the power to be and do all those things God requires us to be and do.

The closer we walk with Jesus—the more we abide—the more the Spirit within us produces life. The person alive in Christ, the one truly walking in meekness rather than pride, is the one who responds, "Here I am. Send me!" whenever the Lord calls. God has great things for us to do, as long as we remain humble and willing to do them.

Being alive in Christ means that what Christ has been and done for us, we must be and do for others. The way of compassion is not always an easy road, but it is the one to which we are called all the same. How have you been doing at being Christ to others during this study? Are there any areas in particular in which God has pricked your heart?

SMALL-GROUP MEETING

In preparing for this week's session, give some thought to how God has changed your own life; are you living fully alive in Christ? Ask for God's continued guidance and support, and ask him for a greater revelation of the Holy Spirit.

INTRODUCTION

Welcome, welcome! We have arrived at week three of *Irresistible Invitation: Responding to the Extravagant Heart of God.* Shall we open in prayer? (*prayer*)

Can anyone recite last week's memory verse? Please take a moment to write it on the lines provided in your workbook.

Before we watch the DVD message from Maxie Dunnam, think of a very dark place and consider how much light a single candle can provide there. We can be that candle. No matter how dark things seem around us, the light that Christ puts in our hearts when we become fully alive in him can affect others far and wide. Let's watch together, then discuss the main themes.

VIDEO SCRIPT

Hello again, and welcome to another meeting of your small group. In the first two weeks of this church-wide study, we've discussed God's infinite goodness and extravagant love for us, and how we receive his gift of love by accepting Jesus' death and Resurrection as a reconciling act for all eternity. As you progress through this material, I hope you are finding ways to bring these ideas home to your lives, making them personal, incorporating them into your daily life of action and relationship.

As a former seminary president, I could probably be arrested for what I'm about to say, but here goes . . . It's easy for churchy theological talk to seem meaningless to our everyday lives. Sometimes as Christians, we talk a simple truth into a cloud of confusion so thick that it becomes impossible to understand. And if we shroud the truth of our faith in big words like *salvation, justification, sanctification,* and *glorification,* it's hard to connect it to the nitty gritty details we face every day.

This spiritual disconnect happens when we listen and nod during worship services on Sunday, then leave everything behind in the pew when it's time to go home. It can also happen when we gather in meetings like this, and instead of telling the painful truth about our struggles, we choose to hide behind a wall of self-defense.

So this week is where we really begin to bring these *out-there* truths home to our personal lives. Yes, there's a big word that professors and theologians use to describe this practice: sanctification. I prefer to think of it as the ongoing process of becoming a new creation in Christ.

The more I learn about following Jesus, the more I'm convinced that this experience of being fully alive in Christ and accepting the Holy Spirit as an indwelling, ever-present help and comfort is the key to effective living.

Now, this isn't just a wild theory of mine—there is Scriptural basis for it. Profound Scriptural basis.

Although Paul was an educated man, very brilliant, his letters to the early Christians speak of his personal experience of God at work in the mundane circumstances of life. And his words are for us today as clear and as challenging as they were in that first century.

Listen to what Paul says in his words to the Colossians. This is from *The Message* translation:

> The mystery in a nutshell is just this: Christ is in you, so therefore you can look forward to sharing in God's glory. It's that simple. That is the substance of our Message. We preach Christ, warning people not to add to the Message. We teach in a spirit of profound common sense so that we can bring each person to maturity. To be mature is to be basic. Christ! No more, no less. (Col. 1:27–28)

It's hard to misinterpret Paul's words—they're so direct and no-nonsense. Our calling as believers is to experience changed lives, and that kind of life transformation can happen only one way—through Christ.

What a countercultural message Paul presents—that being mature means being *basic.* Isn't it funny how, in our twenty-first

century information age, we regard those with the broadest knowledge as the most intelligent? The paradox of Christian living is so
profound that it seems too simple. Yet, it is true: *only Christ!*

Paul also offers advice on how to embark on a new journey as
partakers in Christ's Resurrection life:

> So if you're serious about living this new resurrection life with
> Christ, act like it. Pursue the things over which Christ presides.
> Don't shuffle along, eyes to the ground, absorbed with the
> things right in front of you. Look up, and be alert to what is
> going on around Christ—that's where the action is. See things
> from his perspective. (Col. 3:1–2)

Seeing the world from Christ's perspective seems intimidating at first, if not downright impossible.

We live in an age of incredible abundance, and we're overwhelmed with distractions from the moment we wake up in the
morning until we close our eyes at night. Rather than simplifying things, this abundance complicates our lives: upsize or
downsize, public or private school, cable or satellite, Ford or
Chevy, Pizza Hut or Papa John's, Coke or Pepsi. When we walk
down this path, the game of life sucks us in. It requires real
discipline to turn away from that disorganized, compulsive, and
selfish way of living.

So where do we turn for relief? In the Bible, Jesus gives us a
specific word of guidance: "Seek ye first the kingdom of God." We
know the rest of this verse by heart–say it with me. "Seek ye first
the kingdom of God, and all these things will be added unto
you." But do we really practice it when the rubber meets the
road? And, if we did, what would seeking the kingdom of God
before all other things look like in our lives?

One key to realizing this lofty idea of living each moment "in
Christ" is in seeking him in the little things. We often think of
God extending us an invitation to life, as we've been talking

about in this study. But have you ever considered that God is waiting for you to extend him an invitation?

Have you thought about asking God into the car with you as you sit in traffic, or into the chaos when you're arguing with your spouse? The beautiful truth is that God is already there, waiting for you to enter into conversation, hoping to reveal himself to you through the still, small voice that you've probably been hearing all along.

The big point is that the presence of God in Jesus Christ is not to be experienced only on occasion. The indwelling Christ is to become the shaping power of our lives. It's in the daily interactions that we are to personally experience the common-sense presence of God. When we become comfortable praying, reading Scripture, and inviting God into our day, the ongoing process of being conformed to Christ becomes so innate that it's like breathing. We can't imagine moving through our days without it.

Now, as you move into your group discussion time, I want to remind you again of the importance of being open and honest with one another. Sharing the truth of our hearts is where we begin to bring home the essence of the gospel.

As you listen and share with each other today, invite the Holy Spirit to be present in your group. Remember to be sensitive to the leading of God's Spirit, and try to be faithful to the guidance you are receiving. It can be risky to move outside your comfort zone, but I can assure you that you won't be disappointed.

I hope that this exciting process enlivens each one of you, and I pray the authentic love and compassion that can only come from God is transforming your relationships. Blessings!

POST-DVD DISCUSSION

As usual, we'll begin by filling in the blanks. Then we'll take it to the next step with some discussion. Who will volunteer to read?

1. The big word theologians use to describe the ongoing process of becoming a new creation in Christ is _____. (**sanctification**)

   ❋ Why is becoming new in Christ an ongoing process, rather than a one-time event?

2. The key to effective Christian living is accepting the _____ _____ as an indwelling, ever-present help and comfort. (**Holy Spirit**)

   ❋ How do we access the power of the Holy Spirit in our lives?

3. Our calling as believers is to experience _____ lives. (**changed**)

   ❋ How can a life that has been transformed help others see Christ?

4. Jesus has a specific word of guidance for us: "Seek ye first the _____ of God." (**kingdom**)

   ❋ What does it mean to seek the kingdom?

5. The key to living each moment in Christ is seeking him in the _____ _____. (**little things**)

   ❋ Why might Jesus care about the details of our lives?

6. It is in daily interactions that we come to personally experience the common-sense _____ of God. (**presence**)

   ❋ In what ways can we interact with God?

PERSONAL APPLICATION

Ready to get a little bit more personal? Let's go ahead and break into small groups so that everyone has time to share their answers to the key questions. If time permits, feel free to move on to the supplemental questions.

KEY QUESTIONS:

- ❀ What does it mean to live a life full of grace?
- ❀ What are the characteristics of a person who is alive in Christ?

SUPPLEMENTAL QUESTIONS:

- ❀ How can a person be dependent on Jesus?

- ❀ Why is it important that Jesus was both fully God and fully human?

- ❀ What is the difference between being a servant and being a doormat?

LOOKING AHEAD

Can we really be halfway through the study? Next week, we'll tackle the idea of being fit for kingdom living. But let's introduce this week's Scripture first.

> We are God's workmanship, created in Christ Jesus to do good works, which God prepared in advance for us to do.
>
> —Eph. 2:10

Write the verse below:

_____

_____

_____

_____

_____

LEADER NOTES

Once again, take a few moments to review this week's meeting. How are the group members relating to one another?

Are you witnessing respect and encouragement? Are you modeling that yourself?

_____

_____

_____

_____

_____

_____

_____

_____

_____

_____

_____

_____

_____

_____

_____

_____

_____

_____

Week Four

FIT FOR KINGDOM LIVING

The full measure of Christ means that he comes to both free us and fit us for kingdom living. The key to this holy lifestyle is not "giving our sins to Jesus"; rather, it is giving ourselves to Jesus and allowing him to take our sins away. If you are to do "even greater things," you must remember that *you are more than you think you are, and that there are things that you can be and do, but will never be and do apart from Jesus Christ.* If we identify with Jesus and accept his indwelling Spirit, we can face any situation with our heads held high.

God really does want to give good gifts to us, and one of those gifts is to be in relationship with us. We can know the will of God for our lives through the Scriptures, through the wise counsel of godly people, and even through the Holy Spirit. But once we hear that direction, we must be obedient to it if we are to walk in the fullness of Christ.

SMALL-GROUP MEETING

So far, so good. No doubt God is using you to impact the life of each person in your small group. But what about you? How is he using them to impact you? Remember that each session should be as much about learning as it is teaching.

INTRODUCTION

Hello! Let's kick off this week's study of *Irresistible Invitation: Responding to the Extravagant Heart of God* with prayer. (*prayer*)

As usual, it's time to review last week's Scripture. Can anyone recite it from memory? Please take a moment to jot it down in the space provided in your workbook

The DVD message from Maxie Dunnam is ready to go, but here's something to think about before we watch it. Have you ever had something made specifically for you, something that fits exactly you and no one else? It seems like a decadent treat, but that's the way God "fits" us into our new lives with him. We are the only ones who can walk out all of the plans he has for us. Now, let's get to that DVD.

VIDEO SCRIPT

Hello again, and welcome to our weekly gathering. Personally, I hope this week has been overwhelming for each and every one of us—and I mean that in the best sense of the word! The idea that God loves us and offers his incredible love to us through Jesus in every moment of our entire life is over-whelming. Perhaps the psalmist put it best:

> When I consider your heavens,
> the work of your fingers,
> the moon and the stars which you have set in place,
> what is man that you are mindful of him,
> the son of man that you care for him? (Ps. 8:3–4)

When we begin to really *get it*, this idea of God's extravagant love, we can't help but be overwhelmed. It is life-changing news.

You know what I'm talking about. We've all had those moments—the birth or death of a loved one, perhaps an event on the local, national, or international level that knocked us down with its gravity. Such information alters our perception of ourselves and our relationship with the world around us. Whether we confronted deep pain in grief, or felt sheer delight in joy, we've all had to learn how to adapt and live into new realities.

It's the same way with spiritual growth. Those *aha!* moments when we hear a personal insight from God, receive a word of healing from a Christian friend, or sense the very presence of Jesus, need to be woven into the fabric of our daily lives.

So now that we've encountered the living God, the life and death of Christ, and pondered our resurrection into eternal life, how do we order our lives based on this understanding? How do we respond to the overwhelming *aha*, the marvelous realization that God invites us into a life of abiding in his extravagant love?

This is the greatest challenge of our Christian faith: what Christ has been and done for us, we must be and do for others. Can you say that with me? *What Christ has been and done for us, we must be and do for others.*

Okay, well that's it. Have a terrific week . . . No, wait! Before you stop the video because being Christ for others sounds impossible to pull off, let me explain. This is an impossible task. As individuals, we could never accomplish the work of Jesus.

Some people attempt to save the world all by themselves, and they end up all by themselves, exhausted, burned out, and resentful. You may have had such an experience in your own life. Have you ever set out enthusiastically to achieve some major goal, all the while knowing deep inside you were missing the energy essential for the task?

Friends, please find comfort in these words—you were absolutely correct. Each of us is missing the energy or power essential even for the smallest tasks when we set out on the path alone. But Jesus doesn't call us to do his work all by ourselves. The one who loves us does not set us up to fail—he's not that kind of leader!

Jesus' message for all eternity is that we are all invited to join him in his work. He invites us to step into the world at his leading, depending on his guidance and power at every turn, never losing sight of our purpose to serve him. He also equips us with tools to help us discern how we are to follow him. And he gives us power—his indwelling presence energizes us.

What are the tools for discovering how to be and do for others what Christ has been and done for us? In the daily readings, I have shared that there are three seeds we can plant in our daily lives that will produce the fruit of knowing God's will for us. They are Scripture study, Christian conferencing, and divine conviction brought by the Holy Spirit. Whether you've realized it or not, you have been using these tools of discernment thus far in our forty-day study.

By now, you have seen that setting aside time in your daily routine to study the Bible has enormous impact on your growth as a follower of Christ. There is a point at which reading God's Word becomes more like dialoguing with God. The heart opens to receive God's personal message for you within the words of Scripture.

My own experience has proven again and again that this special time with God reveals answers to the challenges I've wrestled with in my life. When I read and meditate on the Word of God, my understanding of who God is and how he works expands exponentially. Daily immersing myself in God's Word continues to shape my self, my life, and my work in a profound way.

Christian conferencing—fellowship—is another way to discover God's will. That is one of the reasons it is so important for you as a group to stay in conversation, not only during this study, but from this time forward. Jesus promised that when two or three gather in his name, he is present also. So be deliberate. Always have a few persons with whom you can share your life.

I especially encourage you to consider Christian conferencing when it is time to make important life decisions. I have often called on other believers for guidance, and I have been richly blessed as a result. Entrusting others to guide you through major decisions is a humbling task and requires no small amount of vulnerability, but the pay-off is great. Pray diligently and seek out trustworthy friends who will offer you wise counsel.

The most delightfully mystical method of discerning God's will is in hearing and following the inner guidance of the Holy Spirit. This might sound like the most difficult tool to use, but it may be the simplest of the three. The root of this simplicity lies in how we are made. Whether we're aware of it or not, we're all hard-wired to hear and understand God's inner guidance. Some people might hear a "still, small voice," while others experience it as an intuition or a knowing. Still others have heard an audible voice, like the story of Paul on the road to Damascus. However we experience inner guidance, if it is truly of the Holy Spirit, it will always lead us into joyful obedience of God's will.

Some of us may already be comfortable with the idea of knowing God's will for our lives, as a result of having had personal experiences in spiritual discernment. For others, this concept may be new. If it makes you uneasy, don't worry. God has promised to be alongside us on this path as we seek and struggle to know and follow him. He is present, and he will guide.

In committing to spend time reading, praying, and sharing in your group and at home, you are well on the way to claiming this transcendent reality for yourself. I invite you this week to consider trying one of these three forms of spiritual discernment as you discuss within your group.

Perhaps you will experience a fresh awareness of the Spirit of Truth moving among you as you join in fellowship together. I pray that you'll be overwhelmed—*did you get that?* overwhelmed—by the awareness of God's extravagant love for you, and accept his life-giving invitation anew.

POST-DVD DISCUSSION

Below are this week's fill-in-the-blank questions. Let's start by completing them, and then we'll move into deeper discussion of each one. Is there a volunteer who will read the first one out loud?

1. When we begin to fully understand God's extravagant love, we can't help but be _____. **(overwhelmed)**

    ❀ What could stand in the way of accepting such a great love?

2. The greatest challenge of the Christian faith is this: what Christ has been and done for us, we must _____ _____ _____ for others. **(be and do)**

    ❀ Why is it important for us to extend the reality of Jesus to others?

3. Jesus doesn't call us to do the work _____; instead, he invites us to join him. **(alone)**

    ❀ In what ways can we join Jesus in his work?

4. When we read and _____ on the Word of God, we expand our understanding of God and how he works. **(meditate)**

    ❀ Why is the Bible considered living and active?

5. Another way to discover God's will is through Christian conferencing, also known as _____. **(fellowship)**

    ❀ What does Jesus mean when he says that where two or three are gathered in his name, he will be there also?

6. Whether we're aware of it or not, we are all hard-wired to hear God's inner _____, through a "still, small voice," an intuition, or even an audible voice. **(guidance)**

❋ Why does God speak to different people in different ways?

PERSONAL APPLICATION

Remember, it's important that everyone has a chance to share. Let's divide into our small groups so we can talk a few things out. If time allows, move on to the supplemental questions.

KEY QUESTIONS:

❋ What does it mean to be free in Christ?

❋ Why do we, as a people, find it so hard to believe that God loves us as much as he does?

SUPPLEMENTAL QUESTIONS:

❋ Is the idea of being "crucified with Christ" uncomfortable or exciting to you? Why?

❋ Was there ever a time that you suffered that you knew God was with you? How did you know, and what effect did it have on the situation?

❋ What are the keys to an effective prayer life?

LOOKING AHEAD

Next up in our study of *Irresistible Invitation: Responding to the Extravagant Heart of God*, we'll consider the church as a home of grace. Let's bring this week to a close, however, with a new memory verse.

I tell you the truth, anyone who has faith in me will do what I have been doing. He will do even greater things than these, because I am going to the Father.

—John 14:12

Write the verse below:

_____

_____

_____

_____

_____

LEADER NOTES

In your weekly review, consider this: how are the members of the group doing with the Scripture memory verses? If participation is low, pray that each member would discover a deep love for the Word of God.

_____

_____

_____

_____

_____

_____

_____

_____

_____

_____

_____

_____

_____

Week Five

THE HOME OF GRACE

Remember the picture of the church as the dwelling place of wonder, as well as the home of grace. As the body of Christ, we must see through the eyes of Christ, speak with the voice of Christ, and heal with the hands of Christ. Then, and only then, will we be able to reach a dying world with the saving grace of the gospel. God planned for us to live in communities of grace where we pay attention to others and learn to trust people who aren't like us.

Authentic and strength-giving holiness does not begin with us. For holiness to be happy, it must be connected with the Holy Spirit. When the fellowship of the church comes alive by the presence of the Holy Spirit—inspiring and empowering people to care for one another—the congregation as a whole becomes the witness. When you look around your congregation, do you see evidence of each person being involved, and expecting the Holy Spirit to show up and help them with the tasks at hand? If not, what can you do to better help that happen?

SMALL-GROUP MEETING

As you've been praying for each member to develop a love of the Word of God, consider adding some extra encouragement this week in regard to the memory verse. If you desire, speak briefly about the importance of hiding the Word in our hearts so we can use it as a sword and claim its many promises for our own lives.

INTRODUCTION

Once again, welcome! We've got a lot to cover today, so let's go ahead and open in prayer. (*prayer*) Who's got the Scripture memory verse this week? Let's all write it down in the space provided in the workbook.

Now, before we get to Maxie Dunnam's DVD message, here's something worth some thought: the Bible teaches, in John 13:35, that others will know we are Christians by the love we have for each other. We're supposed to create such a wonderful community that others will want to be part of it. How good at that do you think we are?

With that in mind, let's move on to the DVD, and follow that up with some discussion.

VIDEO SCRIPT

Greetings friends. I trust you are well. In going over the material for this week's study, I realized I was beginning to tire a bit, and didn't have quite the zeal of the past weeks. So a pastoral word to you: as we enter the last weeks of our journey together, it's important to remember to take care of yourselves. Rest in the love of family and friends, and refresh yourselves with the knowledge that Jesus is our Shepherd, our Guide. Keep reading, keep working, keep talking with each other. Stay on the journey. It is in these weeks that the fruits of your commitment will reveal themselves.

In our study this week we've learned how the church is called to be "the home of grace." Doesn't that sound like a cozy, wonderful place to be? I'm sure you have your own mental image of what your "home of grace" might look like. When I imagine this phrase, I picture a flickering fire within a quaint hearth. The fire lights up a room furnished with soft chairs and stocked with good books—a place where I could retire after dinner, relax, and renew after a hard day's work.

Ideally, the church should be a home of grace that emanates the warmth and love of Jesus, welcoming all who seek peace.

Well, friends, I have some good news and bad news. While we are all invited to make ourselves at home in the presence of God, sometimes the church—our "home of grace"—isn't the most comfortable or welcoming place to be.

I'm not talking about the facility or décor—the church is more than bricks and mortar. The most elaborate buildings can be as cold as ice without God's Spirit alive in the congregation.

The home of grace to which Jesus invites us is framed with the vitality of relationships and cemented with the outpouring of love from one heart to another, as John Wesley so beautifully described, "one loving heart setting another on fire."

Serving others and living in continual openness to divine guidance can not be contained in a building, and is more than any institution. Yet within our church home, each of us is called to live out God's will for our lives by giving of ourselves—our gifts and service—to be for others what Jesus is for us. Put another way, the call is this: what Christ has been and done for us, we must be and do for others.

Sometimes that call to offer grace and love to others can make us very uncomfortable. Has that ever happened to you? It has happened to me more than once.

Imagine this scene from the Gospel of Luke. Jesus is dining at the home of a Pharisee, and the table is spread with an attractive array of dishes. Everything is prim and proper, and people are using their best manners, until a woman breaks in upon the meal. She doesn't exactly fit in with the dinner guests—she is a social outcast, a prostitute whose sins, unlike those of the dinner guests, are well known. She bursts in the room and kneels at the feet of Jesus. Her tears rain down on him, covering his feet, because of the love and kindness he has shown toward her. Then she opens an expensive alabaster jar of oil and pours it over Jesus' feet, drying them with her hair.

My wife and I have hosted some interesting dinner parties with some distinguished guests, but nothing remotely like that has ever happened. In that situation, it's easy to imagine myself responding just like the Pharisee Simon in the story, reprimanding Jesus, saying, "Do you have any idea who's touching you? If you knew this woman, you wouldn't let her come near you!"

The uncomfortable fact is that we are all happiest in our comfort zones, and we like it when others stay in their zone—comfortable or not. There are certain unwritten rules we expect everyone to abide by, and we all feel uneasy when someone crosses a social boundary. We design our lives for our own comfort and pleasure, filling our homes with things we desire, and arming our spiritual security systems against undesirable intruders.

How far we've evolved, huh? Jesus encountered this kind of conflict everywhere he went. As the Son of God, he empowered the outcasts of society to turn from their wickedness and follow him, often right into the homes of society's elite. He invited people out of their comfort zones with his compelling, magnetic presence, and their choice to accept or refuse his invitation has become the stuff of Biblical history.

This is exactly the kind of discomfort we are called to experience as Christ's body in the world. In order to be a true church, the home of grace, we are not allowed to stay safe and secure behind our walls. To remain vital, we must venture out into new territory, crossing boundaries, and yes, taking risks on behalf of the gospel. As agents for Christ in the world, we must move beyond coffee hour, making casseroles, and the afterthought of writing thank-you notes.

This can be a frightening prospect if we've never tried it. Being called to share with others who might be different from us, to love them, and serve them in the name of Christ might, and I would suggest most certainly will, upset our usual routine. So be prepared. We'll have to give up our same-old habits in order to step out and risk serving not as we choose, but as Christ calls us.

There's yet another kind of discomfort we will need to become familiar with: it's called *conviction*. What that means is that the Holy Spirit often creates a kind of spiritual discomfort within us as a way of directing us to notice something important. It is the Spirit's way of getting our attention and calling us to action.

I've been there, and whether or not you've realized it at the time, so have you. It's that feeling in your gut telling you to speak up, tell the truth, act with love, or share with someone, when it would be much easier to let the moment pass. At the same time, in one part of our mind is the voice of reason, directing us to ignore that inner leading. Don't listen to it!

We can rationalize ignoring the voice of God, but the truth is we miss so many opportunities to bless others and be blessed in return when we move through our days on autopilot.

As we grow more comfortable listening for God's guidance, we begin to welcome that sense of holy discomfort. When we feel deeply convicted and risk acting on our conviction, we experience a peace and freedom that truly "passes understanding."

We all know that our faith is built on paradox. The paradox in risking obedience to God's guidance is this: when we take a leap of faith for Christ, he always meets us in midair. Whatever our situation, Jesus offers his infinite supply of grace so that we may have the strength to do his work. We find comfort, healing, and love in his presence as we reach out to the hurting world.

So as you share within your group today, look deep inside yourself and pay attention to any feelings of discomfort. God may be leading you to share something personal, speak to a certain person, or do something that might seem trivial, but will leave beautiful ripples in the world.

If you will begin to follow those special leadings, you'll be inviting God to be present in your time together. Then you will truly experience what it feels like to reside in the dwelling place of wonder, the home of grace, the body of Christ.

POST-DVD DISCUSSION

Let's fill in the blanks first, then take a closer look at each concept. Who is ready to read the first one out loud?

1. As the Son of God, Jesus invited people out of their _____ _____ with his compelling, magnetic presence. **(comfort zones)**

   ❀ Why was it important for Jesus to draw people out of their everyday experiences?

2. In order to be a home of grace, the church must cross _____ and take _____ on behalf of the gospel. **(boundaries/risks)**

   ❀ What boundaries could potentially hold back a church?

3. Sharing, loving, and serving others might upset our usual _____. **(routine)**

   ❀ In what ways can we make ourselves more available to be used by God?

4. Sometimes the Holy Spirit causes discomfort within us through _____. **(conviction)**

   ❀ What is the purpose of God's conviction in our lives?

5. When we ignore the voice of God, we miss opportunities to _____ others and be _____ in return. **(bless/blessed)**

   ❀ How might God instruct us to be involved in the lives of others?

6. When we take a leap of faith for Christ, he always meets us in the midst of our situation and offers his infinite supply of _____. **(grace)**

❋ Why is it important for us to take the leap before
   God will meet us there?

PERSONAL APPLICATION

I hope that, by now, this time of breaking into small groups
has become a richly rewarding part of *Irresistible Invitation:
Responding to the Extravagant Heart of God*. Ready to get to it this
week? Remember to make sure each person has a chance to
share before moving on to the supplemental questions.

KEY QUESTIONS:

❋ What do you think comes to mind when the average
   person in today's society hears the word "Christian"? Is it
   different than what the Scripture expects, and if so, how
   and why?
❋ How could a church that fully understands and lives out its
   role impact its members, its community, and its world?

SUPPLEMENTAL QUESTIONS:

❋ Why is it important to have a faith that's both public and
   private?
❋ What is the difference between the church as an institution and the church as an organism?
❋ What is the role of the Holy Spirit in a church that is alive?

LOOKING AHEAD

Next week, the final week of our study, we'll consider what it
means to be partners in the gospel. First, though, let's introduce
another Scripture to help us hold this week's lessons in our heart.

Dear friends, let us love one another, for love comes from God.

—1 John 4:7

Write the verse below:

_____

_____

_____

_____

_____

LEADER NOTES

Take a moment to thank God for all that he has done so far through *Irresistible Invitation: Responding to the Extravagant Heart of God.* The study isn't over yet, but it soon will be. Ask God to continue working in each member's heart, even after the study is complete.

_____

_____

_____

_____

_____

_____

_____

_____

_____

_____

_____

_____

PARTNERS IN THE GOSPEL

Joining a church often involves taking a vow to uphold the church in areas like prayers, presence, gifts, and service. Willing hands to serve and loving hearts to love—that's what it means to be partakers of grace and partners in the gospel.

Praying for others will bring us to love them. Loving them will lead us to serve them. Serving them will be the open door through which God can move in to save, heal, and make whole.

Worship allows us to connect with the One who made us. As we pay attention to God, we may be drawn out of ourselves into a living relationship with God from which we can never return.

The discipline of generosity—the actual giving of money—is essential for spiritual growth. Tithing is the biblical pattern established for practicing generosity in the use of our money. Returning to God a portion of that with which God has blessed us must be at the heart of our understanding of the tithe.

When we serve others because we are servants of Christ, our lives become spontaneous expressions of the cross. We all need to give—and receive—acts of kind service.

The invitation at the close of this study is to receive the extravagant love of God—an invitation that, when considered fully, is well nigh irresistible. If we respond to that invitation, we begin to live our lives in Christ, with the exhilarating possibility that we can one day say with Paul, "I no longer live, but Christ lives in me" (Gal. 2:20). Are you ready to turn the page?

SMALL-GROUP MEETING

Well done, good and faithful servant! There may have been a bumpy spot or two, but you've made it through. At this point, pray that God would use this week's meeting as a jumping-off point for an even deeper walk with God. If your church is holding some sort of commitment Sunday in conjunction with the study, strongly encourage your small-group members to take part.

INTRODUCTION

We have arrived at the final week of our study of *Irresistible Invitation: Responding to the Extravagant Heart of God.* I hope, however, that we'll treat this as a beginning rather than an ending as we step through the next door God has for us. Shall we open in prayer? (*prayer*) Now, who can recite the memory verse for us this week? Let's all write it down on the space provided in the workbook.

As we prepare to watch the final DVD message from Maxie Dunnam, consider this: without each instrument playing its part, there is no symphony. The conductor can't make music all alone. So why do so many of us expect the pastor to play all the parts in the music of the church? Could it be that it really is up to each one of us, individually? Let's hear what Maxie has to say.

VIDEO SCRIPT

Welcome back, friends. It is not without some sadness that I greet you today, since this is my last time with you. That is, maybe the last time before we gather for worship around God's throne in God's heavenly kingdom. At this last gathering of our study on God's extravagant love, it seems like a good time to gather close with respect and love for one another.

I want to talk with you in this sacred moment about making pancakes. That might sound strange, I know. Yet you'd be amazed at all the places where we encounter the living God if we only open our eyes.

Brother Lawrence is one of the saints with whom I've kept company through the years. He lived in Paris in the seventeenth century. One day, before he became a monk, he experienced a moment of insight into God's extravagant love while looking at a barren tree in winter. This simple yet extraordinary revelation led him to join a monastery, where he lived a quiet, humble life for the balance of his eighty years.

After he died, some of his brothers discovered a manuscript that contained his thoughts about God. Today, his writings are known as the very helpful book, *The Practice of the Presence of God.*

One of Brother Lawrence's responsibilities within the monastic community was cooking. You can imagine an assembly of hungry monks just finishing a fast—an inspired chef would have been essential around the monastery. Now, some of you may grumble about mundane chores like cooking, especially when it's Thursday night and you're deep into leftovers, but not Brother Lawrence. Listen to what he had to say about making pancakes:

> Nor is it needful that we should have great things to do. . . . We can do little things for God; I turn the cake that is frying on the pan for love of Him, and that done, if there is nothing else to call me, I prostrate myself in worship before Him, who has given me grace to work; afterwards I rise happier than a king. It is enough for me to pick up but a straw from the ground for the love of God.

It's too easy to fall into the trap of thinking that, if we've had a life-changing encounter with God, our circumstances will also change dramatically. Sometimes, however, God gives us the beautiful transformation Brother Lawrence experienced—love in the kitchen, grace over pancakes. Our circumstances don't change—*we do.*

For Lawrence, practicing the presence of God was a reality that infused his every breath. He didn't need to travel to exotic places or meet powerful people to know his Savior: he simply sought to fix his thoughts and his feelings on the presence of Christ in the small things. Washing dishes or scrubbing floors, Brother Lawrence approached every task as an act of selfless worship before a loving God. That worship bridged the gap between man on the ground and the sovereign Creator of the universe.

You could say that this study has been designed to help build bridges for each of us. Not the kind of bridges we drive across, but the mental, emotional, and spiritual bridges between God's infinite love for us, and our individual existence.

My hope is that each one of you has rediscovered the extravagant love of God during our time in this devotional study. Although it may seem like the end of something, dear friends, believe me, it is truly the beginning.

Now I want to invite you to come with me. Let's take that extravagant love one step further. Let us respond to God's invitation like Brother Lawrence, putting our understanding of God's love into practice. It's easy to know something on an intellectual level, but if we don't practice it, it becomes meaningless.

Consider running a marathon, for example. I admire and respect people who have the strength, the will, and the discipline to even attempt such a race. The amount of endurance and stamina required is incredible. For those of us who've never jogged a mile, we can read books about marathons, watch videos about marathons, even attend a race and cheer on the runners. But we'll never really know what it feels like to train for many weeks until, on race day, we lace up our shoes, pin a number on our shirt, and cross the finish line to our personal best. We can know all about marathons, and yet never experience one if we don't make a decision to put our knowledge into practice.

The irresistible invitation to enter God's kingdom is also all about practice and action. We can choose to stand on the sidelines, watching others love and serve in the name of Christ, or we can step up, open the door, and enter into a new kind of life with God.

We've all been invited to join with Jesus, who shares with complete selflessness the infinite supply of love and grace from the Father. And, to fulfill that love, we have to do our part. If we don't speak up and accept his invitation, then we'll never know what it's like to truly experience his presence on a personal level.

I hope you are already reaping the fruits of a new discipline as a result of our time together. I pray you are enjoying the sweet fellowship of Christian hearts and leaning into God as you decide how to live each day. My prayer is also that you have been able to connect your faith in God with each moment of your life so that you can say, like Brother Lawrence:

> This King, full of mercy and goodness, very far from chastising me, embraces me with love, makes me eat at His table, serves me with His own hands, gives me the key of His treasures; He converses and delights Himself with me incessantly, in a thousand and a thousand ways, and treats me in all respects as His loved one.

Now it is time to move onward together in a new understanding of what it is to live as disciples of Christ and agents of God's love in this world. You have read, prayed, and shared about growing into the fullness of God's extravagant love. You are ready to open the door to a new way of life. Remember the road we've traveled. We have explored:

- Opening ourselves to God in an ongoing conversation called prayer;

* Studying and reflecting on God's Word in the Scriptures;

* Focusing on Jesus' Resurrection as our hope and purpose in life;

* Allowing the Holy Spirit to take up residence in our hearts;

* Following God's guidance in our daily decisions;

* Experiencing relationship with God and his people in communities of grace; and

* Becoming a partner in God's work in the world by giving ourselves to others in the name of Jesus.

It has been my honor and privilege to accompany you on this wonderful journey into the heart of our faith. Now the opportunity to become a partner in the gospel is yours. Will you live out your life in holy recklessness from this day forward? I'm counting on it—but more important, Christ is counting on it.

I look forward to hearing great things about the work that you are doing in the love of God, the grace of Jesus Christ, and the fellowship of the Holy Spirit. May God bless you so that you are able to bless others.

POST-DVD DISCUSSION

Once again, let's fill in the blanks for each statement, then dive in for further study. Who will volunteer to read today?

1. This study was designed to help build mental, emotional, and spiritual _____ between the God who loves us and our daily experience. **(bridges)**

    * How can a better relationship with God lead to better relationships with those around us?

2. It's easy to know something on an intellectual level, but if we don't practice it, it becomes _____. **(meaningless)**

❋ What is the difference between knowing something in the mind and knowing it through experience?

3. The irresistible invitation to enter God's kingdom is about _____ and _____. (**practice/action**)

    ❋ How do we, as Christians, continue to practice our faith?

4. We have to _____ our _____; if we don't speak up and accept God's invitation, then we'll never know what it's like to truly experience him and his presence on a personal level. (**do/part**)

    ❋ What are the responsibilities of being a Christian?

5. Now that we've read, prayed, and shared about growing into the fullness of _____ _____ _____, it's time to open the door to a new way of life. (**God's extravagant love**)

    ❋ How can we show others what's different about God's love?

6. Will we live our lives in holy _____ from this day forward? (**recklessness**)

    ❋ How could the church's witness to the world be different if Christians walked in wholehearted devotion to God?

PERSONAL APPLICATION

Next, it's time for our personal application. Let's break into our small groups and dig a little deeper. Don't forget: each person should have a chance to share their answers to the key questions before the group moves on to the supplemental ones.

KEY QUESTIONS:

❋ How can service to others translate to freedom for ourselves?

� Why does God talk more about money than any other
subject in the Bible?

SUPPLEMENTAL QUESTIONS:

� Do you believe there are things that will not happen if we
do not pray? Why or why not?

� Why does God want us to pray?

� What are some of the challenges we face in being Christ to
others, and how can they be overcome?

LOOKING AHEAD

Here's a promise from Scripture to encourage you as you
complete this journey. Let's commit it to memory now.

> He who began a good work in you will carry it on to completion
> until the day of Christ Jesus.
>
> —Phil. 1:6

Write the verse below:

_____

_____

_____

_____

_____

As we bring the study of *Irresistible Invitation: Responding to the
Extravagant Heart of God* to a close, let's review the memory verses
from each section. Keep these Scriptures close, and as you move
into the next phase of your relationship with God, use them to
help recall all you have learned in the past six weeks.

Blessings to you!

LEADER NOTES

Congratulations for making it through! Once again, thank God for his faithfulness to you over the last six weeks. How was the experience different than you expected? In what ways do you think God could use you next?

APPENDIX
FILL-IN-THE-BLANK ANSWER KEY

WEEK 1
1. trust
2. pray
3. God's blessing
4. Passionately seeking God
5. good
6. loves me/miracle

WEEK 2
1. cross
2. sins
3. past
4. shepherd
5. relationship/voice
6. pasture

WEEK 3
1. sanctification
2. Holy Spirit
3. changed
4. kingdom
5. little things
6. presence

WEEK 4
1. overwhelmed
2. be and do
3. alone
4. meditate
5. fellowship
6. guidance

WEEK 5
1. comfort zones
2. boundaries/risks
3. routine
4. conviction
5. bless/blessed
6. grace

WEEK 6
1. bridges
2. meaningless
3. practice/action
4. do/part
5. God's extravagant love
6. recklessness

IRRESISTIBLE
Invitation

RESPONDING TO THE
EXTRAVAGANT HEART OF GOD

PARTICIPANT'S WORKBOOK

IRRESISTIBLE INVITATION
RESPONDING TO THE EXTRAVAGANT HEART OF GOD
PARTICIPANT'S WORKBOOK

Copyright 2008 by Abingdon Press

All rights reserved.

This book is printed on acid-free, elemental-chlorine–free paper.

Original art, cover, and page design by Joey McNair

Participant's Workbook
ISBN: 978-0-687-64869-6

Unless otherwise noted, Scripture quotations are taken from HOLY BIBLE, NEW INTERNATIONAL VERSION®. Copyright © 1973, 1978, 1984 by International Bible Society. Used by permission of Zondervan Publishing House.

Scripture quotations from *The Message* Copyright © by Eugene H. Peterson 1993, 1994, 1995, 1996, 2000, 2001, 2002. Used by permission of NavPress Publishing Group.

08 09 10 11 12 13 14 15 16 17   10 9 8 7 6 5 4 3 2 1

MANUFACTURED IN THE UNITED STATES OF AMERICA

CONTENTS

INTRODUCTION

J ust picture it: a big, beautiful house on a hill. It's different than the rest in the neighborhood somehow, with beautiful gardens, spacious rooms, and all that you could possibly want—but more than you probably think you could ever afford.

Maybe you've heard about the gatherings that go on there, joyful occasions that draw people from far and wide. Maybe you've heard how guests were treated like kings and queens, and even though you'd been invited yourself, you never thought you'd fit in, so you didn't go.

Well, friend, another invitation has just arrived. How will you respond?

What that "house" represents is the fullness of relationship with God. It's not just about accepting him as your Lord and Savior. That's just the start. It's about the richness of a life lived with abundant grace, love, and communication with the very One who made you.

From the outside looking in, that house may appear too good to be true. But once you step inside, you'll discover an amazing truth: it feels just like home. This is, after all, the place you were made for, a daily existence that goes beyond just "getting by." It is a place of acceptance, of purpose, and of fulfillment—and the door is standing wide open.

Over the next six weeks, we'll be approaching that door together. Through questions, discussion, Scripture, and personal application, you'll have the opportunity to discover new truths about God and his extended hand toward you. It doesn't matter whether you're brand new at all this or you've been walking with the Lord a while;

there's always more to know. Keep in mind, though, that you'll get out of it what you put into it. If you're willing to wholeheartedly commit to prayer, study, and conversations with others about what you're learning, there's no telling the depths of transformation God can bring to your life.

STUDY FORMAT

This workbook is designed to be used in tandem with *Irresistible Invitation: Responding to the Extravagant Heart of God* by Maxie Dunnam. That text is grouped into six parts, with forty days' worth of personal readings and introspective questions. It is hoped that as you read through the book and work on the study, you'll take these questions seriously, reaching into the very corners of your heart with thoughtful consideration and prayer, asking God for his revelation and guidance.

If you'd like to take notes on what you discover along the way, you'll find journal pages at the beginning of each part of this workbook. These Insight/Application sections are to help you reflect on what you read and what God is revealing to you through this study. They are for your private observations; what you write down won't be shared with your small group.

This workbook is designed to be the compass for making sure you get everything out of each week's study that you possibly can. Keep it handy while you read the daily book chapters, bring it with you when you attend your weekly small-group session, and expect God to move as he ties it all together.

Here's how the six weeks will unfold. You will begin each small-group gathering with a short DVD message from Maxie Dunnam. Then you'll go over the main points of that week's chapter using a fill-in-the-blank format to initiate some preliminary discussion.

Dividing into smaller groups or pairs will then give you the opportunity to share on a more personal level. At the close of each meeting, we'll look at Scripture that will help us remember what we've learned.

During our six-week study, you'll notice that other activities in the church body will tie into the weekly subjects as well. That's because we are all in this together. No matter where we are in our walk with God, there's always more to learn, share, and receive.

Week One

COMING HOME TO GOD

INSIGHT

Use the space on these pages to record your personal reflections, thoughts, observations, or revelations that you discover while reading *Irresistible Invitation: Responding to the Extravagant Heart of God.*

APPLICATION

After recording your insight, consider how you might make positive changes in your life or way of thinking in response to what you have read.

This discipline will assist you in remembering and possibly sharing with your group or class some of the reflections that come to you during this forty-day journey.

DAY 1: INCANDESCENT AMAZEMENT

INSIGHT _____

_____

_____

_____

_____

APPLICATION _____

_____

_____

_____

_____

DAY 2: GOD'S CREATION IS GOOD

INSIGHT _____

_____

_____

_____

_____

APPLICATION _____

_____

_____

_____

_____

DAY 3: A GRACIOUS GOD

INSIGHT _____

_____

_____

_____

_____

APPLICATION _____

_____

_____

_____

_____

DAY 4: THE PICTURE OF GOD

INSIGHT _____

_____

_____

_____

_____

APPLICATION _____

_____

_____

_____

_____

DAY 5: COMING HOME

INSIGHT _____

_____

_____

_____

_____

APPLICATION _____

_____

_____

_____

_____

DAY 6: A ROADMAP FOR THE JOURNEY

INSIGHT _____

_____

_____

_____

_____

APPLICATION _____

_____

_____

_____

_____

DAY 7: TAKING IT ALL IN

INSIGHT _____

_____

_____

_____

_____

APPLICATION _____

_____

_____

_____

_____

SMALL-GROUP MEETING

INTRODUCTION

Welcome—we're glad you're here. A place has been prepared just for you. Today marks a special occasion as we begin our group study of *Irresistible Invitation: Responding to the Extravagant Heart of God.* Your group leader will begin with a word of prayer, then we'll turn to this workbook's introduction and study format.

Ready to dig a little deeper? Let's watch a brief DVD message by Maxie Dunnam, author of the book.

POST-DVD DISCUSSION

We'll open our discussion time today with a few questions and statements from the DVD. Let's begin by filling in the blank for each statement, then we'll look a little closer at each concept.

1. For this small group to be effective, it must become a place where deepest truths can be shared with security and _____.

    ❋ Why is it important that what is shared within this group stay within this group?

2. As we go through this study together, it's important that we regularly _____ for one another.

    ❋ How can lifting other group members up to God make this study more meaningful for all?

3. Deeply rooted misconceptions of God (such as thinking of God as an angry judge or score-keeper) can prevent us from experiencing the full measure of _____ _____ in our everyday lives.

   ❋ Where do misconceptions of God come from?

4. _____ _____ _____ is the best direction any of us can take.

   ❋ Why is it important for us to seek God, rather than just waiting for him to find us?

5. Above all, we must remember that God is _____; he is for us, not against us.

   ❋ How could a deep understanding of this truth affect a person's walk with God?

6. We must embrace this powerful understanding: God _____ _____. I am a unique, unrepeatable _____ of God.

   ❋ Where will this understanding take you?

PERSONAL APPLICATION

One of the most important parts of this small-group study is the opportunity for personal application. To make sure everyone has time to participate and respond, we'll break into small groups. Begin with the key discussion questions about this week's readings, and if there's still time after each person has had time to share, move on to the supplemental questions.

KEY QUESTIONS:

❀ What foundational ideas do you have about God? What life experiences or teachings have led to that belief?

❀ What things could stand in the way of a deeper relationship with God?

SUPPLEMENTAL QUESTIONS:

❀ Have you ever been amazed by God? How so?

❀ How could regular study of the Bible affect a person's relationship with God?

❀ What do you hope to get out of this study?

LOOKING AHEAD

During the next week, we'll take a closer look at the life of Jesus and what impact it has on our own lives. In the meantime, however, commit to memory the following verse so that what we've learned this week won't be forgotten.

I have come that they may have life, and have it to the full.

—John 10:10

Write the verse below:

_____

_____

_____

_____

_____

Week Two

A LOVE LIKE NO OTHER

DAY 8: THE HINT HALF GUESSED

INSIGHT _____

_____

_____

_____

_____

APPLICATION _____

_____

_____

_____

_____

DAY 9: WHY WE STILL PREACH THE CROSS

INSIGHT _____

_____

_____

_____

_____

APPLICATION _____

_____

_____

_____

_____

DAY 10: HE COMES AS HE CAME

INSIGHT _____

_____

_____

_____

_____

APPLICATION _____

_____

_____

_____

_____

DAY 11: A LOVE LIKE NO OTHER

INSIGHT _____

_____

_____

_____

_____

APPLICATION _____

_____

_____

_____

_____

DAY 12: THE STONE WAS ROLLED AWAY

INSIGHT _____

_____

_____

_____

_____

APPLICATION _____

_____

_____

_____

_____

DAY 13: THE GOSPEL BY WHICH
WE ARE SAVED

INSIGHT _____

_____

_____

_____

_____

APPLICATION _____

_____

_____

_____

_____

Day 14: To Live in Joy

Insight _____

_____

_____

_____

_____

Application _____

_____

_____

_____

_____

SMALL-GROUP MEETING

INTRODUCTION

Hello and welcome! After your group opens in prayer, take a moment to write last week's Scripture verse on the lines below:

_____

_____

_____

_____

As we begin our second small-group meeting for *Irresistible Invitation: Responding to the Extravagant Heart of God,* here's something to ponder: how is Jesus portrayed in movies and on TV, and how is that different than what the Bible teaches? Does Jesus represent weakness or strength? Futility or hope? Compassion or judgmentalism? How we understand Christ will have a definite impact on our level of relationship with God.

With that in mind, let's continue with a brief DVD message by Maxie Dunnam, followed by a few questions.

POST-DVD DISCUSSION

Begin by filling in the blanks for each statement, then we'll look further at each concept.

1. If we are to truly know God and experience the joy of the kingdom, we must enter through the

    _____.

    ❈ What does it mean to share in the death and Resurrection of Christ?

2. When God gives us new life, all of our
_____ are forgiven.

   ❁ Why is it important for our wrongs to be
   confessed and forgiven?

3. God is able to close the door to my _____.

   ❁ What does it mean to let go of the past?

4. Jesus is often presented as the _____,
   caring tenderly for his sheep.

   ❁ What might be some characteristics of a
   good shepherd, and how might those
   apply to God?

5. The sheep follow the shepherd because they
   have a _____ with him; they
   recognize his _____.

   ❁ What's the difference between knowing
   God and knowing *about* him?

6. Just like the shepherd offers the sheep
   _____, Jesus offers his followers
   a place of provision, security, and rest.

   ❁ In what ways does God provide security
   or rest?

PERSONAL APPLICATION

Now it's time to break into small groups for discussion. Remember that each person should have a chance to participate and respond to the key questions first, and if time allows, the group can move on to the supplemental ones.

KEY QUESTIONS:

❊ Why was the death of Jesus necessary?

❊ What happens if we leave Jesus on the cross without considering his Resurrection?

SUPPLEMENTAL QUESTIONS:

❊ What does it mean to find yourself "not guilty," and how could an understanding of that truth affect your choices in life?

❊ What is the difference between optimism and hope?

❊ Is there anyone here who has not yet accepted Jesus as Lord and Savior, but would like to? (If so, please make the small group or Bible study leader aware.)

LOOKING AHEAD

Next week, we're going to dive into the concept of being alive in Christ. Before we do that, however, let's learn another Scripture verse to remind us of this week's riches.

> For it is by grace you have been saved, through faith—and this not from yourselves, it is the gift of God.
>
> —Eph. 2:8

Write the verse below:

_____

_____

_____

_____

_____

Week Three

ALIVE IN CHRIST

DAY 15: THE ESSENCE OF THE GOSPEL

INSIGHT _____

_____

_____

_____

_____

APPLICATION _____

_____

_____

_____

_____

DAY 16: ALIVE IN CHRIST

INSIGHT _____

_____

_____

_____

_____

APPLICATION _____

_____

_____

_____

_____

DAY 17: CONSTANTLY ABIDING

INSIGHT _____

_____

_____

_____

_____

APPLICATION _____

_____

_____

_____

_____

DAY 18: HUMBLE AND AVAILABLE

INSIGHT _____

_____

_____

_____

_____

APPLICATION _____

_____

_____

_____

_____

DAY 19: THE SHAPING POWER OF THE INDWELLING CHRIST

INSIGHT _____

_____

_____

_____

_____

APPLICATION _____

_____

_____

_____

_____

DAY 20: WHAT CHRIST HAS BEEN AND DONE FOR US

INSIGHT _____

_____

_____

_____

_____

APPLICATION _____

_____

_____

_____

_____

DAY 21: DYING AND RISING WITH CHRIST

INSIGHT _____

_____

_____

_____

_____

APPLICATION _____

_____

_____

_____

_____

SMALL-GROUP MEETING

INTRODUCTION

Welcome, welcome! Here we are at week three of *Irresistible Invitation: Responding to the Extravagant Heart of God.* After we open in prayer, let's recall last week's memory verse. Please take a moment to write it here:

_____

_____

_____

_____

Before we watch the DVD message from Maxie Dunnam, think of a very dark place and consider how much light a single candle can provide there. We can be that candle. No matter how dark things seem around us, the light that Christ puts in our hearts when we become fully alive in him can affect others far and wide. Let's watch together, then discuss the main themes.

POST-DVD DISCUSSION

As usual, we'll begin by filling in the blanks. Then we'll take it to the next step with some discussion.

1. The big word theologians use to describe the ongoing process of becoming a new creation in Christ is _____.

    ❋ Why is becoming new in Christ an ongoing process, rather than a one-time event?

2. The key to effective Christian living is accepting the _____ _____ as an indwelling, ever-present help and comfort.

�֍ How do we access the power of the Holy Spirit in our lives?

3. Our calling as believers is to experience _____ lives.

✖ How can a life that has been transformed help others see Christ?

4. Jesus has a specific word of guidance for us: "Seek ye first the _____ of God."

✖ What does it mean to seek the kingdom?

5. The key to living each moment in Christ is seeking him in the _____ _____.

✖ Why might Jesus care about the details of our lives?

6. It is in daily interactions that we come to personally experience the common-sense _____ of God.

✖ In what ways can we interact with God?

PERSONAL APPLICATION

Ready to get a little bit more personal? Let's go ahead and break into small groups so that everyone has time to share their answers to the key questions. If time permits, feel free to move on to the supplemental questions.

KEY QUESTIONS:

✖ What does it mean to live a life full of grace?

❋ What are the characteristics of a person who is alive in Christ?

SUPPLEMENTAL QUESTIONS:

❋ How can a person be dependent on Jesus?

❋ Why is it important that Jesus was both fully God and fully human?

❋ What is the difference between being a servant and being a doormat?

LOOKING AHEAD

Can we really be halfway through the study? Next week, we'll tackle the idea of being fit for kingdom living. But let's introduce this week's Scripture first.

We are God's workmanship, created in Christ Jesus to do good works, which God prepared in advance for us to do.

—Eph. 2:10

Write the verse below:

_____

_____

_____

_____

_____

Week Four

FIT FOR KINGDOM LIVING

DAY 22: CHRIST FREES US AND FITS US

INSIGHT _____

_____

_____

_____

_____

APPLICATION _____

_____

_____

_____

_____

DAY 23: CLAIMING THE PROMISE

INSIGHT _____

_____

_____

_____

_____

APPLICATION _____

_____

_____

_____

DAY 24: THE SUREST PATH OF ALL

INSIGHT _____

_____

_____

_____

_____

APPLICATION _____

_____

_____

_____

_____

DAY 25: THE HANDS AND FEET OF JESUS

INSIGHT _____

_____

_____

_____

_____

APPLICATION _____

_____

_____

_____

_____

DAY 26: COMMUNION THROUGH CONVERSATION

INSIGHT _____

_____

_____

_____

_____

APPLICATION _____

_____

_____

_____

_____

DAY 27: PLANTED BY THE WATER

INSIGHT _____

_____

_____

_____

_____

APPLICATION _____

_____

_____

_____

_____

Day 28: Choosing to Be Whole

Insight _____

_____

_____

_____

_____

Application _____

_____

_____

_____

_____

SMALL-GROUP MEETING

INTRODUCTION

Let's begin this week's study of *Irresistible Invitation: Responding to the Extravagant Heart of God* with prayer.

As usual, it's time to review last week's Scripture. Have you memorized it? Take a moment to jot it down.

_____

_____

_____

_____

Here's something to think about before we watch the DVD message from Maxie Dunnam. Have you ever had something made specifically for you, something that fits exactly you and no one else? It seems like a decadent treat, but that's the way God "fits" us into our new lives with him. We are the only ones who can walk out all of the plans he has for us.

POST-DVD DISCUSSION

Let's begin by completing the questions below, then we'll move into deeper discussion of each one.

1. When we begin to fully understand God's extravagant love, we can't help but be _____.

    ❋ What could stand in the way of accepting such a great love?

2. The greatest challenge of the Christian faith is this: what Christ has been and done for us, we must _____ _____ _____ for others.

✻ Why is it important for us to extend the reality of Jesus to others?

3. Jesus doesn't call us to do the work _____; instead, he invites us to join him.

    ✻ In what ways can we join Jesus in his work?

4. When we read and _____ on the Word of God, we expand our understanding of God and how he works.

    ✻ Why is the Bible considered living and active?

5. Another way to discover God's will is through Christian conferencing, also known as _____.

    ✻ What does Jesus mean when he says that where two or three are gathered in his name, he will be there also?

6. Whether we're aware of it or not, we are all hard-wired to hear God's inner _____, through a "still, small voice," an intuition, or even an audible voice.

    ✻ Why does God speak to different people in different ways?

PERSONAL APPLICATION

Remember, it's important that everyone has the opportunity to share thoughts and ideas. Let's divide into our small groups so we can talk a few things out. If time allows, move on to the supplemental questions.

KEY QUESTIONS:

❁ What does it mean to be free in Christ?

❁ Why do we, as a people, find it so hard to believe that God loves us as much as he does?

SUPPLEMENTAL QUESTIONS:

❁ Is the idea of being "crucified with Christ" uncomfortable or exciting to you? Why?

❁ Was there ever a time that you suffered that you knew God was with you? How did you know, and what effect did it have on the situation?

❁ What are the keys to an effective prayer life?

LOOKING AHEAD

Next up in our study of *Irresistible Invitation: Responding to the Extravagant Heart of God*, we'll consider the church as a home of grace. Let's bring this week to a close, however, with a new memory verse.

I tell you the truth, anyone who has faith in me will do what I have been doing. He will do even greater things than these, because I am going to the Father.

—John 14:12

Write the verse below:

_____

_____

_____

_____

_____

Week Five

THE HOME OF GRACE

DAY 29: THE DWELLING PLACE OF WONDER

INSIGHT _____

_____

_____

_____

_____

APPLICATION _____

_____

_____

_____

_____

DAY 30: THE BODY OF CHRIST

INSIGHT _____

_____

_____

_____

_____

APPLICATION _____

_____

_____

_____

_____

DAY 31: WHAT DEFINES CHRISTIAN COMMUNITY?

INSIGHT _____

_____

_____

_____

_____

APPLICATION _____

_____

_____

_____

_____

DAY 32: THE PEOPLE OF GOD

INSIGHT _____

_____

_____

_____

_____

APPLICATION _____

_____

_____

_____

_____

DAY 33: ESSENTIAL CHARACTERISTICS

INSIGHT _____

_____

_____

_____

_____

APPLICATION _____

_____

_____

_____

_____

DAY 34: THE PRIESTHOOD OF ALL BELIEVERS

INSIGHT _____

_____

_____

_____

_____

APPLICATION _____

_____

_____

_____

_____

Day 35: A Church Shaped by the Great Commission

Insight _____

_____

_____

_____

_____

Application _____

_____

_____

_____

SMALL-GROUP MEETING

INTRODUCTION

Once again, welcome! We've got a lot to cover today, so let's open in prayer, then write the Scripture memory verse for this week.

_____

_____

_____

_____

Before we get to Maxie Dunnam's DVD, here's something worth some thought: the Bible teaches, in John 13:35, that others will know we are Christians by the love we have for each other. We're supposed to create such a wonderful community that others can't help but want to be part of it. How good at that do you think we are?

With that in mind, let's move on to the DVD, and follow that up with some discussion.

POST-DVD DISCUSSION

Let's begin by filling in the blanks for each statement, then we'll look a little closer at each concept.

1. As the Son of God, Jesus invited people out of their _____ _____ with his compelling, magnetic presence.

   ❋ Why was it important for Jesus to draw people out of their everyday experiences?

2. In order to be a home of grace, the church must cross _____ and take _____ on behalf of the gospel.

   ❀ What boundaries could potentially hold back a church?

3. Sharing, loving, and serving others might upset our usual _____.

   ❀ In what ways can we make ourselves more available to be used by God?

4. Sometimes the Holy Spirit causes discomfort within us through _____.

   ❀ What is the purpose of God's conviction in our lives?

5. When we ignore the voice of God, we miss opportunities to _____ others and be _____ in return.

   ❀ How might God instruct us to be involved in the lives of others?

6. When we take a leap of faith for Christ, he always meets us in the midst of our situation and offers his infinite supply of _____.

   ❀ Why is it important for us to take the leap before God will meet us there?

PERSONAL APPLICATION

We hope that, by now, this time of breaking into small groups has become a richly rewarding part of *Irresistible Invitation: Responding to the Extravagant Heart of God*. Ready to get to it this week? Remember to make sure each person has a chance to share before moving on to the supplemental questions.

KEY QUESTIONS:

❋ What do you think comes to mind when the average person in today's society hears the word "Christian"? Is it different than what the Scripture expects, and if so, how and why?

❋ How could a church that fully understands and lives out its role impact its members, its community, and its world?

SUPPLEMENTAL QUESTIONS:

❋ Why is it important to have a faith that's both public and private?

❋ What is the difference between the church as an institution and the church as an organism?

❋ What is the role of the Holy Spirit in a church that is alive?

LOOKING AHEAD

Next week, the final week of our study, we'll consider what it means to be partners in the gospel. First, though, let's introduce another Scripture to help us hold this week's lessons in our heart.

> Dear friends, let us love one another, for love comes from God.
>
> —1 John 4:7

Write the verse below:

_____

_____

_____

_____

_____

Week Six

PARTNERS IN THE GOSPEL

DAY 36: PRIVILEGED PARTAKERS IN
THE PROMISE

INSIGHT _____

_____

_____

_____

_____

APPLICATION _____

_____

_____

_____

_____

DAY 37: PRAYERS

INSIGHT _____

_____

_____

_____

_____

APPLICATION _____

_____

_____

_____

_____

Day 38: Presence

Insight

_____

_____

_____

_____

Application _____

_____

_____

_____

_____

Day 39: Gifts

Insight _____

_____

_____

_____

_____

Application _____

_____

_____

_____

_____

DAY 40: SERVICE

INSIGHT _____

_____

_____

_____

_____

APPLICATION _____

_____

_____

_____

_____

DAY 41: EPILOGUE

INSIGHT _____

_____

_____

_____

_____

APPLICATION _____

_____

_____

_____

SMALL-GROUP MEETING

INTRODUCTION

Well, here we are at the final week of our study of *Irresistible Invitation: Responding to the Extravagant Heart of God*. Let's treat this as a beginning rather than an ending as we step through the next door that God has for us. After we open in prayer, take time to share the memory verse with your group members. You can write it down here:

_____

_____

_____

_____

As we prepare to watch the final DVD message from Maxie Dunnam, consider this: without each instrument playing its part, there is no symphony. The conductor can't make music all alone. So why do so many of us expect the pastor to play all the parts in the music of the church? Could it be that it really is up to each one of us, individually? Let's hear what Maxie has to say.

POST-DVD DISCUSSION

Once again, let's fill in the blanks for each statement, then dive in for further study.

1. This study was designed to help build mental, emotional, and spiritual _____ between the God who loves us and our daily experience.

   ❀ How can a better relationship with God lead to better relationships with those around us?

2. It's easy to know something on an intellectual level, but if we don't practice it, it becomes _____.

❀ What is the difference between knowing something in the mind and knowing it through experience?

3. The irresistible invitation to enter God's kingdom is about _____ and _____.

❀ How do we, as Christians, continue to practice our faith?

4. We have to _____ our _____; if we don't speak up and accept God's invitation, then we'll never know what it's like to truly experience him and his presence on a personal level.

❀ What are the responsibilities of being a Christian?

5. Now that we've read, prayed, and shared about growing into the fullness of _____ _____ _____, it's time to open the door to a new way of life.

❀ How can we show others what's different about God's love?

6. Will we live our lives in holy _____ from this day forward?

❈ How could the church's witness to the world be different if Christians walked in wholehearted devotion to God?

PERSONAL APPLICATION

It's time for our personal application. Let's break into our small groups and dig a little deeper. Don't forget that each person should have a chance to share their answers to the key questions before the group moves on to the supplemental ones.

KEY QUESTIONS:

❈ How can service to others translate to freedom for ourselves?

❈ Why does God talk more about money than any other subject in the Bible?

SUPPLEMENTAL QUESTIONS:

❈ Do you believe there are things that will not happen if we do not pray? Why or why not?

❈ Why does God want us to pray?

❈ What are some of the challenges we face in being Christ to others, and how can they be overcome?

LOOKING AHEAD

Here's a promise from Scripture to encourage you as you complete this journey. Let's commit it to memory now.

He who began a good work in you will carry it on to completion until the day of Christ Jesus.

—Phil. 1:6

Write the verse below:

_____

_____

_____

_____

_____

As we bring the study of *Irresistible Invitation: Responding to the Extravagant Heart of God* to a close, let's review the memory verses from each section. Keep these Scriptures close, and as you move into the next phase of your relationship with God, use them to help recall all you have learned in the past six weeks.

Blessings to you!

WEEK 1: COMING HOME TO GOD

_____

_____

_____

_____

WEEK 2: A LOVE LIKE NO OTHER

_____

_____

_____

_____

WEEK 3: ALIVE IN CHRIST

_____

_____

_____

_____

WEEK 4: FIT FOR KINGDOM LIVING

_____

_____

_____

_____

WEEK 5: THE HOME OF GRACE

_____

_____

_____

_____

WEEK 6: PARTNERS IN THE GOSPEL

_____

_____

_____

_____

APPENDIX
FILL-IN-THE-BLANK ANSWER KEY

WEEK 1
1. trust
2. pray
3. God's blessing
4. Passionately seeking God
5. good
6. loves me/miracle

WEEK 2
1. cross
2. sins
3. past
4. shepherd
5. relationship/voice
6. pasture

WEEK 3
1. sanctification
2. Holy Spirit
3. changed
4. kingdom
5. little things
6. presence

WEEK 4
1. overwhelmed
2. be and do
3. alone
4. meditate
5. fellowship
6. guidance

WEEK 5
1. comfort zones
2. boundaries/risks
3. routine
4. conviction
5. bless/blessed
6. grace

WEEK 6
1. bridges
2. meaningless
3. practice/action
4. do/part
5. God's extravagant love
6. recklessness